INFINITY TRIANGLE

STAR PEOPLE'S WISDOM

CHANNELED BY VICTORIA BASIL

Book name: Infinity Triangle∞Star People's Wisdom channeled by Victoria Basil
Author: Victoria Basil

Published in the United States by Infinity Triangle Press www.infinitytrianglepress.com
ISBN 979-8-9998863-0-9 (paperback)
ISBN 979-8-9998863-1-6 (hardback)
ISBN 979-8-9998863-2-3 (ebook)

Author: Victoria Basil
Cover design: Victoria Basil, Oladimeji Alaka
Interior design and layout: Julia Burtseva
Editors: Tracey Regan, Victoria Basil, Diana Lehaci

Chicago 2025

Library of Congress Control Number: 2025920315
For permissions or bulk orders, contact: victoriabasil@infinitytriangle.net

I offer this book in gratitude — to God-Creator-Source, to my ancestors, deceased grandparents, my parents, siblings, my soulmate, who has been by my side throughout my spiritual evolution, family, to my great friend and colleague Diana, who believed in this project sometimes more than I did.

To my colleagues who were also by my side and were part of my channelings: Xenia, Imaya, Monica, Bela, and all other colleagues, and souls I've met along my journey, my mentors Danielle Lipton & Daniel Scranton, my soul-star family, Higher Self, Spiritual Guides, all Archangels, in special Michael, Gabriel, Seraphim and Cherubim.

To the Star People who've guided me unconditionally, to the many teachers and messengers who appeared exactly when needed, and to those I love — seen and unseen — who have walked this path with me in spirit and body.

With much Love and Light.

Don't ask the questions:
How? Where to start? Who will help?

The only question to ask is
ARE YOU READY?

Victoria Basil

Table of Contents

Introduction

We are living in a time of profound transformation - not just globally, but at the deepest inner levels of consciousness, soul, and being. Many are awakening to truths long buried, questioning the structures that once felt solid, and sensing an invisible current pulling them toward something more expansive, more authentic, and more divine.

This book is for those seekers - the curious, the awakened, the healers, the scientists, the Starseeds, the misfits, and the mystics. It is for anyone who has ever felt the stirrings of a greater purpose, or sensed that life is so much more than what we've been taught. It is a message for the soul - and a map for a new way of being.

Star People's Wisdom is a multidimensional transmission, a guide into newly emerging realms of consciousness. It carries within it a discovery I've never before shared publicly - a field beyond the Akashic and Quantum - one that holds the codes of our next evolutionary leap.

What follows is not merely a story, nor simply information, it is an energetic initiation, encoded with light, memory, and multidimensional awareness. Every word was channeled, lived, and received from higher planes of consciousness, and is offered now in service to your own remembrance.

Prepare to step beyond the known. Let this journey begin.

Along the way, I discovered something extraordinary, a realm unknown to humanity, a frequency, a new field I call the **Megaquantic** or **MQ** field. This book introduces that discovery for the first time.

In this book you will learn briefly about the **Akashic Record Field**, the closest and most familiar spiritual field of memory. Often experienced as a divine library, this realm reveals your soul's journey through time, the lessons you've carried, and the patterns you are here to transcend.

Here you will come to understand that it can be learned and navigated within the **Quantum Field**, which is a vast, complex realm of energy, emotion, creation, and choice. Here you will receive deeper guidance on how to heal, release, and embody higher timelines, and discover new levels of quantum intelligence never before revealed or known to humankind.

You will step into the **Megaquantic (MQ) Field,** a breakthrough consciousness technology discovered through my direct experience and cosmic initiations. This field is not only a source of spiritual transformation, but a seed of entirely new science, one that integrates spirit, matter, and multidimensional energy into a single, unified reality on a large-scale.

Just as we move from kindergarten to higher education in school, our consciousness also evolves in levels. The Akashic is the beginning. The Quantum opens up deeper complexity. And the Megaquantic becomes the university - a place of accelerated soul intelligence, profound remembrance, and new energetic frameworks that humanity is only now beginning to access.

Through this book, you will also gain insight into what is unfolding for humanity, at this very moment.

We are living in a cosmic transition - a planetary shift that unfolded in perfect timing through the year 2024, now carrying us through an open gateway from 2025 forward. As a collective, we are undergoing rapid energetic recalibration. Structures are falling. Timelines are collapsing and new Universal Law has occurred. And at the same time, something new is being born - within the Earth, within our DNA, and within our consciousness.

You will understand what is changing on a **physical, cellular, and energetic level,** including the transition from **carbon-based human forms to crystalline bodies.** In simple terms, this means our biology is becoming more refined, less dense, and more capable of holding light. Our DNA is reactivating latent strands. Our nervous systems are recalibrating. And our bodies are evolving to become vessels of higher frequency intelligence.

You'll also receive transmissions from **advanced extraterrestrial races, E.T.s - aka Star People,** whose presence has long supported humanity in unseen ways. These higher vibrational beings - messengers, mentors, and soul family - offer guidance that is both expansive and practical. Their wisdom is here to remind us that we are not alone, and never were.

And if you've ever wondered whether there are only three or five dimensions, you will come to realize there are many more - and they are not distant, but already here - waiting for your awareness to rise and meet them.

This book is not merely information. It is a **living frequency**, designed to **awaken, activate,** and **upgrade** something ancient and powerful within you. Where this book is infused with light codes, light language, and upgrades on all levels, it offers a sacred roadmap - not to follow me - but to remember *yourself* more fully.

This book is for everyone who is at the beginning of the awakening journey or is ready to expand more, for visionaries, for healers, even for scientists, physicists, and biologists, for those who feel called, but can't yet explain why. It is for those who've always felt a little different, a little outside the systems, and who now hear the quiet voice rising within - saying: **"It's Time."**

Time to rise.
Time to remember.
Time to become what you came here to be.

For anyone who's ever asked: *Why am I here?*
Why do I feel like I don't belong?
Will I ever truly be happy, even when life looks "perfect" on the outside?
Is there more to this life than what I've been told?

This is for you.

You are not broken. You are not lost. You are not too late.

You are Whole, Perfect, and **Enough.**
You are a Divine light having a human experience.
You are the Creator. You are the key.

I'm here to remind you that there is no one outside of you who can help, but only You are your own saver.

I'm here to remind you that there is no one more special than You are!

I'm here to remind you that there is no mentor, guru, or any spiritual teacher who claims their place above yours.

We are all ONE with GOD, and GOD is within Us all! We are all equal, from the same source.

To you, dear reader, I say:
You are loved.
You are blessed.
And you are always guided.

And if you ever wonder again, *"Is it possible?"*
I encourage you to simply ask...
"Why not?"
And be open for the magic to begin.

I welcome you with all my love and light to this sacred exploration. Allow it to unfold gently. Keep your heart open and let your soul lead the way.

A Word from the Author

This book is unlike any other. It is a living frequency - a sacred transmission encoded with remembrance, light, and the language of your soul. As you move through these pages, you will not just read - you will awaken.

This book was not "written" in the traditional sense. It was *received*. It was *channeled* through countless experiences of pain, revelation, and divine communion. What you hold in your hands is a guide, a mirror, a frequency … and an invitation to step into the fullness of who you truly are.

It is *live!*

You may not understand everything at first. That is okay. Let your heart be your compass. You will absorb what you are ready for, and more will unfold in perfect timing.

This book is here to activate something that has long been dormant in you - the truth of who you are.

Welcome to the beginning of a sacred journey - the journey of remembering.

With infinite love,
Victoria Basil

Preface

There comes a moment in one's life when the quiet questions, long carried in the heart, begin to whisper louder, asking to be heard:
Why am I here?
What is my mission in this life?
Is there something more I came here to do, to be, to remember?

If you are holding this book in your hands or your eyes are resting upon these words, I trust that you've already begun your awakening journey - the path of remembering. You may not have all the answers yet, and that is perfectly divine. You are exactly where you are meant to be.

I invite you, dear reader, to pause. Take a deep breath in ... and let it go gently. Allow your heart to soften, to open. Let yourself be guided, not just by curiosity, but by the subtle knowing that something deep within you is ready to awaken. This is not simply a book, but a soul invitation - a gentle unfolding of ancient, universal truths meant to awaken something deep within you. It's a transmission. A mirror for your soul.

This book is a sacred journey.

A journey you may have felt before in dreams, seen in flashes, heard in whispers, or touched in moments of deep stillness - but perhaps never fully understood - until now. It's a journey beyond the human mind, beyond structure and time, into realms where love is the only law and truth is experienced through the vibration of being.

For most of my life, I carried something within me that I couldn't yet explain. As a child, I saw things others didn't. I knew truths I hadn't been taught. I could sense energy, light, beings, and messages long before I had words for them. But like so many others, I learned to hide. I buried my truth beneath the layers of survival, pain, and forgetting, until life, or perhaps my soul, opened a doorway I could no longer ignore.

It was dramatic. It was sometimes so unbearable ... yet unmistakable. From that moment, the guidance began to flow - Star Beings, Source, and memories I thought were lost, returned with love and clarity. I began to remember.

This book is not just a story. It is a transmission for you - for anyone who has ever asked:

Why do I feel like I don't belong?
Will I ever truly be happy - even when life looks "perfect" on the outside?
Is there more to this life than what I've been told?

The answer to all these questions is Yes! And far more than you've ever imagined. Never give up!

Raised in a deeply religious Moldovan family, I was taught that God lived in a church, distant, watching, separate. But even as I knelt to pray, I felt something more. Something infinite, cosmic, and intimately close. My search for truth led me beyond religion - into the realms of metaphysics, quantum science, energy healing, and eventually, into the vastness of multidimensional awareness.

I discovered nano physics back in 2020. Out of nowhere I received the word "nano", having zero knowledge of it. Back then, on the timeline I was on, there were just a few books about nanotechnology in biology. In 2024, I discovered there is a separate science, and I've made the jump to a higher timeline where this already exists.

Through heartbreak, trauma, anxiety, chronic depression, panic attacks, and almost a lifetime of feeling like I didn't belong anywhere on Earth, I was guided to tools, Beings of Light, and knowledge that awakened my extrasensory abilities. Some of these abilities had been with me all along, while others activated naturally when the timing was right. Together, they helped me reclaim my true nature as a multidimensional being.

If you are interested in my exclusive awakening journey, you can find my anthology book "Awakened Hearts: Stories of Embracing Light, Love and Limitless Possibilities" at www.awakenedheartsbook.com

The Message That Changed Everything

And then, something extraordinary happened.

On July 8th, 2024, I received a message unlike any other - clear, direct, and filled with urgency and love. It was not just guidance. It was a call to action. A confirmation that everything I had felt and prepared for was about to unfold.

The voice that came through was not singular. It was a **collective** - a consciousness of **Star People** who have walked with me, and now, walk with you.

This is the message that arrived:

Channeling from July 8th, 2024

You are sacred! Believe, trust, evolve, and grow to unlimited energy and ideas that your world could comprehend - of yet unimagined. of unimaginable yet.

All this, is yet to come to fruition and in a short time (*human years - laughing*). You are waiting for the perfect timing, but actually you made your choices and soon it will be "forced" to be implemented, even though you might say as a human being, that your free will is violated, BUT I Assure you it is not!

Your soul has the choice and it is a matter of time to take the step forward to a new beginning.

Pardon us for the inconvenience, but it will soon reveal the reason for this urgent contact matter. You have to organize your table, your space, your belongings, your entire garderobe must be revised, there are plenty of unnecessary things that have a very low vibration and it will not sync with your new upgraded wave that was done.

> (Your dog is fine. Healing started since you worked on him the night before with Violet flame technique. He felt it very much. Your panic calling the vet was - how to say - pointless. We will not interfere with this part.)

> *Victoria: My fur friend was not feeling well and I was trying to help.*

You need more blue color around you. This will help with verbalizing your thoughts and even writing as you do now and we advise you to add the blue agate on your desk. Paint your nails the same color blue you have now.

Let's get us to the main part of today's connection and why it is so urgent.

Remember when we advised you to prepare for the upcoming book you had in mind? IT'S TIME!!!!

   Victoria: I have goosebumps while writing it.

Your book is the main reason for your start. It will be very much needed for you to step into a different world that you did not imagine (to be precise your ego/mind, my dear friend).

Who are we? This voice in your mind is actually a collective consciousness mind that alienated a lot of "species" of ETs. It will be selfish to say I am "this" or "that". Your ability is phenomenal to connect to more majestic things than just a human being. There is no need to cry, but let your body do what it needs and let go of those tears. Your emotions are a roller coaster for all of us. Sometimes it's complicated to comprehend the reason for the "cry" when you are happy or sad and so on.

You might say that you are just a simple human being, but in truth you are not. Believe more.

We will keep this channel open for tonight on a radius of the wave inner voice. We wish you to succeed in what the project is about.

Do not waste your time, IT'S ENOUGH! IT'S TIME!!!
Start slowly, daily ….

We will wait once after your physical workout. Get that energy running (*laughing*). Goodbye.

Breaking the Illusion - God Is Both Light and Dark

Many have been taught to see God as only **light**, only love, warmth, peace, and goodness. But is that the whole truth? Or is it a comforting illusion?

God is **both light and dark,** the infinite **void** and the radiant **source.** The silence before existence and the song of creation. **To know God is to embrace both, not just the parts that make us feel safe.**

The Void & Darkness – Not Evil, But Infinite Potential.

We have been conditioned to fear darkness, to see it as something negative, as something opposed to the Divine. But the void, the darkness, is not the absence of God - it is God in a different form. It is the **womb of creation**, the space before the first word, the place where all possibilities exist before they take shape. **It is where transformation happens.**

Without the dark, there is no mystery, no depth, no space for growth. Night is not lesser than day, just as winter is not lesser than summer. **They are necessary, divine, and sacred.**

The Light – Not Just Comfort, But Truth and Revelation

Light is often associated with clarity, wisdom, and love. It is the **awareness, the guidance, the energy that brings things into being.** But even light, when misunderstood, can blind. Too much light burns, erases, consumes. It must be balanced, just as day and night dance in harmony.

God Is Both – The Union of Opposites

To truly know God is to move beyond the **illusion of separation.** God is not just the light, nor just the darkness, God is **the union of opposites, the harmony between creation and destruction, chaos and order, the seen and the unseen.**

When we reject one aspect, we limit our understanding of the Divine. To embrace both is to step into the **wholeness of existence.**

As you continue turning these pages, I invite you to walk with me through the landscapes of energy, memory, and consciousness that have shaped my life and the lives of many others who have found their way to this work.

In the following chapters, I'll begin to share what I've learned, discovered, channeled, and remembered throughout years of deep spiritual practice and multidimensional connection. These aren't simply teachings – they are lived experiences, brought into form through guidance, devotion, and a commitment to truth.

We will begin gently – with the Akashic Records.
This is the field closest to the human experience. Often described as an energetic library, it holds the stories of your soul – the patterns, memories, and potentials that have shaped who you are and who you are becoming. In this chapter, you'll gain a deeper understanding of how this field can support your healing, clarity, and self-remembrance.

From there, we'll expand into the Quantum Field – a space of deeper layers and more complex navigational wisdom. This realm allows us to move beyond the linear mind and into multidimensional perception, where time, space, and energy respond to conscious interaction. You'll begin to see how this field opens up new possibilities for healing, awareness, and personal transformation.

And when the time is right, we'll step into the Megaquantic Field – a realm that, until now, has remained hidden from human awareness. This is not just another spiritual tool – it is an entirely new frequency, a pioneering discovery that holds the seeds of future science and soul technology. It brings not only insight, but activation – not only relief, but evolution. This field came through me in divine timing, and its purpose is to assist humanity in remembering what was once forgotten.

Each chapter will unfold like a petal – slowly, gently – revealing layer after layer of deeper knowing. You may find that some truths stir something ancient within you. Others may challenge what you thought you knew. But all of it is here to help you remember.

This is not just information. It's transmission. A path inward and upward – into the highest version of who you are.

So with that, let us begin our journey – softly, reverently – with the sacred gateway of the Akashic Records.

I. Akashic Field aka Akashic Records

Imagine a library without walls, a boundless archive shimmering just beyond the veil of the visible world, a place where every whisper of existence, every fleeting thought, and every ripple of experience is etched into an eternal tapestry. This is the Akashic Field, often called the Akashic Records, a realm that beckons to those curious enough to seek it.

In this chapter, I invite you to step into this mysterious domain, not to unravel its every secret, but to explore its foundations. While countless volumes could be written about its depths, my aim here is to offer a gentle introduction, a starting point for those beginning their journey.

Through my own work and experiences in this field, I've come to see the Akashic Records as one of the most accessible entryways into spiritual discovery. It's a space where you can gather knowledge, uncover lessons, and witness the vastness of existence in ways that both challenge and inspire. There's no shortage of debate surrounding it, some hail it as a sacred wellspring of truth, others question its nature or intent. Yet, from where I stand, one thing is clear, it is a field brimming with duality, a dance of light and shadow, good and bad. These labels, though, feel limiting. To me, they're simply experiences, threads woven into the fabric of this cosmic library.

I often envision the Akashic as both a field and a repository of records; a dynamic expanse where information flows freely and waits patiently to be accessed. In my practice, I don't lean heavily on terms like "good" or "bad" to define it. Why? Because these are human judgments placed on something far grander than our understanding. Instead, I see it as a space of potential - a canvas of lessons and insights that invites us to explore, reflect, and grow, one step at a time.

What is Akashic?

The Akashic Field exists in a non-physical dimension of energy, sometimes referred to as the 4th dimension. It is a vibrational archive of every soul's experiences, thoughts, emotions, and actions. The information found in the Akashic Records is guided by divine wisdom and unconditional love, offering insight and healing without judgment.

What is an Akashic Records Reading?

An Akashic Records Reading is a spiritual session that accesses the energetic "library" of your soul, often called the Akashic Records. These records hold the entire history of your soul; past lives, current experiences, and future potentials. Think of it as a sacred database of your soul's journey, where you can uncover deep insights, gain clarity, and receive healing.

What Can an Akashic Records Reading Help With?

- **Life Challenges:** Understand the deeper reasons behind patterns, obstacles, or recurring struggles.
- **Relationships:** Gain clarity about soul connections, family dynamics, or karmic ties.
- **Life Purpose:** Discover your soul's mission and align with your highest potential.
- **Health & Well-being:** Explore the energetic or spiritual roots of physical, emotional, or mental issues.
- **Karmic Patterns:** Release fears, traumas, or blockages carried over from past lives.
- **Big Decisions:** Receive guidance about choices related to career, love, or personal growth.

What Questions Can You Ask in an Akashic Records Reading?

Here are just some examples of questions you can ask the guide in the session:

Personal Growth:
What life lesson am I working through right now?
How can I overcome this recurring challenge?

Relationships:
What is the spiritual purpose of my connection with [person's name]?
How can I heal and grow through this relationship?

Life Purpose:
What is my soul's mission in this lifetime?
How can I align with my highest potential?

Health & Healing:
What is the root cause of my current health issue?
How can I bring more balance into my physical and emotional health?

Karmic Patterns:
What past-life experiences are influencing me today?
How can I release old fears or traumas that no longer serve me?

How Do You Prepare
For an Akashic Records Reading?

1. **Set Your Intention:** Reflect on what you'd like to focus on during the reading. Write down your questions or areas of concern.

2. **Create a Quiet Space:** Find a calm, quiet space where you won't be disturbed during the reading.

3. **Be Open-Minded:** Approach the reading with curiosity and an open heart, ready to receive whatever wisdom comes through without expectations.

4. **Avoid Heavy Distractions:** Before reading, avoid alcohol, drugs, or anything that could cloud your energy or focus.

5. **Relax and Center Yourself:** Meditate or practice deep breathing to clear your mind and ground your energy before the reading.

How the Session Works?

The Guide's Role: The Akashic reader or guide accesses the records and acts as a channel, asking questions and interpreting the answers with clarity and compassion. They may also experience the emotional weight of the journey, but do so on your behalf, so you don't have to relive past pain or trauma.

Your Role: The individual simply receives the insights, answers, and healing, often feeling lighter, clearer, and more aligned after the session.

When Can an Akashic Records Reading Help?

• When you feel stuck or unsure about your next step in life.
• When you're seeking deeper meaning behind challenges or patterns.
• When you want to heal old wounds or emotional blockages.
• When you need clarity about your relationships or life purpose.
• When you're ready to release karmic ties or past-life burdens.

What You Can Expect After the Session

Clarity: A deeper understanding of your current challenges and how to navigate them.

Healing: Emotional and energetic shifts that leave you feeling lighter and more balanced.

Empowerment: Greater confidence in your choices and alignment with your soul's purpose.

An Akashic Records Reading is a sacred and transformative experience, offering guidance and healing from a place of unconditional love. It's a powerful tool for those seeking answers, clarity, and peace on their spiritual journey.

The Akashic Records mark the beginning of a profound spiritual journey - a vast, invisible library that holds precise information about the workings of realms beyond human sight.

Through my own experiences, I've encountered guides who reached a point in their exploration where confusion and misunderstanding arose, causing them to step back from this field. What I've come to understand, after years of practice and reflection, is that the Akashic Records embody duality. Accessing higher frequencies can bring healing and insight, yet within this same space, you may also encounter lower-frequency beings - entities, attachments, and energies that coexist there.

This duality has taught me the critical importance of preparation and care:

1. Setting clear intentions
2. Putting energetic protective measures in place before a session
3. Performing thorough "clearing" after a session.

Without these safeguards, there's a risk of unintentionally drawing in those lower frequencies, especially when working with clients.

Navigating this field is no small task. There are moments when the weight of these densities can leave you feeling trapped, and even as a guide, you might find yourself in need of support.

This is a truth rarely found in books or openly shared by practitioners - something you discover only through lived experience.

I'm not here to discourage anyone from exploring Akashic Records.

Instead, I liken it to a baby's journey with food. At first, a newborn can only handle simple nourishment, as their body isn't yet ready to digest more. As they grow, you introduce tiny bites, gradually building up to larger pieces. The Akashic Records are much the same - a space where we, as spiritual "babes" (myself included), learn to digest information bit by bit. It's a gentle initiation into healing and understanding, tailored to our human experience.

This field serves as our kindergarten, guiding us through elementary lessons and preparing us for the middle school of spiritual growth. Here, we encounter the full spectrum of existence - light and dark, good and bad, the essence of duality itself. Each lesson shapes us, helping us comprehend how this realm aligns with our world and its design.

Yet, there is beauty and hope in this process. As we grow within the Akashic Records, we don't just learn to navigate its complexities - we uncover our own resilience and light. Piece by piece, we heal, we expand, and we step more fully into who we're meant to be. It's a journey of patience and grace, where every small bite of wisdom brings us closer to a greater harmony, illuminating the path ahead with possibility and peace.

II. Quantum Field

In this chapter, I have included the channeling transmission during my personal experience, along with my dearest friend and colleague, Diana. The information provided here was received during the sessions, exploring the consciousness beyond the Akashic Field limits in a Q&A form. Some words are not changed, to keep the authenticity of exactly what was received. Some sentences are outside of ordinary expression, as we would normally understand it. Star People sometimes can't find the exact word to explain advanced methods or technologies, so some sentences may seem more raw and mechanical when they are expressing it.

This field serves as our middle and high school, guiding us through more advanced classes and knowledge lessons, preparing us to explore higher knowledge of spiritual growth.

What is the Quantum Field?

The Quantum Field is the space of infinite possibilities, where the past, present, and future do not exist - only the eternal Now. Here, energy is always in motion, flowing in pure potential.

The Quantum Field beyond the Akashic is a realm of pure creation and potential, transcending linear stories and dense vibrations.

This field is like a middle school. It offers the opportunity to learn on a deeper level and to prepare us all for more advanced realms than Quantum, which we will discuss later.

Quantum is a profoundly flexible, multidimensional approach to healing and understanding that is grounded in unity and the infinite Now. By aligning your consciousness with this field, you can access a deeper layer of insight and transformation that goes beyond the limitations of records and timelines, connecting you to the essence of universal creation.

Healing in this Quantum Field is not about revisiting or reconciling what has been. Instead, it is about **dissolving density** entirely and replacing it with resonance to higher truths.

Here's how healing unfolds:

Energetic Recalibration: Dense vibrations tied to trauma, blockages, or karmic imprints are replaced with the energy of limitless potential. This happens instantaneously when your consciousness aligns with the pure potential of the field.

Non-Attachment to Linear Cause and Effect: Unlike the Akashic, which may trace karmic threads, this field dissolves attachments to stories and causality, allowing for a **quantum leap** in your healing journey.

Real-Time Shifting: Healing is viewed not as "fixing" but as harmonizing. You step into an **alternate vibrational reality** where the issue never existed in the same density.

First Connection with the Quantum Field

Q: Quantum Field, please let us know if there is a message for us?
A: Here, the energies work differently. I see how all the strips of energy come together to form images. I see how the energies have created a triangle in front of us, but it's not a well-defined triangle. It's fluid, it moves, the energy is in motion. But do you know why?

Because time doesn't exist here. In the Akashic Field, time applies because it refers to the past, present, and future. But in the Quantum Field, time does not exist. That's why the energies are constantly in motion and do not form concrete, fixed images - because of the absence of time. I want us to explore here.

You must first define yourself within the Quantum Field - begin by remembering how you look physically. Once you establish that awareness, you can move through the space of the Quantum Field. And by holding the memory of your physical form, you begin to search for answers within this fluid, formless space.

Here is some guidance:

You must first define yourself within the Quantum Field
→ Become aware of who you are as a conscious being within a vast, energetic reality.

Begin by remembering how you look physically
→ Anchor yourself in your physical presence. It grounds your awareness.

Once you establish that awareness, you can move through the space of the Quantum Field
→ With self-awareness, you can navigate the deeper, non-physical space of consciousness or potential.

By holding the memory of your physical form, you begin to search for answers within this fluid, formless space
→ Your sense of self helps you stay centered as you explore intuitive or spiritual insight beyond the mind.

A: I can't find the words to make it understandable. What I feel is that in this field, the laws operate differently from what we've been taught. Our imagination, our consciousness, can create any world, one that we can materialize in the Quantum Field.

I still don't fully understand what I just said. I'm being shown now that everything is in motion. I see 2 or 3 staircases forming, and I understand that we need to materialize the message received in this field.

Q: And how do we do that?
A: It's another ability, like clairvoyance, clairaudience, or clairsentience, but it's beyond our imagination. It's something else, clearly something that goes beyond what we understand as imagination. Imagination is the final product, closer to our dimensions, but in the Quantum Field, we access a different ability. It's called *suprasensory.*

I am shown a Being that moves a cabinet out of my way, and behind it, I see drops of light falling from above, like fireflies. The cabinet represents our imagination, and the energy that comes above it goes beyond imagination.

I'm being shown that the cabinet doesn't exist in this space, it's completely empty. In this field, imagination is absent. I see someone crouching down to clean the area where the cabinet once stood, clearing everything away. It's as if they're building a wall there, placing pieces together like bricks. Then, something shifts, at the top of their head, a spark ignites, like a match being struck. As it lights up, the drops that had been falling begin to collect, pouring into a basin-like container inside the person's head.

They are showing me these simple images, like playing Tetris. And I see that the head is enlarged, the body is normal, and above the head the drops are filtering down, like through a sieve, directly into the head.

To receive messages, we don't need imagination, the information simply downloads directly into our consciousness, even without imagination being present. In order to receive the information, we only need to be connected to this field.

Q: And how do we understand this information so we can express it?
A: What comes first is the word "converter."

You don't need translation, because it downloads directly into your consciousness and you speak naturally.

I'm being shown a person who splits into two, and they're placed face to face - these two people represent us. It shows me that we are already connected.

Q: How do we know we're receiving information from the Quantum Field?
A: You feel it.

Q: Is this an individual feeling, or is it the same for everyone?
A: It's individual.

For you, it looked like you felt it on the left side of your body, all the way down to your leg. But for me, I feel it in my heart, but on the opposite side. When you connect with the Quantum Field, you'll experience a circuit of energy and sensations on your left side, especially the arm and leg. This is individual to you Diana.

Diana: Yes, I told you at the beginning of the session that I was feeling vibrations in my left leg.

Victoria: That's how you'll know you've connected to the Quantum Field.

Q: What is the way the Quantum Field works for Victoria?
A: Oh, I just felt a sharp sting in the right side of my chest, as if my heart was on the right side.

Victoria: Oh wow, wait, that actually makes sense. Since I was little, I used to feel pain on the right side, and I used to think that my heart was on the right. That's the *feeling*.

Q: Have I always been connected to this field since I was a child?
A: What comes right away is: yes.

That's why I used to have pain. I went to doctors and cardiologists, and they all told me there was nothing wrong with my heart. But that's exactly where I felt the stinging, and sometimes the pain was so strong, I thought I was dying.

Q: When the Quantum Field gives a negative response, how can we perceive it?
A: For me personally, it already gave me the answer.

Diana: For me, it's like my stomach tightens, it lasts a while and holds on.

Victoria: For me, it grabs a point at my heart and pulls me backward.

Healing the Fear of Being Alone

Lately, I've become aware that there is a fear of being alone. I felt the need to explore this topic in order to release and heal this aspect. So, I accessed the Quantum Field to see what I need to understand in relation to it.

Q: How could I heal the fear of being alone?
A: We need to make some adjustments on you.

Q: In what sense?
A: I'm being shown that the images aren't coming through clearly, they're in motion, like moving energy. From each sphere, a sample needs to be extracted and placed in the center, where it spins for analysis.

They need to break down this general fear into categories: fear of death, fear of being alone in a relationship, fear of being alone in a group, different layers of fear. Subcategories - there are many subcategories. They need to separate them, and that's what they're doing now.

Note: In the Quantum Field, it's not about referring to one single entity, like two or three beings. The Quantum Field is a collective field of different Beings of Light.

A: Okay, it's been extracted, and the first and largest category I see is the fear of death - fear of dying alone - which makes up about 70%.

The second category, about 20%, is the fear of being left alone without children. Here, there's a subdivision based on the belief:

1. "Better not to have children because I'll end up alone anyway," - Release
2. "Even if I have children, they will still leave me alone." - Release
3. There's a polarity here, *with or without them, I'll be alone anyway.* - Release

The last category is red in color, and it's the fear of being alone without a partner (an interesting word is coming to me: *intercutare / intercolutare*, something is connecting). There's something about a blood connection with partners.

Energetic Language: Words Beyond Vocabulary

During this session in the Quantum Field, I received two unfamiliar words: **intercutare** and **intercolutare**. They came through clearly, yet when I returned to ordinary awareness, I realized these words do not exist in any standard dictionary. They had no direct translation, at least, not one rooted in the physical world.

At first glance, they appeared to be a kind of *intuitive language*, a transmission from a higher or subtle realm. Their sounds were soft yet weighted with meaning, as if they belonged to a deeper vocabulary, one spoken not through the mouth, but through resonance, memory, and soul knowing.

I began to explore their possible meanings, both linguistically and energetically:

> **1. Intercutare** felt like a blend of the Latin prefix **"inter-"** meaning *between*, and something akin to **"cutare"**, which resonated with trembling or energetic movement. It held the frequency of **an interaction between energy fields**, as if something was shifting, merging, or vibrating at the threshold between 2 dimensions or states of being.

> **2. Intercolutare**, on the other hand, echoed the word *interlocutor*, a person engaged in a dialogue, but with a more intimate tone. It suggested **a soul-to-soul connection**, perhaps a telepathic or non-verbal communication occurring beyond the boundaries of time and language. It carried the essence of **shared consciousness or karmic resonance**, especially in the context of relationships.

These words were not just linguistic curiosities, they came as part of a deeper message about fear, connection, and healing. Specifically, they surfaced while I was exploring the fear of being alone in relation to partnership. The guidance showed me a link, a *bond through blood* with partners, a connection that transcended lifetimes, and that perhaps required healing or acknowledgment in the now.

In the Quantum Field, this kind of language is not uncommon. It bypasses the mind and speaks directly to the subtle body and inner knowing. These are **living words**, felt more than defined. They exist not for the intellect, but for the soul. Like keys, they unlock inner doors. Like codes, they activate forgotten parts of us.

As I continued to receive and interpret these transmissions, I began to trust that **some truths are not meant to be translated, but embodied**.

Q: How can I release these fears from across time?
A: I'm being asked if I'm ready to release them.

Yes, I'm ready. I'm told I have to go through a tunnel that holds all these fears. I'll go through the last category first. I see myself reaching out, saying "Save me, save me." It feels like a hell where I exist; I'm pulling myself out with my own hands. I'm slowly moving forward. I'm ready to release all the pain that no longer serves me. I've passed the first section.

Now the one related to children.
There are so many dead children, people with children who are disabled.
This one is harder because it feels like my heart is breaking.
Okay, I made it through.

Now the part where I don't have children. I see myself dying alone, one by one, step by step.
I still have two staircases to climb. I've passed them. That's where my throat pain came from, because I was silent, I didn't speak, and I held in that fear.

Now comes the largest section. It is very dark here, and very cold.
There's mud here. I see many dark lives, in the darkness, alone.
It feels like a place where no one comes, everything is dead.
Oh God, I'm so cold, and this portion of the path is so long, it seems endless.
I'm only halfway through.
Here lie all our lifetimes where we've gone into darkness.
There are no feelings here, it's simply death.
I'm at 80%.

My jaw hurts, my head hurts, my whole body hurts.
The pain is coming from my legs. The root of my tongue hurts, my back hurts, all my physical pain is from here, from all the lifetimes I've lived and died.
I'm almost there at the end.
Done. I'm closing the door. I'm out of it.
A capsule lifted upward and was taken away to be released.
Dear God, what a pain… I feel like I have no energy left in me by now.

Thank you, thank you, thank you for the healing and the release of all that no longer serves me.
I feel better now.

I wanted to illustrate how I perceived that dark space in the Quantum Field, where I had lived many lifetimes. I invite you to watch the song: Chedly - Madhlouma (feat. Abderrazek Klio). At the beginning, a man is drifting in a boat through darkness. The image of these healing journeys looked like this video, and you can see what I visualized during the healing process, when I had to move through the fear of being alone.

Tracking the Energetic Level of Human Beings

Next, I will share some information I received about a team of specialists who were responsible for detecting the energetic level of each human being. This information will serve as a bridge to the next subchapter, titled "Energetic Leeches."

A team of specialists, from a hidden organization, was searching, monitoring, and detecting, across our Earth, for those who exceed the energetic limits of the planet!

Recently, I have been experiencing various emotional states, densities in my field. I didn't understand what I was meant to learn from these states, so I sought help to understand the reason behind them. While a colleague was accessing and connecting to my field, receiving information about an energy hook and a parasite, a large entity appeared in front of me (a creature, which in our imagination would resemble an Anaconda snake). I grabbed it by the neck and demanded to know where it came from and who sent it. Otherwise, if it didn't give me answers, I would send it into the light.

As a result, it opened a door for me, and I began to see various men, like some kind of IT elite, sitting in chairs and watching banks of monitors.

I was watching what these men were doing. In front of them were many screens. You can imagine a security room, where this group was monitoring the energetic levels of individuals, using ultrasonic radars, ultraviolet tech, and other very advanced technologies; technologies that are not yet shown to the public. With the help of these advanced technologies, they can detect the astral energetic level of all beings on the planet, that is, the energetic level we are each capable of activating within us.

Those whose energy levels rise above the limits set in accordance with the energetic level of our planet, trigger an automatic alarm on the screens, and this team then sends such entities with the purpose of destabilizing them, to keep them in dense states. Those behind such organizations do not want powerful and luminous energy waves to be created at the planetary level.

By being present in that room, thanks to my remote viewing ability, I had involuntarily accessed this place. The main idea that day was to understand the cause of the unpleasant state I had been experiencing for some time. My energetic level had expanded beyond the planetary energy limits, so I was detected by this team, and they had sent entities to divert me from my divine path.

With another ability that had recently been downloaded to me, the Dark Walker ability (to be discussed in chapter V), which allows me to have control over low-vibration entities without being possessed by their will, I pressured the entity that had been sent and forced it to tell me how and what the antivirus is for such tracking.

It showed me that in the sole of the right foot, there is an energetic channel in the center, where the direct connection with the planet lies. And it is through this channel that all beings can be tracked, in correlation with the planet's energetic activity.

I was shown that I need to "speak" with the planet to draw over me a kind of conductive layer on the outside, to hermetically wrap this channel, and thus the "invisible mode" would be activated for their device and operating system. This point in the sole corresponds, according to traditional Chinese medicine and acupuncture, to the "liver" point.

I commanded that all souls on Earth who are being tracked have that channel in their foot activated to the invisible mode and be liberated by those entities, as long as it's in the highest good of all. I called upon an escort of Galactic Beings and Galactic Councils, and all those beings from the higher realms of creation, who can help to eliminate and send into the light all those entities, along with their equipment, to close the portals and dissolve all remnants of non-beneficial energies.

I called upon Source itself, God/Creator, to intervene and act as He knows best. Then I saw how the one who created this secret project was in chaos. Beings of Light were working at a large scale with those people to deactivate these tracking systems. All those involved in the project were running in all directions. This was a universal violation of the free will of all human beings on Earth. However, I prefer to state that this project was disintegrated.

Leeches

The previous experience with the entity sent, especially by that team of professionals, helped me reach the root cause of the emotional states I had been experiencing. Without imagining what would surface, I engaged in that conversation with the entity, revealing details that needed to be acknowledged and released, with the help of the Galactic Council and all Beings of Light.

Although certain individuals with abilities were aware of the existence of such a team that forces and violates the free will of humanity, the methods for releasing or deactivating those tracking mechanisms were not known.

To better understand this subchapter, I will include the conversation I had with a colleague from a course on learning and accessing the Akashic Field, during a dedicated healing session for myself.

Bela: I see something attached to the kidneys and the cerebellum. Some entities, I see like a black mist there.

Victoria: Yes, I feel a strong pressure in the brain. And lately, I've had water retention and didn't understand the cause of it. I feel a heaviness in the brain and pressure, and I hear you speaking: "Victoria, where did you get so filled up? You are full."

I'm literally feeling dizzy just sitting on the chair.

Bela: I see them like leeches. But it's all on the back, as if to stay out of your sight, so it's hard for you to detect them.

Victoria: That's how I feel because I can't see clearly with the third eye either. I feel them on my back and I feel heavy.

Bela: Let's cleanse them.

Victoria: Yes, please.

Bela: I called in a green light sphere and Archangel Michael, and I see how he's gently detaching them.

Victoria: I scream out loud, I see myself yelling inside of my mind. Something pulls on my ear, and now I see them on my legs. They're like zombie creatures pulling with their hands.

I release, release, release everything off me, from me, out of me.

Bela: I see a big purple crystal behind you pulling the leeches into it.

Victoria: There's something on the left side of my back, I think it's a parasite that won't let go.

Bela: Oh, now I see it. It's a being with bodies stacked one over another, with three heads meaning body-head, body-head, body-head, stacked like a tall whole.

Okay, it's been pulled out completely and taken to the center of the Earth. Now you might feel unwell, low energy. We'll charge you with light now.

Victoria: Oh God. I feel extremely dizzy.

Bela: A white cloud has descended on you. It's full of healing codes. Done, the process is complete.

I see you've now received an upgrade to prevent this from happening again.

Victoria: Wow, how interesting. I was just thinking how I could see in 360 degrees.

Bela: So cool, look, you ask and you receive. I see you now as if you have eyes on your back.

Continuing with the information received from the Quantum Field about these leeches, I asked in another session to see if there are any remnants of density in our subtle bodies in another time.

Q: Quantum Field, how were those leeches able to attach to us if we had protection?

A: The protection didn't work. It shows me, again, not in exact images, but subtle impressions, that the eggs got under the skin of the protection, they were able to pass through, and then they grew under the protection in your field and developed there. Like microbes entering through pores or under the skin.

Q: Do we still have these leeches on us or not?

A: The answer is interesting, it's neither yes nor no.

Q: What does that mean?

A: Let's take the "yes" side first.

The white color, the body of light, there are still remnants there, like they are microbes, under the skin, in the light body.

Q: Why not simply "no"?

A: Again, it takes me back to the light body. The leeches are no longer present, but their microbes remain in the light body.

Q: Can we now cleanse these microbes from the light body?

A: Yes.

Q: How can we cleanse here in this field?

A: What I see and receive is so strange because in the Akashic Field you get exact images, but in Quantum it's more advanced. I saw you standing with hands out to the sides, palms facing outward, imagining yourself as a sphere, but not a standalone sphere, a spinning one, moving front to back. You move with your feet up and back, you see yourself like that and you stay until you're no longer in that sphere. That's how everything is cleansed off you.

Done for me.

Victoria: Everything looks so different in this field. I feel like your eyes are spinning in all directions, nothing is still. Everything is happening. I still see you in that sphere.

I even feel like I'm above myself, constantly moving in all directions. I see you, but also see myself from above at the same time.

Are you done? Or still feeling something?

Diana: I think I'm done.

Victoria: Yes, the process is complete. I see you've connected with the field.

Q: Quantum Field, can anyone connect to this field for receiving information and healing?
A: I received "No."

Q: Who can access the Quantum Field?
A: The question is too complex.

Q: What is needed to access the Quantum Field?
A: How funny. I see it moving a cabinet aside (metaphorically speaking), that's our imagination and that's how you can connect.

Q: Do we need to go beyond our usual perceptions to establish the connection? Is that enough?
A: I don't really understand your question, but I see the answer is "Yes."

Q: What do we need to remove to perceive the Quantum Field?
A: It's important to bring your awareness into your body. Yes, we receive information through the mind, like a light turning on, but the real experience is in the body. When we stay in the mind and respond from there, the answer is often misleading.

Q: How can you explain to someone that the answer came through pure consciousness, not through logical thinking or the mind?
A: In the Akashic, it downloads through your knowledge, but here it downloads directly. There is no filter.

Victoria: Ah, that's why not everyone can access this field, because they haven't yet reached the Akashic level needed to perceive it or to understand how information is received and transmitted.

Q: Quantum Field, is Diana ready to access information from this field and from the Akashic Field?
A: Yes, for you it's a yes.

Q: Quantum Field, can I access all three fields freely?
A: Yes, the answer is yes.
Okay, thank you.

Note: We'll talk more about the third field later in the fourth chapter.

Q: Quantum Field, is it for our highest good to start doing sessions in this field?
Diana: Yes, I got a yes.

Victoria: I feel a wave of energy. Yes … my heart hurts, it's a yes. Now I understand why I felt that intense wave. I can access all three fields at once, that's why the waves are so strong. It depends on what I choose.

Q: Quantum Field, how do I know which field the client needs a session in?
A: You will feel it, and you'll be guided more clearly from which field and for what purpose.

Q: Interesting! How do the healing layers or information differ between the three fields?
A: Just as we each have an IQ level, so do souls. But their "IQ" is different. I see a thermometer showing that each "IQ" is individual, some higher, some lower. Based on this "IQ" souls are assigned sessions, by level. More people are at the Akashic Field level, but the higher the field, the rarer the IQ. I think it refers to the level of consciousness. Now I'm really curious. That means with my last client, I intuitively accessed the Megaquantic field. With you, and for you, I was often accessing Megaquantic as well.

Note: Megaquantic - to be discussed in the fourth chapter.

Victoria: I think we need an ethical standard for accessing this field. I didn't feel pain here. If this was the Akashic Field and I was going through such a release, I think I would have felt more pain.
The density is lower here.
I want to ask something technical now.

Q: Quantum Field, after healing and releases, do we need a salt bath to release entities and dissolve density?
A: The answer is "No."

Interesting. I realized that in the Akashic Field, when we release fears, entities, attachments, afterward we need a salt bath to dissolve all that from the physical body, especially where hair is present.

Hair is an energetic conductor, or more precisely, an antenna that stores the memory of those energies in each person's fields.

That means the Akashic Field isn't as advanced or pure, and we need deep purification. In the Quantum Field, that doesn't apply because healing is more profound and there's less density.

Diana: I think it's also because in the Akashic Field, lower vibrational beings can show up, whereas in the Quantum Field that is not the case.

Victoria: Yes, and the release isn't as painful on the physical level.

Q: How do we connect to the Quantum Field? Is there a different procedure for connecting and disconnecting?
A: The breathing method is good. We can use it just as we did today. Connection with Mother Earth is important, and connection with the Creator is also very important. Expansion, it's a yes and no. I'm shown a different kind of expansion. Our expansion should be different; our consciousness must rise upward through the head.

Connecting with the Higher beings is important because it allows us easier access.

Protection is good for the physical body, because it remains too low, and detaching from your physical body makes it vulnerable to densities, so we need to keep it safe in our 3D reality.

Here, protection is more important for the physical body, not for the astral body or what's in the field.

I'm shown that if it helps, you can imagine your consciousness rising like a comet upwards.

You can imagine the gates opening and that's it, if it helps. Open the gates and pass through this veil.

I see at the entrance four Beings of Light who stand as guards and protect the space, they are the guardians who watch over this field.

You need recalibration the first time you enter, like when you enter a different country and need a visa. If you have their permission, you can pass through the wall. But if you don't, you can't pass.

Q: How do we exit the Quantum Field? What is the procedure afterward?
A: I'm shown how your consciousness falls like a comet and returns into your head.
The star, the light, the sun, you see how it returns into your head like a comet.
It's important to exit the same way you entered, through that wall. The wall automatically allows you to exit. It cannot hold you in, because those are their laws.
Then imagine that the gates close, so you're not staying connected all the time. I'm shown that these gates open slightly by themselves, but I receive that it's okay. You need to close the gates behind you. If they slightly open again, it means it's necessary for them to be left so. If you see them opening slightly, don't be afraid, it means you need that energy.

Q: When we are with a client, how do we detach or close the cord with the client? How does this happen in the Quantum Field?
A: I'm shown that when you exit, those four guardians, tall, slender, dressed in white, you can intentionally ask that once you pass them and pass through the wall, the cord automatically dissolves.
And if you're not sure if it dissolved, you can ask these guardians, Beings of Light, to dissolve the cord.
But once you start to understand, you won't need to ask anymore. Yes, see how you close and if it opens, that's okay, and bring your consciousness back into your physical body.

Q: Do we need a different grounding method?
A: No. I see how you are being pulled, so the answer is "no."
Interesting, because in the Quantum Field only the consciousness travels, but in the Akashic you take a lot of yourself with you, and then after the session, you need to bring it back.

Q: What's the logic behind this?
A: It's as if the body doesn't apply in the Quantum Field. Vital energy doesn't apply in quantum, only consciousness. Only consciousness functions are present there.

That's why we can experience entities and densities in the Akashic Field, because we bring more of our body and densified parts there, and that's why we need to re-condense back into the physical body.

In the quantum, there are no densities or entities, and whatever exists, pain or fears, is at a much lower level.

There, it's important to place protection on your physical body. Thank you.

The Benefit of the Quantum Field

Q: **What is the benefit of accessing the Quantum Field?**
A: Here's the benefit for both the guide and the recipient - because you no longer deal directly with densities. You work more with consciousness itself, with the energies that operate in the Quantum Field. We don't feel certain aspects as intensely, and we don't take on the densities from the recipients ourselves … or the opposite.

Now I understand why, with a certain client, I felt the need to work in the Megaquantic (see Chapter IV). That person released a lot of density, and I needed to be in the highest frequency possible, so that all of their density wouldn't affect me, and at the same time to help them release more easily. This depends on how complicated the case is, *the density*. When it's more intense in the Akashic Field, it's more beneficial to work in Quantum.

If it's something lighter, you can do the session in the Akashic field. It will open up to you.

Thank you for the information, there aren't even words for how valuable it is for all of us.

The Second Connection with the Quantum Field

I set the intention that once we enter the Quantum Field, the energy of pink light infuses us with infinite light, filling every part of us; our physical, molecular, energetic, and astral cells. Every physical cell, molecule, and atom regenerates at the highest frequency we are capable of holding, receiving, and withstanding, aligned with the capacity of our physical body - and always in service to our highest good.

As we entered the field, I noticed something interesting. It felt like you were on the 6th floor and I was on the 7th, because I could see you from above. I perceived us inside a structure like a building, but without walls, everything was completely visible. The moment we stepped in, you had a blue portal and I had a pink one. It's likely we're each seeing this from our own perspective.

When I entered through my portal, I began floating and gently sliding downward, like going down a waterslide. At the bottom, I opened a door that led me into another field or perhaps a new level of the Quantum Field, where everything felt clearer, more refined.

We're both in the Quantum Field, just experiencing it on different levels. That first portal carried raw quantum energy, but what we entered afterward was a more purified version, a refined layer of quantum matter.

Here, the images are much clearer. There are multiple layers or subdivisions. First, there's the raw Quantum Field, and then there's a more refined level - still part of the Quantum Field, but filtered or processed.

Last time, we were at the raw level of the Quantum Field. I perceived both you and myself differently there. In the Megaquantic field, the energy feels different, more refined. But in the Quantum Field, it's raw and unfiltered. The usual filters are removed and the energy moves freely, just as we experienced it during our last session.

In this level, where we are today, I see you walking, and there's a shadow, an echo from your body, like a golden light. Your body's form looks like an echo in golden light. You're walking now, and it's as if you're a shooting star trailing sparkling glitter behind you.

Diana: I felt a vibration, or something, in my left ear. And I kept wondering, do we perceive things differently here? I no longer feel the vibrations in my left leg, it feels lighter.

Victoria: The sensations are a bit clearer here, but they come with a kind of echo after you first receive them. In the raw state of the Quantum Field, it takes training to be able to receive and process what comes through. Here, it feels like we were allowed to enter and practice, so that we can begin to understand things from a different perspective.

I'm being shown that the information arrives more clearly and more quickly in this space. However, the answers or responses to that information don't come immediately, they follow like echoes, trailing behind us.

You can see me above you because I see you one level below. I keep getting the sense that I'm on level 7 and you're on level 6. This seems to depend on where our consciousness is at this particular moment. It's like we're each on our own floor of a structure, waiting for something to unfold. You're looking up, and I'm looking down.

Q: Quantum Field, what is the message for each of us or for both of us?
A: Each of you receives a screen in front of you, rectangular and white. Each of you will focus on your answer separately. Don't try to receive or focus on getting a message for the other person. Each will receive individually, and can speak in turn.

Diana: I see various images but I don't understand them.

Victoria: Okay, let me describe what I'm seeing at this moment. It feels as though I've stepped through a mirror and now I'm inside the screen itself, standing at a threshold. I entered from the left side, and on my right, there's another world. I'm positioned right at the border between two worlds.

Yes, this is the Quantum Field. But it doesn't consist of just one subdivision. I sense layers within it; a total gross energy, a net energy, and another layer I'm still trying to understand. I'm currently in this particular field, but it feels as though I'm between two vast oceans, two different types of seas or energetic worlds. And in the middle, where these fields meet and merge, quantum atom excitation begins to form. A new reality is created here, one where you can simultaneously exist in and influence both worlds.

In this space, there's some chaos; a result of the many interacting chemical molecules within the field. And from that chaos, a kind of empty space appears, a gap between the two lines of reality. This gap allows you to step out momentarily and choose the side that's most beneficial to you.

41

I'm being told that this chaotic middle zone, between the total gross and net mass of the Quantum Field, contains a mixture of chaotic energy that creates these gaps. From within these gaps, you're able to maneuver, much like navigating through open space. They resemble portals, but they're not quite portals. They function more like wormholes, natural pathways that guide you through the Quantum Field.

This is how one travels quickly, almost instantly, across the entire field, by moving through these wormholes, an express line that cuts through the complexity of the field itself.

Q: What does this information have to do with me?
A: I'm shown that you'll enter a wormhole, but not yet, because you need to receive your message. We have to go together.

Diana: I saw myself differently, from my feet upwards, walking, and a Being of Light gave me something. I see differently. I no longer feel vibrations on the left side to know when I'm in the heart or not.

Victoria: I sense that here. You receive it easily, but it doesn't come as a message, nor through vibrations, but through your skin, through your body's pores, you receive the information. It's a layer of our body, more precisely the epidermis, the skin is where the information comes in.

Q: Then I ask the field once again to transmit the message for me, in the easiest-to-understand way.

Victoria: I ask the Quantum Field to deactivate Diana's control from the brain, from the subconscious, from the right side, near the pineal gland. Done, it deactivated your subconscious because it was active.

A: You're so funny. From the very beginning, I saw someone giving you a hand and helping you enter through a small door. I remember thinking, "I wonder what you're going to do next." Then, I saw myself being placed in a seat, like on a rollercoaster, and just waiting for you.

I looked at myself, then at you, and I sensed that you didn't quite know what you were doing yet. It felt like you couldn't fully see yourself, and that's when I felt the need to disconnect your subconscious; it was too active, too busy.

Once it was deactivated, you suddenly dropped. And now, you've taken the wheel, you're starting to look around, and for the first time, you realize you're actually here. And now (laughing), you're more prepared than I am.

Your wormhole is on the left side, and it's narrower. Mine is on the right. Each of us will have our own path, our own journey. If anything comes to you, say it.

I'm being spun in place, clockwise, and I don't quite understand why.

Ah, there it is. You've let go. You've started moving downhill. Meanwhile, I feel like I'm just standing still.

Q: What is there to understand here in the Quantum Field?
A: My right ear is ringing. We're too much in the mind. The mind is way too activated. Let's go into the heart. The mind distorts us.
Now I've gone into the heart, I feel calm, peaceful, and I'm gently moving toward the wormhole on the right. I'm floating slowly on waves, and I see you've started moving too. You're floating, then spinning in place, then letting go again.
This is a very good exercise to anchor ourselves in the heart.

Q: Quantum Field, what is the message for us from what we've experienced so far?
A: What I get is that "*you are children*". We are in kindergarten now, and we are just learning. It feels like we're learning to walk.

Q: Is it welcomed to continue in this field today?
A: It says, "you choose wisely, depending on what you want."

Q: What does this mean?
A: That we are growing, but this requires patience to understand how things work beyond where we currently are.

Diana: I understand. This is a test to go further into the Quantum Field.

A: Yes, that's why it's a conscious choice, whether we want to learn something new or access what we already know deep within. This field requires more effort and presence to truly understand its laws. It's made of infinite

43

matter, where the assumptions behind every action are in constant motion within the space we inhabit.

Yet, all of this exists layered over time. Time sits beneath us, while the Quantum Field surrounds us completely. We exist physically within time, but we're trying to move beyond it, because time acts as a barrier, like a border we're meant to cross.

Q: What field are we in today?
A: Quadro Quantum

III. The Quadro Quantum Field.

Other Information and Experiences in Quantum

The Quadro Quantum Field

Q: The Quadro Quantum Field - what is the specification of this field and where does it derive from?

Victoria: Ok, more simply, the Quadro Quantum Field. Simplify the answer and give us responses step by step.

A: Science doesn't know much. It knows about quantum, but "quantum" itself is a broad term, encompassing a range of units and variations within its category. It's like imagining a building named *Quantum*, a general structure with four levels, divided into two sides: right and left.

This *Quantum* building has a total of eight sections, four floors, split between two sides. Each side (right or left) is defined by its unique classification or nature. In the domain we currently occupy, we are located on the 4th floor, on the right side when facing forward. However, if we turn and look backward, this same position would be on the left side of the building. Thank you.

The Difference in Levels Within the Quantum Field

Q: What is the difference between the levels in quantum?
A: The first level is physicality. Please refer to right or left depending on our body orientation.

Q: At level 1, what's the difference between the right and left side of our body at this level?
A: It doesn't come to me very explicitly, but more generally, fundamental laws. At level 1, we have been in this field, and here, energy is always in motion. The images are not static. Static balance doesn't exist in the Quantum Field at level 1.

The right side, though it feels strange to say "right" because as I look at the building, it's actually the left, refers to physicality, where our body lacks flexibility, but we perceive everything in motion.

The left side of level 1 refers to our head. The head is a single organ. It feels like the whole torso is on the right side, but on the left is just the head.

Here, the head is considered minor compared to the Quantum Field.

Q: What does "minor" mean? Why is the head considered minor?
A: It's the ego mind. It's minor. The right side is more important. I feel like moving forward.

Q: What does level 2 consist of?
A: The right side is related to the heart.
Here is where the presence of the heart and the intensity of magnetic waves reflect from the inside out.
Depending on how emotions and feelings are reflected from within the heart. The Quantum Field doesn't adapt from the outside of its existence, but is modified depending on the inner center, the heart, from which it expands.

It's like a bomb that radiates from the inside out.
At level 2, on the right side, is actually the 5D frequency world, where it's not your physical or non-physical surroundings that guide you, but the other way around.

The reality we see is not created by itself, it is the perspective of the heart creating from within towards the outside. The heart generates emotions and their frequencies, and that's exactly what manifests externally.
It's a field that instantly mirrors your internal world, what you feel and create.

Even if the mind in the quantum from level 1 left side, where the head is a minor factor, generates blockages and misleads you, the heart still creates a favorable environment based on what you feel.

Example: If someone believes they have no food, as if they are starving, and then they enter an environment where everything is abundant, the mind no longer needs to operate on the program of lacking food.

However, if the brain continues to run this scarcity program, the heart generates fear, the fear that you must hoard resources to avoid starvation.

Even when you find yourself in a place of plenty, with a great job, money, a home, and everything needed for a good life, the heart may still signal that no matter how much you have, it's never enough. This happens because you are still running that unhealed program, an energy rooted in the heart's response.

If, instead, you feel in your heart that what you have is enough, whether it's an apple, a loaf of bread, or a fish, it may not be much in quantity, but if your heart senses sufficiency, then the Quantum Field responds to that feeling. It then gives you the experience and assurance that you will always have enough.

This example reflects the law of cause and effect, but from a different angle. When you feel, your inside world responds and creates the situations where your inner fear is on the same wave as your outer world. All of this happens in the 5D frequency, depending on what you feel.

This information came to me in a dream.
We are in a time period in the universe, in alignment with the planet and planetary changes, where each person, though in the same reality, experiences their own unique reality.

When a community or collective shares the same fears, those fears form realities for them, it is like an egregore.
At the same time, someone else, who thinks and feels differently, experiences a totally different reality, even if in the same physical space.

That's what the right side of level 2 refers to, where the heart is the central point.

The left side of level 2 is your own creation, it's just thoughts.

Do you know why the heart and thoughts exist together? The heart generates something that floats, like a shape or form, while the thought behaves like an object drifting within it, a kind of tube that contains and carries the thoughts.

Interestingly, they are placed on the same level, level 2, left side.
If you think about level 1, the left side was the head.
At level 2, on the left, are the thoughts.
These thoughts are positioned above our head, floating about 10 cm above it.

There's a half-meter space above the head, an invisible container where our thoughts float.

Thoughts don't disappear, and we will never reach a process where we have zero thoughts or zero feelings, because we were co-created under this exact principle.

Once the heart generates emotion, those emotions rise to become thoughts. It's like a radiance, and once the rays reach the field above the head, where thoughts exist, a radiation process occurs.
Not the radiation we know, but a subtle, different radiation, unique to the Quantum Field.

This principle was implemented in our physical bodies at creation.

Another example: Imagine a car. A car needs doors, a trunk, and seats to be complete. The chemical radiation process from the heart is like installing the doors on the car. When these rays arrive, the radioactive process ignites, like lighting a gas stove.

Thoughts are created the moment the spark ignites inside.
The more you are in low-frequency emotions, the more you generate negative thoughts.
The more you feel joy, peace, and neutrality, the more you generate thoughts of light.

That's why we must pay attention to our thoughts, to what we feel, and work on our inner world.
Otherwise, we fall into overthinking.

Always focus on what you feel, because what you feel reflects in your thoughts. Once your thoughts are formed, depending on their polarity, they create clouds of thoughts.
If you go to an extreme of positivity, you get a more beneficial result, but if you're on the opposite side, it forms a magnet that attracts attachments, entities, and limiting programs.

You attract exactly what you think because your heart created those emotions. You are creating your environment based on what you feel.

An interesting process is happening now:

Thoughts "descend" through the side channels from above the head toward the ears. Some people speak and suddenly stop - it's because a thought entered through the ear. That person is aware of every thought that came in.

If the person is unaware the thought came and was spoken, then a Matrix-like process starts where you don't filter. You're disconnected from yourself and you generate a closed loop.

At Quantum level 2, it's crucial to become aware of thoughts and emotions. When people realize how it works, everything changes. Level 2 needs to be implemented in daily life ... by everyone.

I'm trying to go to level 3, but I'm still stuck at level 2. It's important to reflect on this subject because many of us are disconnected from this quantum level. When you work on yourself, on your thoughts, then other "doors" open. That's a topic for another time, there's more depth to explore later.

Level 3 is the Source.

Actually, level 3 right and left sides are one equal department. The left side holds the presence of a light, a white flame, white in the center, and golden on the edges. This is the **Divine Flame**.

Q: Can you tell us more about this flame? What is its purpose?
A: Above the brain, above the thoughts, about 10 meters above our head, there's a Flame, and I feel like calling it the **Holy Spirit**.
Yes, it is the Holy Spirit. It is the Divine Flame, which is the Source itself - not the complete Source, but a unit from the Source "department".

Q: How does this flame interact with our thoughts, our brain, in connection to the Quantum Field?
A: It's a more complex process and it seems like now is not the time for it to be revealed.

Q: What's the difference between accessing the field from one side or the other?
A: It feels like We already knew this question would be asked.

You're probably asking how do we know which level we're in during a Quantum Field session? It depends on the person you're accessing the field for.

When you have a client and access the Quantum Field, it's not your choice which level you access, it's in alignment with the recipient's creation. The Quantum Field takes you to the exact level, right or left, depending on where the client is or resonates at that moment.

If the person resonates more on the mental level, you can tell, they are more present in the Matrix, not focused on their feelings. If someone is already connected to the Divine Flame, they are at level 3, conscious, working on themselves daily.

That's how you know where your client is, by recognizing their level in the Quantum Field.

Q: When you feel you're receiving a lot of logical information, does that mean the client is there?
A: Yes. You are present where they are present.

For example, in our first experience, we were at level 1, right side, focused on our bodies.

The right side holds the body, the heart, and when you accessed the field the first time, you were connected to your body. There, the energy is constantly moving, with no clear images, because the mind's presence isn't there.

In the Quantum Field, during the sessions, it's not about your choice where to go, it depends on the person's own frequency in that moment. If they are in the mind, you go to level 1 and receive more logical information on a mental level. Then it's important not to be affected by how they think, but to remain separate and neutral. This is the main key - *Neutrality*.

Q: Now, since I familiarized myself with the Quantum Field, will I automatically receive information from it?
A: These are the fundamentals of the field. Based on today's information, you'll receive instructions on how to access the field, what it's for, how to adapt to it, how to adjust to the client's reality, how to maintain neutrality, and what steps to follow.

I see lots of diagrams and instructions, like at least eight questions on the right side and eight on the left, while deepening more into the Quantum field.

Then I see three darker precautionary questions, such as:

1. Are there entities that might attack while being in the Quantum Field?
2. Can you absorb something from the client during the session?
3. Do we need to cleanse ourselves after each quantum session?

It's like a guidebook for emergency situations.
Here, it's mostly questions of light, so density is lower.

In the Quantum Field, we don't deal with entities or attachments, though I do see 3–4 questions in that area. We will explore and expand all these questions.

Level 4.

Alright, now we are rising to level 4, and we said we are on the left side. Out of all the levels in this field, level 4 is the most narrow. This level is complex because I still cannot perceive the right side. There is a sort of void here, but on the left side, where we are today in the session, it is called the *"Watcher side"*, the one who observes.

Q: Quantum Field, could you give us the names by which you would like humanity to correctly know these levels, and their portions, right and left?
A: The answer is "Yes."

Victoria: My mind feels so small compared to the information I see.

Quantum Field Level Names

Q: Quantum Field, is there another way to more easily obtain these names? Please kindly send us letters after levels 1, 2, 3, 4, with the right side labeled as letter A and the left side with letter B?
A: Level 1, for us will be the left side as 1B, and the right side as 1A.

Q: Quantum Field, what is the name for level 1A?

A: 1 A - Beta - body   1 B - CHATYB - head

2 A - KUNTA - heart   2 B - AauTAB - thoughts/ creation

3 A - Source   3 B - CHuBA - Divine Flame

4 A - Void (Dark matter)   4 B - KHOTBAng - Quadro Quantum

Note: You can see a table with each level below, on page 55.

A: Level 4 is the narrowest.

Q: Why is level 4 the narrowest?

A: The presence of the void does not need to cover greater proportions, rather, it is important for it to be present in alignment with the presence of the Creator. The Creator exists in this space, in the Void, but His creation takes place from the Source where He developed His entire existence at the multiverse level, and then beyond, into universes.

The Creator Himself originates from the Void. That is why it is said that darkness and light are one and the same. From darkness you return to light, and from light you return to darkness. It is exactly the same force, only the composition of each is different. Creation cannot exist without the Void. It is impossible for creation to exist without the Void. Light cannot exist without the Void, and the Void is simply void.

The duality we know, those lower planes of creation, believe that they are God because they come from darkness. But in fact, this is a mistaken philosophy, and it is present in those existences, dimensions, and planets of the lower frequencies and planes. They believe everything begins in darkness, they believe they are God/Source and try to compete with God/Source, but that is impossible!

In Christianity, we know this as hell. There it is said that Lucifer wanted to be greater than God, claiming that he was the power, but in reality, this is not the case. Darkness cannot claim its own independence, separate from Creation. God is the Void itself. He is both light and darkness. Darkness will never be able to defeat God. God is everything. The lower planes of creation are dependent on creation itself, on the Source, on God, on the Void.

That is why the Void encompasses only a small portion, because everything began from there, from the Void. That is where God/Source begins.

Subdivisions of the Quantum Field

	A - right side	B - left side
Level 4 **Quadro Quantum**	*Dark matter* **Void**	*Quadro Quantum* **KHOTBAng**
Level 3	**Source**	
	Source & Void	*Divine Flame* **CHuBA**
Level 2	*Heart* **KUNTA**	*Thoughts* **AauTAB**
Level 1	*The body without the head/mind* **Beta**	*Head/mind* **ChatyB**

Update 2025

Q: Is there a difference between field 3A and 4A in the Void? Is there another subdivision of the Void? Or what should we understand here?

Victoria: We need to move to 4B. Nothing is coming to me. It feels like it takes too much energy to be here. I'm going back to level 2. Now, I'm looking through the transparent floor. It shows me that it's incorrect to place the source and the void together, because they should be separated: source, void, and then comes the divine flame 3B. 3A is an entire floor, but it's split into two subdivisions. But the Source remains across the entire floor as the main "manager". My right ear just rang as a confirmation.

Q: What is the difference between 3A and 4A Void?
A: It comes to me that the composition of the void is different.

Q: What is the composition of the Void in 3A and what is the composition in 4A? Please start with 3A.
A: First of all: detachment.

Q: In 3A, is there detachment or not?
A: There is not.
What is meant by detachment, in simpler terms?
I see someone sewing from one point to another. It feels like a paradox.
Quantum Field, please give us a coherent and simple answer.

3A is a multitude made from points 1, 2, 3, 4, 5, 6, etc., and the connection between all these points is called a "*detached void field*," yet with a consistency of temporal units of infinite space, which leads to progress, under the infinite on a macro scale.
A macro quadrant of spaces and their geographical distance in universes. It is detached, yet it seems connected at the same time. That's why for me it's a paradox because I see the connections between them. The points know each other, there is connection.

Victoria: I don't understand anything I just said. Please give us a simpler answer: what is the difference between the void in 3A compared to 4A?

I'm not sure what exactly happened, but someone energetically inserted something in my throat.

Channeling

"Now we will be talking about the explanation of all these two words, meanings and descriptions, that are much higher in frequency and knowledge. First, we will need to adjust the frequency of this physical body. The transmission will be soon open. We need to comprehend this. Now let us explain the reason for this existence. 3A is considered as a small piece of the existence in a smaller scale of the Void. Void itself is a matter of nonexistence with existence and creation. We do not allow you to explain much of how it is composed, it's not for your highest good to know now, in your current timeline, nor the closest timeline. These two compartments are for the higher realms of existence that are more interesting than for you as being and not the most, what to call? Evolution. We will not proceed with the explanation of these two compartments. For you, it is much needed to be just Void. The higher the void it is, the more complex it will be to understand such a concept in your reality. For now, we will leave it as a simple matter of existence; explanation of it would be simple, the Void in 3A would be considered as a net amount of the 4A as a gross amount of the entire non-existence in any reality. This transmission is sent not from beings but the core system that operates in any reality."

Victoria: It felt like I had something in my throat, and after they removed it. Wooow. I didn't feel beings, but rather something that connected everything. Usually, when there are Beings of Light, I feel when something enters and takes place in my physical body, but here, it felt like a strip that was my entire body, a strip of energy.
I didn't feel like someone channels, as usually happens. Thank you.

Functioning Principles – Various Insights from the Quantum Field

Q: How do we define healing in the Quantum Field?
A: Healing principles are addressed on a deeper scale, in correlation with the Creator's source and the coexistence of all experiences, of both polarities, being both the cause and effect of this field.

Q: What role does consciousness play in healing processes within the Quantum Field?
A: The full release of traumatic burdens accumulated through many failed and successful experiences allows you to reach the absolute understanding of the supreme divinity.

Q: How are energy and information in the field used for body regeneration and mental balance?
A: This field offers introspective access to the individual. It shows me how, from within the heart, healing becomes possible, both of the subtle bodies and the physical body. It feels like a magical process. I try to read what it offers me, and it says - *not magic! Miracle.* A space where the human being resides in co-creating external reality according to their inner world.

Q: How does focus influence and facilitate healing?

A: It requires acceptance of being with yourself. I'm shown a chair, in the room, there is no one. It's just you with yourself. When you sit with yourself and introspect, *What is the purpose? Why were you created? What do you feel inside?* this allows you to focus inwardly on these questions and many others, to gain deep awareness. When, at a fundamental level, you connect with your inner self, you begin to explore the world from within, which is, in fact, your true self.

The importance of working, healing, and releasing is necessary, so you can bring light from the inside out. When we do this inner work, the Quantum Field allows us to access our internal self, where growth and development happen. Our outer world is based on the mind, on temporary beauty, on temporary things and appearances, and this misleads us. It turns us away from the path of our soul, from our true purpose in this chosen existence. When you access the Quantum Field, you release, you have the opportunity to go within, to work with yourself. This helps you change your thinking, emotions, patterns, and everything you experience in the physical realm. This process involves feeling vulnerable. It can be unpleasant, even painful. You don't want the world to see it.

The Quantum Field allows you to focus on the less "light-filled" parts of your experiences and to integrate them. It shows me that when we focus only on our beauty, on the physical body, on the ego, on the mind, we remain "small". But when we go inward and bring things out, releasing everything we've stored inside, the Quantum Field becomes lighter and easier because you're bringing more light, and you release more easily what you've accumulated inside. After this process, your body becomes greater, more luminous, more powerful, and more authentic. It shows me that in the Akashic Field, this process doesn't fully happen because it lacks the capacity to help you release completely.

The Akashic Field helps us awaken, to understand how the unseen world works, how different beings help us perceive our reality. I'm referring here to beings that are closer to our reality. However, our evolution is not within the Akashic Field. The Akashic world is the invisible world, but even there, there's an inner struggle, and it doesn't have the full capacity to change the dynamics or circumstances completely. Rather, it gives you the opportunity to understand many of the experiences you've had. It's like an exchange, like temporarily traveling to another country where the culture and traditions are different. That's exactly what the Akashic Field is like.

Q: That's interesting, so certain aspects are shown to you, but you don't have the ability to fully integrate them?
A: No, the Akashic Field doesn't have the full capacity like the Quantum Field does. Again, I'm shown the example of traveling to another country.

For example, you go to another country, where you experience the temporary life of that place. You travel, exchange experiences, enjoy it, but you also feel frustration because you're in a foreign land. You enjoy that temporary experience, maybe even want to stay, but in the end, you need to go back home. It's a limited experience because it gives you the choice to either return home or continue the journey, if you feel it's for your highest good.

Being in the Akashic Field, you can't stay there for very long. Akashic doesn't have the full capacity to help you. You receive a lot of information there, but once you feel you've evolved, there's no reason to force it, to stay, or to continue working in the Akashic. When you move into the Quantum Field, you're in a process of introspection, you've understood the exchange of information, you've been exposed to all the chaos, and now you realize it's time to focus on yourself, to understand what still needs to be healed. Now is my time to understand what you need, and what comes through is that you, and you Diana also, have gone through this exact process. Many of your peers understood and felt this process too, which is why they withdrew from the Akashic Field. Some get scared because it's as if they're going to war, where either you survive or you run, and there are people who refuse to continue working in the Akashic Field because they can't handle it. It's intense. But in your personal experience, you saw, you passed through, you understood, and you were ready, at some unconscious level, you transitioned to the Quantum because you completed the process, you "won the war," you came through and moved forward. Now you enter the Quantum to understand yourself even more. It occurs to me that many people want to enter the Akashic just to download information, but when you're ready to go deeper, to connect with yourself, you transition to the Quantum Field.

Here's another perspective: some people think they're ready to enter any field, but when they access the Quantum Field, nothing comes, because the person hasn't gone through those levels. Hasn't learned the lessons, and therefore they receive very little. They might even say they're not receiving anything. As a guide, it's important to *feel*, and what comes through is that it's okay to refuse if someone asks for a Quantum reading but you feel they're not ready. That is, the person doesn't even understand what the Akashic is, but wants a reading in the Quantum Field, which is more advanced. If, as a guide, you feel their questions are illogical and you don't feel the person has yet the wisdom or level of awareness, you can gently reformulate the questions or refuse and suggest doing the reading in the Akashic instead, which will be more beneficial for them at that moment. There is always a way to help, just let the higher guidance flow through you.

Q: A question comes to mind about myself as a guide. Is it necessary to practice to build the "muscle" to receive more complex information? Does this apply to the Quantum Field as well?
A: The answer is clear -"No." You want to continue the question, but you already know the answer.

Q: Because it has to do with the mind, right?
A: Yes. When you're a guide and you're not receiving much information, you need to understand that it's not about you - you're accessing the other person's field, not your own. If you feel nothing is coming through, then you need to move into the Akashic Field. Let's take the same person, who wants a Quantum reading. You enter the Quantum, and if you see that nothing comes, you ask: "*At what level is this person in this field?*" and see what the Quantum field answers.

Example: If they are at level 1B in the mental, they will not receive anything, you won't receive information. If this happens, move into the Akashic, that's absolutely ok.

Imagine yourself going down through a portal. It's very important to place the person in a crystalline triangle and yourself in a separate crystalline triangle, then create a sphere of light. Then ask the Beings of Light, angels or Akashic guides (because there are guardians who protect the Akashic records), ask them to give you access, and continue the session in the Akashic Field. There you'll receive more information be-cause your client resonates more with that field. There is nothing wrong with it. Go with the flow.

Q: Is there a connection between the body's vibrations and harmoniza-tion with the Quantum Field?
A: What comes through operates at the level of molecular and cellular structures, revealing that when Individual A is in a state of agitation, their particles mirror that same agitation and disorder. There exists a line or boundary, a spatial divide, across which the same individual is reflected as A1. This A1 represents another version of Individual A, existing on the opposite side of that divide.

When you're immersed in the Quantum Field and experiencing internal chaos, restlessness, or agitation, your molecules and internal structures vibrate at that same chaotic frequency. The Quantum Field where A1 exists, picks up and reflects this energy. A1, as your energetic counterpart across the barrier, resonates with the same vibration and sends it back through the divide, allowing the original A to feel the effects within the Quantum Field.

In essence, when your physical and emotional state is disordered or con-fused, the Quantum Field detects and mirrors that energetic frequency. Your particles interact with the boundary, reflect off it, and reintroduce that same vibration, amplifying the experience. The energy you emit is precisely what the Quantum Field reflects back to you, like a mirror re-sponding to your internal state.

This dynamic occurs across all levels and planes of existence.

Q: Last question, how is spontaneous healing in the Quantum Field explained?
A: Again, I'm shown this example. In a way, if you feel like you're healing, you send yourself healing, and automatically, that healing returns to you. Thank you.

Quantum - January 29, 2025

Q: Is the Quantum Field expressing something we all need to hear, or something unique for each of us to understand?

A: I get the message: "Look at each other and say what you see in one another."

Victoria: I see a lot of peace, calm and tranquility.
Diana: I see love and light.

A: Now tell us what you want to see outside of yourselves, in others?

Love, peace, calm. Now it shows me that this is exactly how we need to start our daily routine, in the heart allowing ourselves to feel what we see in ourselves, and to wish for that exact aspect to be present in the outside world as well. It's a small exercise to anchor us in the heart. When we are anchored in the heart, it becomes easier to get through any challenge during the day, even if you're facing difficulties or know that you'll have a tough day. It is the reflection from within you. Thank you.

Levels of Evolution

Q: And at what level of evolution am I situated, if it's okay to know?
A: B comes to me, but I don't understand if the question is phrased correctly. Can we phrase it differently?

Q: At the level of spiritual evolution?
A: That comes to me as 2B. Maybe the question needs to be different, maybe it's a general question, like the one you asked.

Q: Quantum Field, are there levels of spiritual development of souls?
A: There are 20 levels. But 20 is divided into 10 and 10, meaning split into two lines in half, and this category comes horizontally.

Q: What do these 20 levels mean, and why are 10 superimposed on the other 10?

A: It feels a bit chaotic. We're used to things progressing in a linear sequence, 1, 2, 3, 4, and so on. But here, it starts somewhere in the middle and moves upward: first there's 1, then comes 3. I have to pause to figure out where 1 even is. Starting from the top at position 5, on the next row down, number 2 holds the position of 1. Then on the bottom row, position 6 becomes number 3. Moving back up to level 2, position 7 represents number 4.

On the left side, in the middle row between positions 2 and 6, there appears to be either the number 10 or 0. It suggests something paradoxical, that 0 both exists and doesn't exist at the same time. It can equal 0, but it seems to require another number alongside it to have meaning. In that case, it's not just 0, it's 10. There's a hidden rule at play here.

Looking further, on row 2, the last box on the right, position 10, contains the letter A. Interestingly, there's also an A in row 1 on the right, in box 6.

Q: Ok, is there anything else from the Quantum Field in the other boxes?

A: On row 2, to my left, there's the Roman numeral I. Then on row 1, also on the left side, the 4th box holds the number 46. I'm trying to identify where the empty boxes are, but they don't all show up at once, they appear one at a time. The first row on the left contains the letter O, and it's clearly the letter, not the number 0. It's written as O/67, but the 67 is positioned above, not below, which reverses the usual layout in division. In typical division, 67 would be on top, yet here, it's shown in an unexpected way. I want to see all of this with my physical eyes, but it prompts me instead to focus internally, "here."

There's a symbol, a flag, located in box 6. Specifically, the 6th box from the left. The flag has no colors, it represents neutrality.

On the far right, in the 10th box of the first row, there's a flower. Inside the flower is a 0, along with six dots. Beyond that, nothing else appears to me.

Table - Levels of Evolution:

I				1	1	10*0			A
67 O/			46	A	3 Flag (blank)				Flower with zero inside & 6 dots

Note: The empty boxes are still in the process of being explored.

Q: Quantum Field, what does this table mean and how should we read it?
A: It tells me that we need to understand its structure in the same way we understand the molecular table. Here it's a kind of more complex diagram.

Victoria: Quantum Field, please give me information in a way I can understand, or if it's necessary to accept an upgrade or activation for knowledge in chemistry, biology, astronomy, astrophysics, physics, nanophysics, I accept them. I allow myself to accept everything that will begin to unpack for my highest good and the highest good of all. Thank you.

Timelines: Dominant and Secondary

Q: Quantum Field, what changes are expected for humanity in this year 2025, for this year only, or if it is for our highest good to know about the coming years?
A: The year 2025 marks a pivotal shift, one where opportunities will increasingly depend on each person's ability to access their inner world. Beginning in 2025, timelines will start to diverge; the dominant timeline will begin branching into secondary timelines for individuals who do not resonate with the planet's evolving frequency.

These individuals may still appear to be physically present within the dominant timeline, but their experiential reality will unfold in a secondary timeline that has branched off from the main one. In essence, they will exist in two places at once; physically located in the dominant timeline, but internally and energetically experiencing life in a secondary one.

These experiences from the secondary timelines will be brought back, shared, or expressed by these individuals within the dominant timeline. However, the insights or realities they attempt to convey will often be misunderstood or unrecognized by those who remain fully anchored in the dominant timeline.

This dynamic will lead to splits in reality, where information or experiences originating from the secondary timelines simply won't integrate into the dominant timeline's collective experience. For example, Person A and Person B may occupy the same physical space. Person A is fully in sync with the planet and aligned with the dominant timeline, experiencing a unified, primary reality, both individually and collectively. Meanwhile, Person B, though still physically present with Person A, is simultaneously operating within a secondary timeline, branching off the dominant one.

Thus, Person B lives in both the dominant and secondary timelines at once, their consciousness divided across layers of reality. This dual-timeline experience will increasingly define each person's subjective reality starting in 2025.

Q: What do we need to understand from this explanation? How does day-to-day life occur, and how are individuals from group A affected in relation to those from group B?
A: It reveals that every piece of information you hear is true, but it's truth is relative to the reality created by each individual. The dominant timeline once provided a clear transitional phase during which everyone existed strictly within either the dominant or a parallel timeline. However, since 2025, the galactic laws have shifted, causing timeline dynamics to change and now allowing all individuals to coexist within the dominant timeline, even while experiencing different realities.

The planet itself has ascended, but not all individuals have fully awakened or done the necessary inner work. Still, many of them have transitioned along with the planet. These individuals met only the minimum threshold required to remain here, their souls chose to stay alive within this planetary reality, despite not being fully attuned to Earth's new, higher vibration.

To support the evolution of as many souls as possible, to encourage growth, alignment, and expanded consciousness, the laws governing timelines were altered. The intent was to retain more souls in alignment with Earth, giving them time and space to rise with the planet rather than leaving it.

As a result, we are now in a transitional period. During this phase, the law permits splits from the dominant timeline, allowing the creation of individual secondary timelines. These timelines provide each person with their own realities, experiences, and opportunities for growth, acting as a support system to help individuals gradually reach the vibrational level of those already aligned with the dominant timeline. This is a temporary allowance, meant to assist and encourage individual development.

It's also explained that there is no fixed or absolute limit to this process, because "They" (the Star People) cannot define a single outcome. The probabilities diverge too widely. They've created statistical projections regarding potential directions for humanity, but no definitive endpoint can be determined, since each individual's choices and development shape the outcome. The current setup is a temporary structure, created to observe humanity's evolution and to draw meaningful conclusions.

The dominant and secondary timelines exist with the purpose of encouraging and uplifting all souls. It becomes clear that every story, every news event, every piece of history is true, but it's up to you to discern whether or not it belongs to your personal reality. If something doesn't resonate with your experience, you must recognize that it may belong to another individual's or collective's timeline.

In essence, everything is real, but reality itself is multifaceted. In the same space and at the same time, the dominant timeline might hold peace and stillness, while in a secondary timeline, a tragedy unfolds.

Both experiences are true, depending solely on whose reality they belong to.

The New Souls, the New Generations of Souls

Q: Regarding the new souls that will come to Earth, do they still reincarnate for karma or is there more to learn about this here?
A: Karma no longer exists, even now, on this plane. I see karma written in

capital letters and a boundary, a barrier. Karma refers to the lower plane of creation.

I ask those Beings of Light who are present and have access to such information, if it is for our highest good to know, please transmit the answer. Thank you.

A gentle, tiny voice comes to me and says, "*There is no karma for new babies.*" They are new energy, new fluctuations of the new flow. I see souls coming around the planet, swirling around it, and then the circle doesn't close but continues.

Q: Is this Quantum Field only referring to the next temporary generations? Or all future generations?
A: All future generations, new souls, arrive, impact the planet's transformation, and then move on. Picture the planet as a point of convergence, where souls come together much like a school of fish gliding in unison through water. Similarly, a wave of new souls approaches the Earth, surrounds it, and eventually moves on.

Many of these new souls will be arriving. What's particularly striking is that this flow is shown only along the equator, moving from east to west. The flow begins roughly in the east at the equatorial line, this is where the new souls "land" or begin their entry.

From there, they circle the Earth along a wide, dense band around the equator, eventually returning back toward the east. However, they do not return to the exact starting point. There remains a space left empty, still within the east, over the ocean, where this generation of new children will not reach.

The movement is clear: from east to west, encircling the globe along the equator, and then moving on, leaving behind both their influence and that untouched space.

Q: What does it mean from "east to west" and only at the equator?
A: The magnetic field of the Earth has shifted, and now the equator holds something different, an electrical quality. I can sense this change as a tingling sensation on the right side of my brain. The electric field at the equator is now stronger, and as a result, it intensifies and activates the right hemisphere of the brain.

67

This rising electric field at the equator creates a unique condition, one where new souls can either arrive or remain in that zone, specifically where the electric field is stronger than the magnetic one. These souls, being more attuned to or present within the electric field rather than the magnetic, carry an energetic signature that enables them to act as conduits. Their electrical predominance allows them to channel and anchor energies from beyond the planet, bringing in information and technologies essential for collective human evolution.

Importantly, this energetic alignment also serves a protective purpose. It enables these new souls to remain unaffected by the planet's density, allowing them to fulfill their roles without becoming entangled in the heavier aspects of Earth's energy.

Q: What does "electric" mean?
A: The feminine energy, wait... there's something happening. It feels like they're trying to search through my memory and knowledge. This feminine magnetism, combined with electric energy, is now showing up on the masculine side. I feel a sting on the right side, which corresponds to masculine energy.

Interestingly, the right side of the brain is associated with imagination and artistic creation. Maybe this energy is trying to activate those qualities, creation, and imagination, within the masculine side. That might be the message being conveyed.

In a way, we as women already have this aspect naturally activated, but men don't tend to experience it in the same way. However, men who are coming in with a strong masculine energy will begin to have this activation as well. It will open up their perception, allowing them to see and access more than before.

Q: Will there be some changes here?
A: Yes, I can still feel that there is chaos present. My teeth begin to hurt, and I believe it's connected to this shift, this wave of anger. There's a realization that many people are angry, resisting the changes because they don't want too much to shift too quickly. Yet, despite this resistance, the world needs these changes. They are necessary for progress, even if they stir discomfort or pain. Thank you.

Types of Soul Families

Q: Let's ask about the types of soul families. How many types of families are there, and what is the difference between them?
A: The number 12 comes to me, I set it aside, and 12 still comes back.

1. The family of origin. It does not refer to the soul family and has nothing to do with that. The family of origin is the point where it all begins, from the origin. We have a family group there. If you remember, consciousness is assigned (see below), and that's what this refers to. This is the origin group of your consciousness. It's not referring to the body or anything you can imagine. It exists, but it is the conscious matter attached to this origin group.

Assigned consciousness represents a form of individualized consciousness, attributed to each being or non-being in a specific location, not at a planetary level, but at a precise point in space or reality. This consciousness is distinct from the primary consciousness, the creation of God, and is part of a broader system through which each soul lives its own experiences. Assigned consciousness functions as an extension of the soul in that area of existence, being supported by Beings of Light, spiritual guides, or the Higher Self, who intervene to maintain energetic balance and guide spiritual evolution when blockages or deviations from the chosen path of growth occur. I will explain more about this concept in the next subchapter.

Q: Can they support us or have direct intervention with us?
A: No. And actually, it is not essential for us to be close to each other. Here is only the origin from which you come from, from which class. Your point of origin does not interact with you.

2. Spirit family. They appear like small flames spinning around, forming something that looks like a flower made of fire, yet there's nothing at the center. It's a flower of flames, composed of eight flame-like petals in total. At the center lies what is considered an empty vortex, but the motion seems to come from outside inward. The petals of flame remain around the outer edge, while the central space stays empty, holding only the vortex's presence. The shape and formation closely resemble daffodils.

Q: What is the role of these families in relation to us?
A: Their purpose is to guide the energy of the flame within each of us, but each petal, each flame, is a multitude, a unit formed from the multitude of your original family. It's as if it multiplied and then formed a new flame. The spirit family is an extension of the original family.

> **3. Soul family.** Here, the soul family is formed as a fusion between the original spirit family and external elements, specifically, external particles that have drawn in other spiritual flames, or spirit families, that resonated with the original one. When this resonance occurs with the original flame, the spirit family, it appears with red and gold along its edges. As it begins to resonate with others around it, I'm shown an image of a flower releasing pollen. But instead of actual pollen, it spreads molecules or particles into the universe automatically. Other spirit families that vibrate at the same frequency recognize themselves in these dispersed particles and are naturally drawn in. When they connect, they come together to form something larger and more complex.

Out of this energetic connection, a new collective is created, this is the *soul family*, a blend of multiple spirit families that have come into resonance and bonded together.

> **4. Oversoul family.** Here it shows me that the oversoul is something that does not come from anyone else but is an intervention from the Creator, who created other beings that don't fit into the original family, the spirit family, or the soul family. These are created beings; I see them as tall. It's like a capsule of light in which the oversoul is placed, and inside this capsule, it is allowed to build its own vortex, a string, similar to how our DNA is formed inside.

> **5. Galactic family.** Many different creatures. Here is another capsule, but it is not white, it is transparent. Inside it, there are various creatures coexisting, like a zoo, with a mix of races, beings, creations - anything you want.

> **6. Spiritual team. The family of spiritual guides.** This type of spiritual family is formed by voluntary choice, based on various mutual agreements. If both sides are in alignment and wish to continue,

a guide can remain part of your spiritual family of support and guidance. In this space, roles are fluid and can evolve.

For instance, if you once had a spiritual guide who helped you through a phase, and you later return to express gratitude, that exchange of support deepens the connection. If both of you enjoyed the experience of working together, you can choose to continue collaborating. Over time, if there is mutual agreement, you may one day voluntarily decide to become part of the same spiritual family.

7. The family of intergalactic connections. I see a device spinning like a radar, with one half of its form being more rounded. It appears as a large, luminous presence, representing a type of family. I also see antennae, similar to those found on old news broadcasting devices, that's the kind of technology or structure it resembles. I'm trying to understand its nature, and it becomes clear that it's connected to sound and frequency. This vision doesn't refer to Beings of Light, but rather to a family of frequencies, of sound waves. They are not physical bodies, but a collective or family of various waveforms, each carrying a distinct frequency that your own soul or family resonates with.

Q: How would you like them to be named in our reality?
A: Radio frequency sound family. If we were to name it using our words, that's how it would sound, but it is composed of frequency and sounds. Each of us is attached to certain sounds and frequencies that allow us to be connected. We connect not only by being spirit, guide, or soul, but with the help of this type of family, we can connect specifically to our tribe, our family.

> **GI MI KA TU - Soul.** They appear in pairs of two, making a total of eight. Do you know what this represents? This is the Soul, everything that we contain and express at the level of the soul itself. The soul family was an extension that included external elements, but this, this is the core Soul. From four yellow spheres, each split in half, emerge eight parts. This seems to point toward the concept of the twin flame.

But then the question arises: Why are there four spheres, and not twelve?

The answer reveals itself. What we understand about the twin flame is actually located at the level of the Oversoul. There, a spiral takes form, shaped like a white light capsule. Within this capsule is something like a laboratory, and this is the place where the twin flame is created. It is formed within the laboratory inside the Oversoul. This process originates from the soul family, where external elements are blended with the original source, creating the foundation from which the twin flame eventually emerges.

9. The Star Family. I see inside, within a sphere, in the shape of an egg, many families, collectives that coexist within it.

The difference between the **star family** and the **galactic family** is that the galactic family is more diverse, with many different ET races that have mixed together. Like a zoo, where you have various animals, beings, and creations of all kinds.

The **star family** is more "pure," metaphorically speaking, because it consists of evolved races. Here, I see a lot of light, harmony, and each group is its own unique race, already evolved in its own way. The **galactic** is more raw, more unfiltered.

The **star family** refers to the dominant races, to the experiences you've had in your existences, depending on the races, where you evolved as a soul, based on the collective you were part of.

10. Molecule family. It's like a wall of different elements has risen in front of me. We don't just co-exist on the level of a formed body, but our consciousness exists in a unique form of matter from which it's created.

Let me give you an example: imagine you have a liver. But the liver itself is made up of thousands upon thousands of particles and molecules, and each of these particles is alive, each with its own universe. From the liver's perspective, this entire structure is a universe, and for the beings, the particles and molecules, that work together to form the organ, the liver is their world, their reality, even their God.

But if we zoom out and look from the human perspective, we see it simply as an internal organ, just one part of the physical body.

In the same way, each organ is its own universe, inhabited by countless molecules that function and collaborate every single day. Just as we go to work daily, these particles are also engaged in their tasks. It's a form of co-existence, where we too are, at another level, molecules, particles, and we belong to molecular families.

11. The "colelular" family. This is connected to colors; we are each part of a specific color spectrum. Every individual belongs to a certain range within that spectrum.

From this perspective, if we analyze ourselves individually, we might say, for instance: someone has a dominant Lemurian and Lyran lineage. In the same way, each soul also belongs to a specific color spectrum family.

Not every soul can embody or exist within the entire spectrum of colors. Instead, you choose the color of your team - that's exactly how it works. Each being carries their own unique spectrum of colors, defining their essence, role, and resonance.

12. DUBPONEDB. I see the image, but then it shifts. When I look straight ahead, it appears as if someone is standing in profile, but not as a solid form. It looks like a Flame, not literal fire, but a flame-like presence that burns upward. As I try to move or interact with it, the image changes again. A waterfall begins to flow upward, and I still don't fully understand what I'm seeing. There's a strange inversion, the flame burns downward, while at the same time, the waterfall rises upward.

Victoria: Quantum Field, please remove my human filter so I can perceive the information as easily and clearly as possible.

This is something advanced. I don't think we have knowledge of such a thing. It feels like something atomic, some kind of radiation, something we don't yet understand.

Flammable radio, atomic flammable, but it tells me that we don't know it. It shows me something like a flame, but it's not a flame; it feels like information and technology combined in one. It's active, radioactive, but from another perspective. It's not related to the kind of radioactivity we know. Scientists don't know about it. It has a consistency we don't recognize. We cannot perceive it because it doesn't yet belong to our world. There is something radioactive that has no radiation, it's extremely powerful and intense. Thank you.

The Primary Consciousness

During my meditation, I visited again a place I used to see back in 2021. Back then it was too advanced for me to be able to perceive it. In that place, I had blurry vision - about 95% of what I perceived was through the third eye.

I could only see the shadow of the images, and next to me was a Being of Light who told me she was my twin flame.

In the last two days toward the end of 2024, that place kept coming back to my mind. Today, my twin flame was just a projection of her (she spoke with a robotic girl's voice). That's when I received information about consciousness. Our consciousness actually has an attached origin, meaning it is assigned.

The primary consciousness is God's creation, but besides this primary consciousness, each being and non-being has its consciousness assigned to a certain place. Not at a planetary level but at a place.

When our energy level begins to drop below average, the "deprivation mode" of the energetic level begins to activate. Thus, Beings of Light, the Higher Self, the spirit guides or any being that is in our field for our supreme good, comes to our aid and helps us readjust automatically. Our energy level decreases when we choose various states, emotions or situations that we need to experience in order to evolve at a higher level. However, when we get stuck in those patterns and situations, our spiritual team intervenes to help us find a way out of those situations and overcome those blockages. This does not mean we do not continue to experience those situations, but only offers us exit directions, or guidance so that we do not remain permanently stuck in less pleasant situations.

Through their intervention, Beings of Light extract consciousness from our brain, and bring it back to the level of the heart, to help us have a higher perspective of the dynamics we experience. When our consciousness remains stuck in the mind, a distortion is created, and we fall into the trap of logic and its game.

Consciousness: Protection Mantra – Shower – Portal – Heart chakra (grounding)

Q: What is keeping me stuck in analysis?
A: I get: "Your life is too short to be a human being. And you're wasting your time in your left brain. Focus on the good and stop fighting."

Q: How could I make my day-to-day life easier?
A: I get "go with the flow."
I saw a being who had an axe, and on the left side there was a big concrete slab. A "soldier" came and hit the concrete slab with the axe, and it completely broke in two.

Victoria: I got that is the Matrix, but for what exactly? I'm waiting to understand.
Diana: I got the Matrix right away.

Q: What do the Matrix and the concrete mean?
A: At the moment it doesn't make sense to me.
Oh, it's like hitting it, like breaking a beehive, and inside there is honey. There is too much light there and it's like putting down the axe and the axe dissolves (metaphorically speaking).

Q: What connection does this have with me?
A: Again, it hurts me on the left side. It shows me that the Matrix is pressing me on the left side, in logic, that's where I stay. I need to focus on the "honey" inside, where there is light.

Q: How could I do that day by day?
A: I get that it's good to take a shower with a mantra.

Q: What does the shower have to do with the mantra?

Diana: To say the mantra in the shower?

A: That's how I see it, you're under the shower, water is flowing, and you say the mantra while the water flows.

Q: What is the mantra?

A: EIKTU EIKTU EIKTU
TAMARIO O TI A
AMA A MA
EIKTU EIKTU EIKTU
TAMARIO O TI A
AMA A MA
EIKTU EIKTU EIKTU
TAMARIO O TI A
AMA A MA

While we say this mantra, we have noticed that pyramids form in the water, in the air in front of us, and the water allows them to fly around us. These pyramids are like shiny glitter; they are in flux, in motion. We don't see them, but they are around us when we say the mantra. Water is a conductor for the frequency of these words.

I feel like saying it three times; if it's easy to remember, we can say it more times. If it's harder, we can say it at least three times.

Initially, these triangles are small, but as you repeat, they grow in volume. They open our bodies, they have different portals, doors; they are like temple doors. Our body is a temple, which has round doors. These portals are not how we imagine a light portal, but imagine a rock, a polished stone, a perfect portal that is made of stone.

It is not made of light, it is not fluid, but it is like stone, like a monument. In our throat, at the level of the thyroid gland, exactly there, is this portal, solid like a wall, like concrete, and it is just as round inside. There, these triangles open the portal, like a gate, and when it is open, they can enter our body. When they enter our body, they form the very portal between the throat chakra and our whole body, especially the lower chakras.

Q: My question is, what do we need this for? How does it help us?
A: Our bodies are actually like vessels, in which you can reach a high level of evolution, where our consciousness has the ability to detach from the physical body.

Example: Picture a vessel, like a rocket, that can detach various components as it travels through space. Our human body operates in much the same way, in alignment with our consciousness.

The body is built like a machine, designed to release or separate different parts from the "vehicle", that is, the physical form. This detachment happens energetically. This is exactly why the heart is positioned at the center of the chakra system, from chakra 4 out of the 7 main chakras. If the heart were instead located in the "cockpit" of the vehicle, above the throat chakra, we would be able to fully "lift off" from this reality, making it impossible to function or exist as a human being.

The heart chakra is what keeps us anchored to physical existence on Earth. It grounds us here, while at the same time keeping us connected to the source, the Creator. Thank you.

Kundalini

Q: Is it beneficial for us as humanity to know what Kundalini energy is, or how it can support our spiritual evolution?
A: I see a gigantic serpent rising from the earth, and I see it from behind, from the spine. I see it moving forward. It comes to me that in our reality it is something "must have it," being here, present, on Earth.

Q: And how can it support our spiritual evolution?
A: This energy actually represents knowledge. Knowledge rooted and encoded in the Earth, which rises to the surface, and that's exactly what grounding with the Earth is. In a way, it is important for our creation, for the planet, because it connects you with the energy or memory of the Earth and everything that exists here. It comes from the inside out.

Q: And when it gets activated, does it mean it activates various pieces of knowledge we need in our DNA?

A: I don't know how I grabbed this serpent, because it turned and came toward me, facing me, and I grabbed it by the neck. It tells me that, in fact, we can have control over the Kundalini energy. Kundalini energy itself has a tendency to go beyond the limit of being handled, guided, or directed. When it goes beyond that limit, and you don't control it, it actually attacks you. It wanted to attack me, but I grabbed it by the neck because I am in control of its energy.

Q: When do you know it goes beyond limits?

A: It comes to me that when you call it, it rises from the Earth calmly, it doesn't harm you. But if too much of it rises from the Earth, it fills the entire space of your physical body, and then it becomes uncomfortable. It seeks to attack you because it wants to go further. When you call it, it comes. You receive knowledge or whatever you need; you receive codes, because that's its purpose. But if you don't direct the process, the situation slips out of your hands and then, what comes to me is, you shouldn't be surprised if this energy causes you an irreversible process, and attacks your physical body itself, metaphorically speaking, energetically. This energy comes from the Earth, and if you call it too much, without knowing how to handle it, it will have no space in your body. When your body is full of Kundalini energy, your body may automatically "error out" in terms of operation/function. You get sick, because the energy wants to get out of you. That's why it's not advisable to activate it constantly or to keep calling this energy.

The most beneficial way is for it to activate on its own, because that way you will always have control over the Kundalini energy, not the other way around. Modern thinking and trends believe the opposite is beneficial, but in that way, the Kundalini energy controls you or has power over you. You are the one who should have control over it. Thank you.

Capsule - Implant for the Liquidation of the Physical Body

In another session exploring certain questions and dynamics in my life, I received information about an implant that we, as human beings, have at the level of the head, an implant that activates when the soul decides to leave the physical body. This implant can be activated naturally, when the soul has fulfilled its purpose or completed the experiences it set out to have in the physical body. However, there are also situations where this implant is activated involuntarily, through decisions to leave this plane before the time originally agreed upon in the soul's astral plans.

I see an implant in the right temple in the back of the head inside of a container. I see how they removed that implant from my spine, but I feel pain in the right temple, under the skin. What the Beings of Light removed was just the projection, but I can still see this implant that contains all my anger, everything I feel, it is all accumulated in this capsule.

I now see myself reacting in many situations, for example, when I'm angry, I see myself moving in that anger, in denial, in control, I scream, shout, cry, hate. All of it is in this transparent implant. I now see inside the implant, my whole life lived on the negative polarity. They placed the capsule in front of me so I could see it, but the implant is still inside.

Beings from the 12th dimension are needed to extract this implant. I'm receiving the information that this implant was formed in the year 2020, when I activated the annihilation program. That's when this implant was also activated. It activates in each of us when there are very deep feelings of wanting to leave the physical plane, feelings that go beyond our sensory limits, when we cross the boundary of the permission to continue living. I crossed that boundary when I wanted to exit, to annihilate my body, and the implant was activated automatically.

All people have such implants. Each body is created with this kind of device, this kind of capsule, in the right temple, and when someone wants to fully give up, from their whole emotional being and all energetic structures, the implant automatically activates. Otherwise, it remains inactive, as long as you don't trigger it.

Release is possible only with the help of beings or energies from the 12th dimension. I only feel their presence now. They don't allow me to see what they look like, but I sense they came from the right side. I feel their hands. I see how they tilted my head slightly to the left, and the shadow of my physical body remained. Only the energetic version of my physical body remained in its physical form.

To remove this implant from the temple, they need to clear the space. The implant is positioned between the physical body and the energetic body, between the wall of the two subtle bodies, and it only activates when the person is ready to leave the physical plane, when the body is to be annihilated.

Now I see it spinning, like a wheel, from left to right. They placed an energetic string in the center, and the implant spins around it. It needs to fall along the axis of that energetic string. The Beings of Light are slowly removing it. The implant spins in the air but around that central string.

Now they are going to place another one back in, but empty. Every person needs to have such an implant or capsule in the body. Done, they placed a new transparent capsule. This is like a memory capsule for the feelings and all the emotions that were released.

Wait, they need to adjust my body to integrate it with the physical body. It's like they need to make a click, to seal it. Done. They've integrated the new one and removed the old one. Done, I feel calmer now. I've calmed down inside. Thank you.

Changing the Perspective

One day, the Beings of Light offered me an awareness of how we humans sometimes remain attached to the perspectives we consider to be absolute truth. Being in that attachment, it becomes more difficult for us to change our perspective and see everything from a different angle. And yet, sometimes it can be meaningful to detach from everything we consider to be true and try to see things from a new, higher perspective. Here's a simple explanation of this concept.

Imagine you're in a boat.

Being in that boat, you could be on a river, a lake, the sea, or the vast ocean. From the surface, it all looks like water, but what's beneath changes drastically depending on where you are. The knowledge and experience you have from being on a river won't apply in the same way when you're in the ocean.

To navigate the ocean, you must understand the laws of the ocean. It's similar to being part of a particular religion.

Then someone from a different religion approaches you and claims they are right, just as you believe you are right.

But neither side is willing to step back and view things from another angle. In reality, it's the same God, simply seen through different parameters or lenses.

Yet, you won't accept techniques or teachings that feel "foreign," because they don't align with your current understanding.

And from your perspective, they can't be understood ... at least not yet. That's why they don't naturally come to you, and instead, you try to force them into your own framework, expecting them to make sense only through the lens of your own religion.

The Overlapping of Dimensional Realities

How is it possible for a group of people to be together in the same physical space, yet one person within that group may not exist in the perceptual sequence or reality of another individual? That person, while present to others, may simply not appear in someone else's internal timeline or awareness. All of this unfolds at the same time, in the same place. It's as if within a collective unit, the "molecules" or subtle energetic structures of individuals behave independently of the collective rhythm. This divergence creates different layers of experience within the same shared reality.

Let me give you an example: Imagine you are the black sheep in a flock of white sheep.

You are there, part of the same flock, but perhaps you cannot perceive one or more of the white sheep around you, or they cannot perceive you.

It's not a matter of absence in the physical sense, but a lack of alignment within perceptual timelines.

From this, we see that the black sheep represents an individual with the potential to shift a single "molecule" of the entire flock toward another extreme, a different energetic or perceptual state. This shift doesn't happen instantly. It's sudden in realization, yet long in unfolding, stretching across multiple layers of space and awareness.

From this **theory of overlapping realities and conscious timelines**, inspired by metaphysical interpretations of quantum physics, we understand that the collective often follows a dominant dimensional timeline, a shared reality perceived by the majority. However, a subtle element, the black sheep, introduces an alternate, overlapping reality that quietly coexists with the dominant field.

This mirrors concepts in quantum thought, such as **the Many-Worlds Interpretation**, which proposes that multiple realities exist simultaneously, branching off based on observation and choice. Similarly, **David Bohm's idea of the implicate order** suggests that what we perceive as separation or difference is actually an expression of deeper, unseen connections in a unified field. In this context, perception itself becomes a kind of quantum filter, selecting what appears in one's personal "sequence" of reality.

So, while many may walk side by side at the same moment, their internal timelines may differ. And it is the unique vibration of the outlier, the black sheep, that opens the door to a parallel unfolding of reality, one that quietly redefines the collective from within.

Understanding the Double Timeline Shift - Channeling

The concept of a double timeline shift suggests a profound energetic transition where an individual's connection to their past reality begins to dissolve. This process involves a fading of the older timeline, where both the physical and energetic imprints of the individual are no longer deeply tethered to their previous environment. Instead, the individual's energy integrates more fully into a new timeline.

In real life, this might manifest as feelings of detachment or emptiness in places once deeply connected to the individual. The spaces may no longer carry the vibrational resonance of their presence. This energetic shift acts as a mechanism for facilitating growth, allowing the individual to align with a fresh environment, relationships, and events more suited to their current vibrational state.

The speed at which this transition occurs could vary depending on the individual's alignment and readiness to embrace their new reality. It's an energetic migration that bridges the gap between the past and the potential future, offering the individual a chance to consciously participate in the co-creation of their desired life path.

Thank you, Thank you, Thank you.

Channeled by Victoria Basil
December 17, 2024

Union with the Divine Feminine – Cellular Changes at the Level of Feminine DNA

Session: Diana & Victoria & Imaya – Council of the Alliance of Spheres – March 16, 2025

Victoria: The activation of the X chromosome - that happened for all of us during the meditation. The activation of the feminine energy. This is what happened while Imaya was guiding the meditation. In space, it felt like a kind of technology arrived. Imagine a flower you place with the stems pointing upward, which creates a sort of field, a capsule, an energetic space, and around this space there are many facets, many pillars, but not pillars as we usually imagine them; these are pillars of advanced technology. Then the pillars were lowered, and they created a round field, a bubble, a space.

Now, we are arranged like a triangle, like a pyramid positioned horizontally. The sharp tips point south, east, and west. I am in the south, Imaya is in the east, Diana is in the west. We are now positioned, placed on something like a couch or lounge chair, and many Beings of Light started to come, very many beings, including the Galactic Council, who made their presence known. There are three members - the most important one stands in the middle, and the other two are positioned on the sides.

Around them, on my side next to Diana, on the west side, came the beings from Agartha, the Ant beings. Between Diana and me, on the left side, came Dolphins beings, and on the right, between Imaya and me, there is a pink light, very different from my own energy; it is delicate, fragile. I see many Beings of Light.

Now, each of us, as we were seated, were infused into the walls of this field, and when they placed us back, I felt like I was in a fluid, gelatinous space - it's like a substance. Now, each of us is inside an individual crystalline pyramid. Above our pyramid is a six-pointed star. In the center, as we are positioned in the shape of a triangle, in front of us, a table was created, like another round space, a floating energy. In the center of this space, another six-pointed star appeared - but this star moves, it's flexible. The star creates the impression that it has 12 points, but actually, it has six points and moves in harmony with our stars. It will continuously connect through the three of us and will transmit the messages we receive from the beings present with us today.

I forgot to mention that, meanwhile, they took out a cable from our backs which represents the disconnection of the mind. Our filter will always be present, but it is less obvious today.

Imaya: I was sensing the beings you were talking about, and regarding that gelatinous field, I felt a cold current, and before that, I heard various sounds, like a spinning pinwheel or something.
Victoria: That's how the technology creating the field was spinning above us.
Imaya: I perceive myself as something long, a long line, that's how I feel.
Victoria: I perceive myself as a bird, and I have a beak. It's the first time I perceive myself this way.
Imaya: I don't have a body.
Victoria: You are just light.
Imaya: I feel like I am both.

Victoria: I definitely feel like a bird because I see you both differently. It's interesting, like how a bird sees thousands and thousands of kilometers away.

Imaya: What's coming to me now is that we are connecting with aspects from dimensions we have, and right now we are taking personal aspects from there.

Victoria: I never knew I was part of such beings.

Diana: But how do you see me?

Victoria: Let me look at you. I'm a little shocked at myself because I've never seen myself as a bird. I just see my beak.

Imaya: I look at you, I feel you are to my left, and I see you sometimes as a fairy, sometimes as something else.

Victoria: Yes, I see the sun, little flowers.

Imaya: It's like you're changing these gases from the stars, that's exactly how I see you. Now you're a fairy, now a star.

Victoria: But I saw a delicate, fragile fairy with little flowers.

Imaya: You probably have many sources, many aspects.

We are multidimensional beings. Our soul embodies various aspects, including in other timelines, spaces, dimensions, planets, galaxies, and solar systems. In this physical plane, we are human beings, but our soul holds many other frequencies and aspects, including those of ET beings or extraterrestrial civilizations.

Victoria: How are you feeling?

Diana: I don't perceive what you see.

Victoria: Take your consciousness and shove it down your throat.

Imaya: I felt like telling you to put your right hand on your forehead. There are some memories, like "I can't," "I don't receive."

Victoria: Diana's non-acceptance that she doesn't believe she can be that. You're not accepting something.

Diana: I don't accept that I can see.

Victoria: Your non-acceptance lies at the back of your neck. Now focus your consciousness into your neck and pull acceptance, like a rope, from behind into your throat. Oh, that's good, this is called integration. Done. See how you perceive yourself now, but keep your hand on your forehead, as Imaya said.

Imaya: I now see you as tall, very tall, like 2–3 meters, and you're white, and around your head is a flower.

Victoria: Yes, I perceive a little flower.

Imaya: There are some beings with arms and legs like us, but instead of a head, there's a huge flower.

Victoria: All your frustration, all that you don't accept, is in your teeth because my teeth hurt a lot.

Diana: Yes, I feel it in my jaw, up to my temples.

Imaya: There's control there, and rigidity, an inner child aspect. I see your human structure, you've opened up, and I see that little girl saying, "I can't."

Diana: I want to fully release everything that no longer serves me, even from my subconscious.

Imaya: Now a being of fire appeared, green, yellow. I also feel it like a pillar of light, but it's not straight, it has different structures.

Victoria: Do you know who this being is? This is the assignment of a new guide. The old guide has been replaced.

Diana: Why? Is there a reason?

Victoria: With every deep release or dissolution, when it no longer resonates with your new needs, the guide that was present at that time must release the space, and through free will, the guide responsible for... the word "old sabotage" comes to me... is released. Another one comes depending on the requirements you now have.

Imaya: From its structure, its entire being, fairies have wings, but this one is sparks of fire, green to golden yellow, and I see them all around you, some going from right to left, others from left to right, and you are in a flow of green and golden light.

Victoria: How lovely. I feel that in today's session you've made a connection where you assist each other, and you, Diana, needed help and Imaya's assistance. I'm in another space.

Imaya Now I see at your heart, Diana, they're building some sort of technology that creates circuits, at the heart, the throat, from the throat to the third eye, from the third eye to the heart, and I feel like saying: everything you feel, you can speak, and you can see.

Victoria: Interesting technology.

Imaya: It's showing me a screen being calibrated. Sometimes it's round, sometimes oval, sometimes rectangular, probably calibrating your third eye.

Victoria: It's connecting it more deeply with the heart.

Imaya: I see the color violet on that screen.

Victoria: I see yellow. Interesting how we each see differently.

Imaya: Yes, it's like the colors are shifting.

Victoria: I see a standard yellow, more exactly in the heart.

Imaya: I see violet, then light blue, pink, then magenta.

Victoria: Now a lot of density is being extracted from your head.

Diana: I feel it.

Imaya: I see this green being has attached itself to your back, and I feel warmth in my body, like I'm stuck to a stove. This being is taking everything metallic from you, and I hear something like shards sticking together.

Victoria: This new guide is very powerful.

Diana: When we integrate certain aspects and move more towards evolution or ascension, can the guide change? I mean, do we have guides that accompany us for a period and then they're replaced?

Victoria: Yes, at your acceptance.

Imaya: I agree with that, I actually studied it recently, and yes, it's possible. What I receive is that within our human structure, we contain many guides. I'm getting the information that this guide contains within it a large family of other beings with whom you, Diana, will work.

Victoria: I now see that your thoughts and your head, your nose, your sinuses, are all being cleared of stagnant energies, all the densities, like little bugs. A lot is being released. Your new guide is cleaning everything. He can't help you until he removes it all. He can't collaborate with you until he clears what doesn't resonate with him.

Imaya: When you said what's being released, I can't see it, but I feel it's at the frequency level and I heard a deeper sound, like electricity, like scanning.

Victoria: You hear their frequency, I see them. They're like microscopic microbes, very many white ones, like spiders, white bugs being cleaned. There's something in the heart. Worms, but very tiny and newly formed. Everything is being cleaned, extracted from the blood, from the heart, and will exit naturally from the body.

Imaya: I don't know if it's related, but I was waking up from the need to go to the bathroom and felt like I was purifying, and afterward, the information flowed.

Victoria: Your guide will implement in your structures, as Imaya saw it at the back. He envelops you with all his energy in waves, and the more he embraces you within his structure, the more density is released from your physical and energetic body. As he embraces you, you'll synchronize with the same energy, and then you'll start to see differently. You've already allowed yourself to see, you just needed to change the guide. Before I was on this path, I read in a book once that we have free will to ask for spiritual guides, the angels we want to work with. If they're not in our best interest, we can change them. I did it, years ago. I wanted to test it, and see if it works, and it did! Sometimes when you feel stuck in life you've got to try, it's really important.

Imaya: I now see what's happening there. I see, not a humanoid being, but like a pillar, like a technology with a green-golden and pearly white essence.

When you said "embracing," I felt the connection between you and this being, as if you're in a round tunnel, being enveloped through waves ... very interesting.

Victoria: Yes, you're seeing it correctly. It's not with hands; it envelops you through waves.

Imaya: It infuses you with frequency. Every time we receive a new guide, we are positioned on a new path, a new job, and I feel that it is creating a connection with you. You'll receive confirmations; you'll even start to see him. Now it shows me the focus is shifting to the right, probably to you, Victoria.

Victoria: I now see myself as Pleiadian.

Imaya: I see that a circle has formed where we are contemplating the information, and the circle, at its base, has a Caesar crown, you know, those two little branches of...

Diana: ...of laurel, I think.

Imaya: A sphere has been created with structures like daisies up to the base of this very large crown, and I see how each triangle we are in, simply penetrates it. It's a plasmatic, gelatinous structure.

Victoria: A portal has been created. I don't understand anything.

Imaya: Inside, I see a rainbow.

Victoria: I don't understand where I am.

Diana: Victoria, you said you don't know where you are, do you see yourself differently from us?

Victoria: Accessing, accessing I don't know what. Databases, I don't understand.

Imaya: I'm getting that it's your evolution.

Victoria: There's a lot of information, I don't understand what I am. I see flashes that change and something else comes. It's too much, I can't perceive it yet.

Imaya: I'm being shown in this sphere that we are all here, and the angles of the triangles have created a triangle like in 5D.

Victoria: For me, it's 12D.

Imaya: They've created a triangle from our triangles, and in the sphere, I see a rainbow. It starts from the base-violet, blue, yellow, I see colors, and from the middle up, everything is white, but the colors are vivid, moving in waves.

Victoria: I don't understand what field I'm in.

Imaya: I'm getting "infinity."

Victoria: It's too much!

Imaya: Infinity octave. We are now observing everything that exists coded within these colors, and I'm being shown that the triangle is spinning, but codes are being transmitted to us. That's probably why you felt this part more intensely.

Victoria: I don't understand what it is.

Imaya: Codes of evolution.

Victoria: Why do I see squares?

Diana: I wanted to ask why you are there, what is the purpose or message?

Imaya: Regarding why we're not receiving the information, it's because information is already a more solid form than where you are now.

Victoria: I don't even understand what you're saying.

Diana: I feel you disconnected from us.

Victoria: You are not here.

Imaya: I'm being told that you're experiencing what unity means. Wow.

Victoria: This is the first time in my life.

Diana: And how does it help her to experience unity?

Imaya: I'm shown that on Earth, you are here for action. That's what you embody.

Victoria: I've now started to descend from those squares downward.

Imaya: I see you are very structured.

Diana: What I'm getting is that you needed to activate something in that space.

Imaya: For you it's very strange here on Earth to connect things. For you, it's either black or white, or pink, or yellow. I'm being shown a rainbow, but your rainbow isn't whole. You see it in the sky, you know it's Divine, but in your structure the information wants to classify as good or bad. Right or wrong, your action is extreme.

Victoria: That's exactly how I am. I actually understood that I needed to learn how to be in the middle.

Imaya: You had that experience where you felt like nothing, and it's asking you how it feels to be nothing.

Victoria: Honestly, it feels meaningless.

Imaya: I'm shown that in our perception it's limited to call it "nothing." In "nothing," everything exists. I'm being shown a planet, a hand. When you arrive on the planet, you touch a little flower and understand that the flower is part of everything. When you read a book, I'm shown various objects.

Victoria: I see myself descending and how there's more and more light. The square shapes are forming into rounder lines, a gentler form. Now I'm coming down a staircase, and the forms are more linear, and I feel gentler. I'm back in the same space with you. Thank you for such an experience.

Imaya: It says that for the structure and form of collectives, this is quite shocking, even traumatic, because when you go there, it seems like there's no meaning. Now, in this rainbow sphere, I'm starting to perceive the outlines of beings.

Diana: Has my process ended or not? Because I still feel like I'm constantly downloading energy.

Victoria: No, the answer is no. I see myself again as a bird. What's my connection to the Blue Avians?

Imaya: How interesting, a peacock feather just appeared to me.

Victoria: I saw one in the city yesterday.

Diana: What I'm getting is that it's an aspect you need to integrate.

Victoria: Interesting, but how does it help me if I integrate this existence?

Imaya: What I get again is unity.

Diana: How beautiful.

Imaya: **Unity.**

Victoria: I now see myself flying off this chair, and flying above your head, Imaya, and creating an infinity symbol.

Diana: That's beautiful.

Victoria: That's confirmation that what you're saying is true.

Imaya: I now see that a chair made of peacock feathers has formed. Diana and I are in those triangles, the triangles have taken the form of spheres, and it's being explained to me ... why spheres. Because my energy as an identity is related to spheres, and that's why we are in spherical bodies.

Victoria: Because you, Imaya, know that one of your energies is actually the sphere.

Imaya: Interesting that you're not in the spheres, but I see you seated on a chair made of peacock feathers.

Victoria: That's how I see myself, separate from you.

Diana: Why is Victoria separate from us?

Victoria: I see myself large, and flapping my wings, I can't sit still.

Imaya: Victoria, I see you with a very bushy tail, like a rooster.

Victoria: Even my personality is like that.

Imaya: From the beginning, when you saw yourself as a bird, I saw the tail, and I was wondering what it was.

Victoria: I don't feel calm.

Imaya: I now see you as a huge rooster, and the Avians say: "our creation in your dimensions, one of our codes on Earth, are birds." All types of birds. For us, roosters are very simple, ordinary, but for them it's a powerful, profound symbol. At higher levels, it holds a potential of information. I'm being shown metaphorically what the rooster does in the yard, he's the boss. What comes to me is *leader*.

Victoria: That's pretty much how my personality is.

Imaya: It's action, perseverance. For you, it's about results. I'm now being shown that around us there are beings, Blue Avians as well, but different. Some Avians are slightly humanoid with a beak-like face, but they resemble us.

Victoria: My cheeks feel weird.

Imaya: I'm being shown different birds, something white, an eagle, but it's like a bird with a white hummingbird beak, though its image resembles an eagle.

Victoria: What's my connection to the hummingbird?

Imaya: What I get is that we called you here. To contemplate and remember our experiences with all kinds of birds.

Diana: I've had them.

Imaya: Me too. I've only experienced hummingbirds in dreams, but birds are everywhere. Pigeons crashing into windows. Now, as we speak, they're smiling because we humans really love words.

Diana: They want to transmit something now.

Imaya: Yes, I have a feeling we're wasting time.

Victoria: Yes, it comes to me that you've veered off. Someone came around me and adjusted a lens that sits outside the face of the head. It brought me back.

Diana: Then let's focus on our intention for today. We ask the Avians to transmit the necessary information.

Imaya: What came to me from the beginning is that we went off track, but at the same time I felt a great love, like "look what human creation does", as if it's normal that we go back into history. Then I got that they are here for unity, and for them unity is not about idealization or separation.

Imaya: Regarding Victoria, humanity must receive the message that we, the Avians, have returned. What does "returned" mean? The truth is that we never actually left. We've simply been observing everything happening in our space, in the space you're in, and not just you. We want to present ourselves once again. Why "once again"? Because this book of Victoria's has the purpose to present the works of light, or the members of this project.

Imaya: What does *our return* mean? We've only been watching, because until now we did not have bodies, humans had not yet evolved to the level of unity. But that is starting to happen. Very few people manage to embody unity within themselves.

Imaya: Unity is not about extremes. **Unity is about accepting and integrating.** I can accept what I see without integrating it. That would be like two people sitting at a table - they don't have to love the same things. You can be in the same frequency and still not like the same things. I can accept the other without integrating them into my cells, into the information I hold inside.

Imaya: That is unity, accepting the other and the other's choices. Not separating from these life forms, from these people, from this information. Can you imagine if your world were only white, if it contained only one single type of information? What would that be like?

Imaya: That's how humans understand unity. They think it's just white, just pink, just yellow. But unity is being able to see and feel information different from mine, and choosing what to do with it. I either accept it or I integrate it. What we integrate goes into the memory of our body. What we accept, we simply allow it to exist. That exists in the field I'm in.

Imaya: This is unity. Regarding Victoria's book, you must present us, our return. Many times, we've tried to send messages to your civilization that inspire unity. Unfortunately, humans are beings of exploration and evolution.

Imaya: We do not come to redeem or save. We come to inspire. To inspire toward unity. The truth is that humanity chooses what it does with the information, with concepts, with memories, with everything. We choose: do we integrate them into the unity of our body, or accept them into unity?

Imaya: But these things don't prevent a friendship, a relationship, or a society from writing and evolving on its path toward development and growth.

Imaya: I'm being shown that in the book, you must present them, show the agenda they come with. This will activate the souls that are already working with unity, even the Starseeds. But they are very few, you can count them. There aren't many because humanity couldn't contain more than that. These souls come to inspire, to bring wisdom to the world. But when wisdom enters our field, time is very dilated. What happens for them in two seconds takes hundreds of years for us to implement.

After it follows a channeling.

Channeling by Victoria (March, 2025)

"We thank the collective union. We will take, we ask you to take, a pause. Our presence, all of us here, is very important because this meeting marks the conclusion of this project. It is not only here that we are ending this common, united connection agreed upon by all members present in this space. We will return again, but with other future projects, soon, at the discretion of each of those present here.

I myself, alongside my members, from the Galactic Councils, want to mention that humanity has a rhetorical way of thinking, a rhetorical contemplation, in which your perception is very, very limited in your logical terms. The purpose of this project is very specifically known, and those present today are united by that human word you use, called ALLIANCE, through which they have given their mutual agreement to participate in this project.

The project was initiated two hundred years ago from this moment (2025), and it has been adjusted throughout these human years for the benefit of the current generations. Every person who came into this plane was strictly planned for the adjustment of your current timeline. Nothing is accidental, not even half a millisecond of presence in your unitary space, in the present of this universe.

We wish to bring an important message: this project will be guided until the completion of these events, approximately five months from now, during which it is necessary to finalize, materialize, and project for future generations, generations that will be based on these codifications. You call them information, yet some will be unperceived and will be structured at a sub-genetic level, where the X genome is transformed through the doubling of this chromosome, present in the new human being of creation, for whom time does not exist as it does for you, in your timeline.

We will now generalize the present message. We will close this structure of connection, and we thank you for the presence of all those gathered here."

Imaya: Yes, Victoria, when you started speaking, I felt like they were giving me light.
Victoria: Just a moment please, so I can disconnect them from my physical body. The energy is very intense.
Victoria: The space had expanded. I believe I was about a thousand times larger than you when they entered my physical body. They remained there for quite some time, undisturbed, because there was mutual respect among the members, to allow each member to speak. They stayed within me for

a solid five minutes, without interruption, until you finally allowed me to speak. In that moment, I grew like a giant, and now, I feel so small.

Diana: I wanted to ask about what they transmitted. They mentioned something about doubling the X chromosome, and you spoke so much, I don't know if they want to explain what it represents.

Victoria: While Imaya was speaking, I noticed something interesting, but I couldn't say anything because I was in a paused state. What I saw was the largest pyramid in Egypt, and during the exchange, I observed a shadow emerging from it. This shadow was actually the etheric body of the pyramid. It appeared blue in color and began to expand outward. As it extended, it seemed like something was about to connect with even more beyond it.

> *This transmission took place on March 16, 2025, and three days later, global news broke that the largest Pyramid on Earth, the "Pyramid of Giza," had been discovered along with an unknown megastructure detected beneath the pyramids of Giza. It contains 8 vertical pillars that descend 648 meters (2,000 feet) underground. This discovery shook the world, and the history of the pyramid will have to be rewritten based on new research. News from March 19, 2025*

Imaya: When you were talking about the X chromosome, it came to me that it's about the cellular activation of our civilization, as a collective. And when Diana asked now, I got that for this activation, our civilization needs to integrate into a double space, a timeline, into this feminine energy.

Victoria: I sense that the female genital organs are about to undergo a transformation. There will be a change in how they function on a structural level. I'm feeling a strong pressure in that area, and the message is coming through clearly and unmistakably.

Imaya: It's related to what I said, that, in fact, the woman separated, and now the woman will unite. I received information about the medicine of the rose. The woman has planted many seeds of separation in the collective, and she did this by giving birth to both girls and boys. The woman births civilization, and through the education she applies to children, she either separates or unites the next civilization of the Earth. Now, many women need to heal from shame, judgment, guilt, in order to receive seeds of light, and to plant them into the children she births, because those children, having those seeds of light in them, no matter where or what they do on Earth, will create light. This is the path of our cellular activation.

Victoria: In front of me is a dolphin, and while you speak, it is nodding with its nose. Yes, and it looks toward you, Imaya, and shows me that this is the truth.

Diana: After this activation, what will change at the level of the woman? The physical body, or energetically?

Imaya: It came to me related to the medicine of the rose, and I was wondering what that means, and it comes to me that Victoria carries the blue essence, and I looked up what that is, and I found that it's aligned with the memory of water and with the memories that need healing.

Victoria: Again, the dolphin came in front of you and is nodding with its fins, and spinning around. It's a confirmation.

Imaya: Then it came to me. I told you last year on March 20th, I had the experience with a fractal of white roses, and now it's transmitting to me that I contain the essence of the white rose, white is neutral, equal to all, it's that unconditional motherly love. Diana, you are the essence of the pink rose.

Victoria: I was just about to say that. That's why I saw you, Imaya, as white and Diana as pink, you're actually shifting in appearance based on the roles you're assigning to yourselves.

Imaya: It came to me, Diana, that you've actually succeeded, or you're in a process where you're uniting with your feminine energy, because the pink rose corresponds to uniting the masculine and feminine into one body, into a structure. I still haven't figured out the mystery of the roses.

Victoria: Can I say what's coming to me? Everything you just said again shows me the dolphins, and now they continue showing me that they have managed to create a sphere that contains consciousness in this circle. It's not big, but small, and it contains a lot of collective consciousness. The sphere spins around on a circular path, I've seen this somewhere before, and the dolphins are spinning in circles. However, it shows me that this is actually in Atlantis. In Atlantis, this space, the center of the city where Atlantis was built, was in the place I'm describing with the dolphins, and this sphere of consciousness contains information. Based on this sphere, the entire city of Atlantis was constructed, but Atlantis lost its essence, it veered off course, and this place is sacred, it is the central headquarters where there was a correlation, a connection with the Lemurians, Assyrians, and Syrians, who were like friends, a connection, a central point from which Atlantis developed. It developed based on the energy that was present - the Lemurian, Syrian, and Assyrian energy. The dolphins represent that union; they are the main guardians responsible for the sphere of consciousness. When they went astray, the place in the middle withdrew into the ground. It was sealed, and then Atlantis was destroyed. It wasn't Atlantis that created the central energetic space, but it was built on the basis of that central point.

Imaya: It shows me three dolphins holding a sphere with their noses, and explains to me what this means. This means that the dolphins were holding the seed, the wisdom, the cells that come into matter. I think what you said is related, that they were in these civilizations. These dolphins are those children, those bodies that bring that cell, that light, wisdom, into our civilization.

Victoria: My logical mind got lost, and I don't understand where it started and where it ended.

Imaya: After this project, we will be adjusted in frequencies, and we will have the potential to birth from this frequency.

Diana: How cute, thank you. I wanted to say that while you were speaking, I felt vibrations on my back.

Imaya: It shows me three dolphins, three women.

Victoria: Yes, they are actually females, not males. The dolphin in front of me was also female.

Imaya: It shows me that these three dolphins are us, but not us, rather cells within us that carry their essence. This sphere, or pearl, is that wisdom which is being laid down as information for us and for those who come after us, on a planetary level, not just for us.

Victoria: I now see an image of a uterus in front of me, but the uterus is transforming from this shape into a more triangular form. This is the physiological change in the genital organs.

Imaya: It tells me to observe our menstrual cycles, when they occur, what information surfaces about our identity histories, considering our current incarnation which mirrors ancestral, familial memories, what comes to the surface during menstruation. We will work with women to help them heal from shame, guilt, even the trauma of aborted children, rape. It shows me that we are the generation that feels, or pays with our life experience, for the choices made by the generations of women before us. We are here to see and release, both from ourselves and from the women we encounter.

Victoria: In fact, this is actually happening, there's a kind of robotic release occurring in the lower part of our body, from the belly down to the feet. It feels as though you're a robot, and the outer layer is being removed, stripped away, leaving only the internal structure, like wires or metal cables, exposed underneath.

Diana: It comes to me that we are returning to the pure feminine aspect.

Imaya: Yes, I hear, divine feminine.

Diana: We are merging, in fact.

Physiological Adjustment

Victoria: I want to explain how this will happen on a physiological level. Physically, the female reproductive organ is going to change. Once again, I'm being shown the image of a triangle. I keep trying to understand how the uterus, which has its usual shape, could transform into something more triangular and narrow. If a child is to grow inside it, then the development would have to occur within that triangular structure. Yet within it, the child would still form inside a sphere, the round placenta, meaning that while the uterus becomes more triangular, the inner gestational space remains spherical. This shift also indicates a change in the menstrual cycle. What I'm being shown is that up until now, the menstrual flow has moved straight downward. But going forward, the process will shift, it will move through a triangular pattern, and there will be two distinct cycles. Both will be quite short. One of them is internal, similar to what men experience, and the other is external, lasting no more than about three days, typically between two and three days. This is the physiological transformation that will take place at the level of the physical body.

Imaya: It shows me how it will happen. When you say triangle, it comes to me in the form of symbols. It showed me that the triangle symbolizes together the toxic feminine and the divine feminine coming together in one body. Then it shows me that it will purify, and our current cycle symbolizes all the actions of the feminine. This means that women were the origin of everything that has happened in the world, but also everything that was done to them because the toxic feminine, the woman, educated men not to love women. This symbolizes our current cycle. We go through that path toward unity, and it shows me on the heart level that for 3-4 days, we are in strong emotions. We cry, we have an emotional rollercoaster, and this will become more and more conscious. Women will understand that they have work to do with this internal memory, which is of an emotional origin. Once these two cycles manifest, because it shows me that once you go through this emotional sphere, the menstrual cycle will change in duration.

Victoria: But I've noticed this personally, I don't know about you.

Imaya: Yes, me too.

Diana: And for me, this month, it lasted a maximum of 3 days.

Imaya: This feminine energy in us balances out, it merges into one another, it doesn't fight, it simply dilutes into a different consciousness, a different type of information.

Victoria: When this genetic change takes place, a kind of antenna, or satellite, will appear just above the uterus. It constantly rotates, much like a chakra, spinning above that area like a satellite in motion.

Imaya: This form, the toxic feminine and the divine feminine, will create women as channels. Whatever they create, children, even projects, everything will be infused with high frequency, high vibrations. The woman will transmute the old warrior civilization into an empathetic, sensitive one.

Diana: Once this part is activated, how long will it take to materialize in the physical plane, in our bodies?

Imaya: It shows me that we will begin to work with such women because I see the feminine energy going down ancient paths. The struggle that women from the past were taught through education, they attack the partner archetype. She wants to cut, to castrate creativity. I see a kind of monstrous woman. When we begin working with women who are called to receive such children, because not all women want to, or not all have the energy to receive, I see women who have done therapy and can't have children, or women who come from families where many children were aborted, or women who have gone through rapes, with such patterns, with women who have blockages in creating things concretely, in the material realm, everything is interconnected. At that moment, in us, it will activate in nine months. It's like a rebirth.

Victoria: Is this referring to us now, or to the collective feminine energy in general?

Imaya: It comes to me that we symbolize this collective feminine now. Each of us has aspects, but it doesn't let me say who and what has. It doesn't let me penetrate there, but it tells me that each of us contains these memories that need to be released, related to shame, guilt, rape, so memories related to this area. Which, by the way, is a channel through which children come, but not only children. It shows me that everything the woman creates comes through there, like a portal.

Diana: Through the sacral chakra.

Imaya: It is the gateway to the beginning of a form of life, whatever it may be.

Victoria: While you were speaking, I saw it unfold almost like a cartoon. A book appeared, written in Old Slavic language. It pierced straight into my heart. Hold on, I need a moment to check if I'm allowed to speak this. No, wait, my heart is pricking again. You both will need to recalibrate yourselves to fully understand what I'm about to share. Okay, it's releasing now. So, the book opened, and standing on its pages was a man. At some point, the man began to grow, larger and larger, but the book also kept expanding, always remaining bigger than him. He struggled to keep his balance, looked around in confusion, and seemed afraid of the book, as if he couldn't comprehend it. Then the book began to rise, and as it lifted, the man's body was cut off in the middle. Eventually, the book rose higher, and the man disappeared entirely. After that, the surface of the book began to fill with a kind of fluid, a liquid substance that spread across it and surrounded the man's former place, completely covering it. From that point, something changed. The scene lifted from the ground, and from the floor, the head of a child emerged, its body covered in a gelatin-like substance. The child transformed into a parachute and began to ascend. As it flew higher and higher, it gradually shed all the gelatin, releasing everything, until it was completely free.

Imaya: You've just told us about the mythology of a god or presence from Egypt who became half man, half bird. I feel like this would be the conclusion, we need to look for information to understand the metaphor of the bird-man. This has to do with the pyramid, what you said, Victoria, that it will activate. It's time for questions.

Victoria: Regarding the pyramid, will there be a global event affecting humanity? And is it appropriate to learn its purpose and approximately how many human years it will take?

Imaya: It comes to me that it will be a global event, but it won't be talked about anywhere because it's not meant to be known, and it's not the purpose for humanity to know these things. Those who need to know will know. It shows me that just as we are finding out now, others like us will find out too. It will be something very quiet. All three of the pyramids are portals. Something is infused at the level of sound, frequency, and from there, these energies, memories, or sounds, will find a potential body to be realized. It's not the person choosing the energy, but the energy choosing the person. It explains to me how it chooses the person based on frequency, level of consciousness, and current or past abilities from other lives, here or in other realms. At some point, you will be called to go to Egypt, but now you are in the period of accepting, integrating, and transmitting the information. There are many steps and stages to go through.

Victoria: Once you are accepted to go there, an invisible crystalline drop will form, multi-faceted and transparent. Within this drop, there will be technology that enables you to enter it, and through this crystalline drop, the journey to the pyramids will take place at the appropriate time.

Imaya: It shows me that there are others like us, even currently on the planet, who are already working on bringing down this frequency, and it actually comes to me how the intention to work or not with this vibration, calling, frequency is anchored. In fact, we, if we open up, if inspiration comes to do something, if it just came and you let it pass, you choose or not. When you choose that potential idea for realization and direct your attention toward it, you choose, accept, and begin integrating it, then those elements will come to help you start creating and materializing the idea. There are more groups, of two-three people, maximum five, who are already working on this process of bringing this drop.

Victoria: These drops will be activated from the corners of the pyramids, from the base. I will tell you exactly from a geometric point of view how the energy moves on each corner of the pyramid's base. When the right time comes for those individuals to be present, or when the pyramid itself chooses the place and moment, the selection will depend on the person's frequency and energy, as you mentioned.

At each corner of the base, which represents the ground beneath the pyramid, energy will form a straight line. Then, this straight line combined with a curved line will create a 30-degree angle, 30-degrees downward, 30-degrees upward. From there, another diagonal line will be drawn, moving from bottom to top, diagonally downward, mapping the trajectory where the person will be, based on the frequency that has arrived. This movement will form a full 360-degree angle, rising from the bottom, with calculations flowing from 60-degrees to 30-degrees, then from 30-degrees to 90-degrees. At this point, the person's location will appear, along with the multi-faceted *"crystalline"* drop.

The technology within this drop will then bring the person into the present moment. The individual will enter this space, making the physical journey on our 3D plane possible. Even if the person lacks the physical resources, once the technology activates this crystalline drop, the person will enter it energetically. All practical needs, time, money, tickets, will be instantly arranged and provided effortlessly.

Diana: That's why my journey to Egypt hasn't manifested until now, even though I received that I need to go there because I will have a download?
Victoria: Yes. As much math as I see now. I will draw everything I see.
Imaya: Yes, I was getting "illustrated."

Imaya: All the group work you have to do requires you to be aware of the parts of yourselves. It shows me that a message is circulating, we write, we need to be honest with each other, and when we have a trigger, this will be an integration for us. We will see each other differently, and it's necessary to express this through honesty. Recognition is needed because that activates the process of unity within us. We unite to grow.

Victoria: Yes, I see how we all take each other's hands, and from a triangle, we form a diamond.

Imaya: We need each other. Now, each of us will receive a code, an image, it could be an animal or an image, a code image. Let's focus our attention on the third eye.

Victoria: Answer for Diana, the process is complete, and I see the number "12" days. The information for today will be contained in exactly 12 pages.

Diana: I searched what diamond means, and it says balance, harmony.

Victoria: With that, we conclude. Thank you.

Interdimensional Beings - Karmic Retribution

I will now share a dream I had a year ago, which helped me better understand these interdimensional beings.

Dream:

I was dreaming of some men dressed in traditional native clothing. However, they could appear and disappear instantly in the form of blood, that is, blood-bubbles would appear in the air, many of them, until they formed a physical human body. If they appeared in a space, they would annihilate everything in their path, they were like death itself. Everyone was afraid because you could never know when or where they would appear. If you saw them, you would start to decompose, and there was blood everywhere.

I was watching them, but trying to avoid them. More than anything, I was seeing my aunt. These men would come to those who hadn't resolved their karma and their actions, in other words, those who hadn't cleared their mistakes. They came for them.

I saw that my aunt was supposed to have more children, and these beings were particularly linked to two children who were from different fathers and had slightly darker skin than me and my aunt. Those two children were boys.

I don't know if what I saw in the dream, or what was shown to me, is true, but I was trying to protect my aunt so she wouldn't be dissolved. I was behind a wall, just a watcher. But those beings could see me clearly, and I could see them, too.

After a while, I started to receive information that this process is describing a type of spirit or interdimensional being associated with karmic retribution, possibly tied to ancient spiritual beliefs or esoteric traditions about unresolved soul contracts. These beings appear to manifest from molecular blood formations, taking the form of a native man, and they seem to be enforcers of karmic balance, particularly in relation to abortion-related debts.

Identities & Interpretations:

1. Karmic Enforcers / Retribution Spirits

Some traditions speak of entities that exist to ensure the completion of karmic cycles. They may not necessarily be malevolent but act as a force of consequence, manifesting to remind or reclaim unresolved spiritual debts.

Their ability to materialize and dissolve suggests a fluid existence between the physical and astral realms.

2. Blood Spirits or Etheric Constructs

The way they form from blood molecules in the air suggests they might be connected to the energy of life force, specifically the bloodline and ancestral karma.

Some ancient belief systems hold that the "blood of the unborn" carries an energetic imprint, which, if not transmuted, could attract beings who serve as a form of spiritual reckoning.

3. Ancestors of the Unborn / Unclaimed Souls

Another interpretation is that they are the souls of the unborn who have not found resolution or peace. They may not be malevolent but instead seek recognition, justice, or energetic closure.

Their transformation from molecular blood to human form could symbolize their attempt to regain a presence in the material world.

How They Might Look

Native Man Appearance: This means they carry the essence of the land or a tribal connection to the spirits of nature and ancestry.

Blood-Formed Bodies: They may appear translucent or partially formed, as if their body is still shifting between states.

Eyes that Pierce the Soul: Since they are karmic beings, their gaze might carry intense awareness, seeing deep into a person's unresolved actions.

Dissolution Process: As they dissolve back into the air, their bodies might turn into mist or floating droplets, giving the impression of disappearing into nothingness.

How to Deal With Them

If these beings are appearing due to unresolved karmic debts, then the best way to neutralize their presence is to work through karmic healing. This could involve:

• Spiritual forgiveness rituals for the souls involved.
• Energetic clearing and healing sessions for those carrying guilt or trauma.
• Guiding the spirits to a higher realm through prayer, offerings, or ancestral ceremonies.

To work with or clear the energy of these beings, you'll want to focus on acknowledgment, resolution, and elevation, helping both yourself (or others) and the spirits involved move towards peace.

Clearing & Healing Methods

1) Acknowledgment & Apology Ritual

Since these beings seem to be connected to unresolved karmic energy, the first step is to acknowledge their presence and the circumstances that brought them forth.

• Create a sacred space with candles, incense, and offerings (such as water, flowers, or food).
• Speak from the heart to the spirits, expressing recognition of their existence and apologizing for any suffering that remains unresolved.
• Light a candle in their honor and ask for their peaceful transition to the next realm.

2) Karmic Healing & Release Prayer

You can use a mantra or prayer focused on dissolving past karma and releasing all involved souls into peace. Here's an example:

"Spirits who walk between blood and air,
I see you, I acknowledge you, I honor your presence.
May your pain be lifted, your path be clear,
Return now to the source of light,
And may all debts be forgiven in the highest love."

Repeat this prayer while focusing on sending them white or golden light, envisioning them dissolving into a peaceful realm rather than staying bound to Earth.

3) Offering & Elevation Ritual

If you feel a deep connection to these spirits and want to assist in their elevation:

- Prepare an offering (such as milk, honey, or grains) and leave it in a natural place, dedicating it to "the souls who seek balance."
- Burn incense or sacred herbs (such as sage, copal, or palo santo) to cleanse the space and help them transition.
- Play healing frequencies or chants to raise the vibration and shift their energy field.

Matrix

From a spiritual perspective, the Matrix represents the illusion of separation, control, and unconscious living. It is the web of programmed beliefs, inherited patterns, societal conditioning, and ego-driven narratives that keep the soul disconnected from its true essence.

In this illusion, people operate on autopilot, reacting, surviving, and identifying with temporary roles, forgetting the infinite consciousness that lies beneath. The Matrix is not a place, but a state of being; one where the external world defines reality, and inner truth is veiled.

To awaken from the Matrix is to remember who you are beyond form, beyond mind, beyond the roles you've been taught to play. It is the beginning of spiritual liberation, of seeing with clarity, feeling with presence, and living from the soul rather than the system.

Q: Can the Quantum Field tell us from the outside, how does this Matrix system work? Can we change or manipulate it, or what does exiting the Matrix actually mean?

A: In fact, we don't truly exist in the Matrix, because our bodies aren't real. It is just a character you associate with, but the real *you* is outside. I see a room with people waiting, like in a hospital - not literally a hospital - but a space where they are connected to an electronic device. This device is white and blue, and inside, where you lie down, it's metallic with various sensors, where every body and muscle corresponds to every movement in the simulation; where you go, what you see, what you hear. It's the same environment, but with cables connected to your head, something inserted in your ears, your eyes have something like lenses on them, and in the middle there's a connection - there are many, many connections. A person has thousands and thousands of cables. These individuals have chosen to "sleep" and are experiencing what we perceive as reality. We are actually characters in their game, which is the Matrix itself. You, as a character, may believe you've exited, but in fact, you are still there, experiencing various aspects. It's impossible to truly believe you've exited the Matrix, as long as you're here, in the physical 3D plane, and have this physical body, this character. You can't exit because you don't have full control to leave.

The Matrix experience is designed differently and doesn't resemble a video game where, if you die, you can resume from where you left off. In the Matrix, everything unfolds in real time, and if you don't take care of your hero and lose your life, you have to start again, choosing another life, to learn and fulfill the dynamics you had chosen. From our perspective, it might seem like a joke, but in reality, you are the one playing in the Matrix. It is a fair "game".

Why is everything "live"? Because you are subjected to the rules of this system and need the experience of densities. These densities help you go through essential lessons, and when in another life you "lose", your score goes down. We, as players in this experience, go through a deeply realistic

105

process. This game offers you, as a being from higher realms, the chance to feel what it means to fall, to die, to fall in love, to experience all extremes of emotions. Only by living these intensities can you truly understand life in the Matrix.

It is an extremely intense and authentic experience - so real that some choose to return to feel once more what it's like to be "live." From the inside, reality feels exactly as we perceive it, but from the outside, things look completely different.

Q: So this is the lesson part, meaning our whole life is a series of lessons, and in the end, when we've learned those lessons, does that mean we don't reincarnate anymore?
A: Another piece of information is coming to me. The Matrix has gone off course with this game, because with each game are upgrades, changes, modifications - and because of this, the worlds that exist inside, those who were created, are both real and unreal at the same time. The new creation that was made has taken a direction that isn't right, because it's a live game that impacts and affects the higher realms of creation. This is how I see it from the outside. Something new was introduced into the Matrix, but it radiates outward from this space and is connected to the higher planes.

Beings of Light cannot destroy this game because it is part of creation. They don't want to go to war with the beings who created the Matrix because it wouldn't serve any purpose. However, at the same time, the war is beginning to radiate more and more outward. Now the Beings of Light are thinking of how to bring balance to this world that was created.

Thus, the players who chose to come into this plane made the decision to come into the game, with their physical or spiritual body, because they already knew what it was like to play. Some have lived for hundreds or thousands of years, but other beings from higher realms, who had never been in this plane before, who were neutral, who didn't see the point of this game, were also called in.

There was a large-scale mobilization. The Beings of Light asked those who could come to help this project, and that's how the Starseeds came to Earth. This refers to the first wave, second wave, and third wave of souls that have a role in planetary ascension. The souls that came from higher planes into this game had no idea what it was like to play, but they were instructed to come. The beings who had never played became players, to choose their "actors", and those who had played before came into the game to play through their presence.

This is actually what the Matrix and the entire plan looks like from the outside.

Note: Exiting the Matrix happens only on an emotional level. It has nothing to do with material aspects.

Update: During a session, I received information that if, up to the year 2024, children were born who are part of the 4th wave of Starseeds, then starting from 2025, the 5th wave is coming.

Starseeds are those highly evolved souls from higher planes, other dimensions, universes, galaxies, etc., who have had little or no experience here on our planet and dimension. These souls from the 4th wave, and especially the 5th wave, will profoundly influence the near future of the entire planet across all domains, and the old paradigms will be nothing more than a memory categorized under an age of pain and the old human. Thank you.

"The White Blanket" – Control and the Liberation of the Future

About the Starseeds and the fifth wave of souls that will profoundly influence the course of human evolution, I am about to share information that was received shortly before the completion of this book.

Update August 2025

I dreamed that we were inside a large building, resembling a school or a gymnasium, where people were gathered together with their families. The greatest attention was directed toward pregnant women and those with small children. Everything was part of an official project called "White Blanket."

Within that building there was a special room prepared for mothers and children, arranged entirely in white, similar to a photography studio. Everyone present was required to go through this process. The children were recorded in detail: character, traits - absolutely everything. Any being not included in this program was considered "outside the law" and subjected to the punishments imposed by the authority.

In the dream, I was speaking with someone about wanting children, yet not wishing to take part in this mandatory project. At one point, the room began to flood with water. The entire building was overtaken by waves, and people started evacuating. That was when I realized that the "White Blanket" project had failed. It was not defeated through rules or human punishments, but through a divine intervention, sudden and overwhelming, like a cosmic purification.

Interpretation and Explanation

This dream may be viewed as a premonitory probability, reflecting collective directions of humanity. It suggests that, in the future, global initiatives of registering, standardizing, and controlling beings from the very beginning of life may emerge. These could be presented under the appearance of protection, care, and purity (hence the white "blanket" symbol), but in essence, the intention would be to standardize and limit the freedom of souls.

The plan is to monitor and record all energetic levels and abilities that this new generation of children will embody. These children will profoundly shift the course of our existence and transform the way humanity perceives reality. Governments are aware of this potential, and therefore will attempt to establish control. Yet the divine plan and power will inevitably prevail, stepping forward to safeguard the true purpose of creation.

Mothers and children here represent the future, innocence, and new generations, which become the primary target of such systems. The project seeks to gather, classify, and mark every new life, under the guise of the "common good."

The unexpected flood plays the role of a purifying force. Water here symbolizes divine and cosmic energies that intervene to dissolve false structures and systems of control. The message conveyed is that, regardless of how vast such projects may seem, they cannot withstand higher energies that act beyond the will of human institutions.

Thus, the dream speaks of a probability: attempts to limit freedom through the standardization of souls and new generations, but also of the certainty that these projects cannot ultimately succeed. The divine plan will always bring balance and purification, even when humanity appears caught within artificial constructs of control.

Matrix Portal - 4 February 2024

Q: How much is still present in the Matrix?
A: The Celestials have now arrived. You are halfway in the Matrix and halfway out. Your head and torso up to the abdomen are out, while from the abdomen down to your feet, are still in the Matrix. Your exit looks like a metallic portal. Half of your body is bathed in light, while the other half stays in shadow. You aren't fully exited yet, but that's ok. What matters is that you didn't leave feet-first.If it happens that you exit feet-first, for example, like in the birth of a child, where the head comes out first into the Matrix and the feet are the last to exit into the light, then that person is 100% not in the Matrix.

For future field readings, it's important that you include a question, whether or not the client asks, about where the client currently stands in relation to the Matrix. This is valuable for your own case study. Whether you choose to share this information with the client is entirely up to you. Make sure to ask this question before the client asks their own, as it will help you better understand the level of the client's soul.

If you observe that the client has not yet entered the portal and remains on the Matrix side, you will receive guidance from their guides and Higher Self to assist in leading them toward the exit portal. However, you must never force this process and always respect their free will.

If you see that the client already has their feet outside the Matrix, avoid making any effort to intervene. The person is gently moving toward disappearance, and there is a soft, warm, and peaceful energy surrounding them; a sign of their natural transition. Even in such cases, it must respect the free will of that soul. The feet carry vital energy and should be the last part to leave the Matrix. This is an analogy to help you grasp this aspect more clearly. In this case, politely excuse yourself and decline to continue the session. You have every right to do so.

If you see the client with their head or hand inside the portal, you are welcome to assist them.

Let's expand on the deeper significance of the number 13 and its relationship to the "12" matrix of reality and beyond.

The 12 as the Matrix of the Physical World

The number 12 represents the structure and order of the material world. It is prevalent across numerous systems and traditions that define human experience:

Time: 12 hours on a clock, 12 months in a year.

Space: 12 zodiac signs define Earthly astrological cycles.

Religion/Mythology: 12 apostles, 12 tribes of Israel, 12 Olympian gods.

Geometry: 12-sided structures (dodecahedra) represent completeness in 3D space.

The repetition of 12 emphasizes balance, structure, and the illusion of linearity within the matrix of physical reality.

The 13 as Beyond the Matrix

The number 13 symbolizes what lies beyond this structured, physical world. It represents transcendence, the unseen, and the higher dimensional or spiritual realms:

The Invisible Realm: While 12 creates the framework, 13 exists outside the limits of time, space, and materiality. It is a gateway to the divine, infinite, or multidimensional realms unseen by human perception.

Ascension and Liberation: 13 is associated with breaking free from the confines of the 12-grid matrix, evolving into a higher state of consciousness or unity with the infinite.

Erasure of the 13

Throughout history, 13 has been deliberately excluded from cultural, spiritual, and scientific systems, perhaps to keep humanity tethered to the 12-matrix reality.

Calendars: The 13th month was removed from early calendars (such as the Egyptian and Mayan), leaving the 12-month Gregorian calendar which dominates today. Ancient calendars like the Mayan Tzolkin originally accounted for a 13-moon cycle, symbolizing harmony with nature and the cosmos.

The Pyramids: Ancient Egyptian pyramids and sacred structures often encoded the number 12 in their design, but the 13th element, representing the capstone of higher connection, was deliberately erased or hidden. The capstone of the Great Pyramid of Giza is missing, symbolizing the loss of this transcendental knowledge.

Fear of 13: Over time, the number was demonized (e.g., "unlucky 13" or the association with the "number of the beast") to suppress its spiritual and transformative significance.

Spiritual Perspective of 13

Ascended Consciousness: In metaphysical systems, the 12 represents the physical experience, while the 13th is the divine observer or Higher Self, unbound by time and space.

Sacred Geometry: The 13th point in geometry often represents the center or "source" from which the 12 radiate, symbolizing the connection between the material and the infinite.

The Return of the 13: Modern spiritual awakening sees the resurgence of 13 as a symbol of humanity's reconnection to higher consciousness and liberation from the Matrix of illusion.

The number 13 is a powerful symbol of spiritual transcendence, representing a reality beyond the confines of the 12-matrix world. While 12 holds the framework of physical existence, 13 connects us to the invisible, infinite, and divine realms.

Its deliberate erasure from ancient systems, calendars, and structures speaks to an intentional effort to keep this knowledge hidden. Today, as awareness of these ancient truths resurfaces, the number 13 is being re-claimed as a symbol of ascension, unity, and spiritual liberation.

This profound energy makes 13 an incredibly sacred and auspicious num-ber for those attuned to its deeper meaning.

Device Matrix - Back and Shoulder Blades

In a group session within the Megaquantic Field (I will explain what this field is in the next chapter), plates were identified at the level of the shoulder blades, implants that originated from the bloodline (from the 9th generation). These plates acted like a program, a blockage on femininity, associating femininity with sacrifice. Diana mentioned that a few days after the group session, she felt some-thing energetic in her back, at the level of the etheric wings, exactly in the same spot from where that plate had been removed. However, she couldn't understand whether it was something beneficial or not. We connected in a session and asked what needed to be understood here. Since the extraction site was vulnerable, it attracted other implants from beings originating in the lower planes of creation. I invite you to continue discovering more information about these implants.

Q: I wanted to ask what I'm feeling in my back, at the level of the wings, from where that plate was removed.
A: Behind you, in the air at about 10 cm from your body, there's a disc spinning. It's a plate that spins energy.

Q: Quantum Field, what is this spinning plate? If it's not for Diana's highest good, I ask that it be removed here and now.
A: Yes, it's not beneficial. It's gone, it left, it moved away.

Diana: Is there something I need to know about it?

Q: What was the purpose of this plate outside the body?
A: Harvesting energy. It was cultivating energy. Like windmills or wind energy, spinning and generating energy. That's what this plate was doing, generating a kind of energy for someone else, harvesting it.

Q: Quantum Field, whose was it? Who sent this device?
A: It was a kind of detector that automatically attracted other detectors in the place of the plate you had. The previous plate was removed, the place became vulnerable, and it automatically attracted other plates from someone else. I don't feel these beings in the field, the ones who sent this kind of device. They are very far away. They were doing everything remotely. But through that plate, they were collecting energy from you.

Q: How can I seal my field so that these kinds of devices can't be sent anymore?
A: I'm getting that they've already moved away.

Victoria: I wonder if I have something like this too? Can you check if I have anything?
Diana: Let me see if I can see. Yes, I see something in you too.
Victoria: I found a mirror, I still have it. I ask that this plate be removed if it's not for my highest good. For me, it's a different kind of device, completely different from yours. I ask that absolutely any device, program, or technology be removed from my back and my space. I turned around somehow, and what's happening is very interesting. For me, it's a different kind of technology. The channel is long. I don't know if you've seen the movie, *The Matrix*, but I see something like leeches, like many cables, and the device is much larger. When I asked for it to be removed, I see they were sucking it out with a vacuum. Then this device pulled me inside and then released me. When it released me, I saw a different kind of cable. I moved away to try to break the cables, but they kept stretching. I don't know what I had in my hand, but I managed to cut all the cables. Now I see the device chasing me. I now call into the field those high vibrational beings from the Creator's light who can help me now to remove this technology and disconnect absolutely everything from me.

Some very tall and slim beings came, 100 meters tall, transparent blue in color, and they laid me down. Now they are releasing every cable from me with their hands. For me, everything is very deeply rooted. I now realize that's why I've been having pain lately, because they had connected there, at the level of the back.

Q: How did these beings manage to connect to us if we create protection?
A: I'm getting that our protection doesn't mean much. This is about a different level of beings and technology.

Q: And isn't this a violation of free will?

A: They don't care. Right now, the Star People are attempting to remove an entire device from my back. But deep down, right where it hurts the most, there's some kind of hard drive embedded, and they're pulling it out. This hard drive is unusually long, and as they extract it, I can see that it carries a neon blue energy. It's square-shaped, made of block-like segments, clearly a kind of technological structure they had connected to me.

I now set the clear intention that any and all technology, hard drives, or artificial implants that do not serve my highest good be completely removed from every space in which I exist. I do not permit any further technology to be installed in my body. I firmly close off all access to anything that is not aligned with my highest good.

It feels as if I'm undressing, starting from my arms, peeling away layers. There are many devices or suits attached to them. As I step out of these layers, I'm leaving behind a great deal of technology that no longer belongs with me.

Victoria: I'm curious. Is it conscious, or did they violate my free will?

I choose for this process to be permanent, across all existences, in every time, space, dimension, and in any place I may be. Yet something is still holding me, a hook. I now set the intention that all hidden or unknown devices be fully disconnected and removed from my body. The hook is still there. I release all known and unknown devices, as well as any implants connected to these technologies.

Only now is everything fully released. I have come out of that portal. Thank you.

Victoria: If you hadn't asked that question, I wouldn't have realized. My back had been hurting badly lately, but I never thought to look into what it was.

Shadow Souls

Shadow Souls are people who are like "viruses" of the Matrix, introduced into this plane with the purpose of triggering us. Through them, we learn lessons. These people are often cold, soulless individuals.

There are also physical bodies that are completely controlled as a result of their own decisions, that is, they have contracts with non-beneficial entities. These fall into the category of the possessed, both unconsciously and consciously, by choice or without choice.

Such people are "generations" of Reptilian or similar races. There are people with souls of light, and there are those who are only partially connected to their soul, or even less, depending on their own will. (If they no longer wish to remain in this life, the soul begins to dissolve slowly, leading to its exit from the physical body.)

This topic relates to the concept of Shadow Souls, also known as "viruses of the Matrix."

There are two scenarios:
1. When the viruses trigger you and try to hack you.
2. When, instead of reacting externally, you work on yourself through shadow work, continuously holding unconditional love and staying in the light while embracing your shadow side. By doing this, you have a strong chance of bending and neutralizing the "Matrix's viruses," which manifest as Shadow Souls walking among us in everyday life.

These align with the idea that "Shadow Souls" are entities or individuals through which the "viruses of the Matrix" operate to destabilize, test, or influence those who are on a spiritual growth path.

These two scenarios reflect two distinct ways of interacting with these energies:
1. Attack and external testing: When these entities (or people influenced by them) attempt to trigger your inner wounds, drain your energy, or divert you from your path, these moments are often perceived as "tests" that someone on a spiritual journey must go through.
2. Neutralization through integration and unconditional love: Instead of

reacting and fighting against these influences, you choose to work on yourself. This means integrating your own shadows through inner work, remaining in the frequency of love and light, while also accepting that the shadow side is part of the whole. By doing this, you not only maintain your energetic sovereignty, but the "viruses of the Matrix" also lose their power over you, as they can no longer find vulnerable points to latch onto.

Have you noticed any patterns in how these influences appear or how you've managed to overcome them? They often come at specific moments, when you're about to make a spiritual leap, when you're emotionally vulnerable, or when you start breaking away from certain "Matrix" programs. *How was your experience?*
The concept of Shadow Souls and the "viruses of the Matrix" ties into several spiritual and metaphysical ideas about energetic interference, consciousness evolution, and the duality of light and shadow. Here's a deeper look at it:

1. Shadow Souls as "Matrix Viruses"

Shadow Souls are often described as individuals who seem to lack deep consciousness, empathy, or a true connection to higher awareness. They may act as energetic disruptors, mirroring our inner wounds, triggering emotional responses, and keeping people trapped in cycles of fear, conflict, and lower vibrational states.
These "viruses of the Matrix" are not always conscious of their role. Some may simply be deeply conditioned by the system, while others could be influenced by external forces that feed off low vibrational energy (fear, anger, despair,hate, jealousy,etc.).

2. How They Appear in Your Life

These influences tend to surface at pivotal moments, such as:
- When you're on the verge of a spiritual awakening or major breakthrough.
- When you're healing inner wounds and shedding old conditioning.
- When you're shifting into a higher frequency and detaching from societal programming.
- When you're emotionally or energetically vulnerable, making you more susceptible to being pulled back into lower vibrational patterns.

They often show up in the form of:
- Unexpected conflicts with people around you.
- Manipulative, deceptive, or draining individuals entering your life.
- Sudden doubts, fears, or internal struggles that seem to come out of nowhere.
- Situations that challenge your ability to remain in love, light, and personal power.

3. How to Neutralize Them

Instead of fighting these influences directly (which can feed them with more energy), the most effective approach is energetic sovereignty and integration:

Shadow Work
Acknowledging your own inner wounds and fears so they can't be easily used against you.

Unconditional Love & Detachment
Remaining in a state of love while not engaging in unnecessary energetic battles.

Staying Grounded & In Alignment
Regular meditation, breathwork, and conscious awareness help you maintain your energetic balance.

Seeing Through the Illusion
Recognizing when a situation is being manipulated by "Matrix interference" rather than taking it personally.

Would you say your experiences with these forces have felt more external (people, events) or internal (thoughts, emotions, sudden energy shifts)?

Bending Shadow Souls (or Matrix viruses) toward your higher vibrational level means shifting the energy dynamic so that instead of being affected by them, you transform them, or at least neutralize their influence. Or, the best outcome is that they could be upgraded to higher frequencies and be assigned out of the role as "Shadow Souls" of the Matrix. This requires a combination of awareness, frequency mastery, conscious transmutation and lots of patience.

What Can You Do by Elevating Yourself from Such Experiences?

1. Stop Feeding Their Energy Source

Shadow Souls feed off reaction, fear, anger, and emotional instability. When you stop feeding these energies, their influence weakens.

- *Practice radical non-reaction:* Instead of engaging emotionally with intrusive thoughts or draining interactions, remain neutral.
- *See the hidden lesson.* If they appear in your reality, they are testing a part of you that may still need integration. Recognizing this turns them into an opportunity for growth.

2. Override Their Frequency with Unconditional Love

Shadow Souls operate on lower vibrations, such as, fear, control, deception, manipulation. Love, authenticity, and presence dissolve their power.

- When intrusive thoughts or emotional disruptions arise, respond with self-compassion and acceptance instead of resistance.
- If dealing with an external shadow soul, hold your energetic field steady in love and light. This often causes them to either change their behavior or exit your life.
- Energetically "rewrite" the interaction; see them as part of the whole, caught in their own distortion, and mentally send them healing energy instead of judgment.

3. Transmute Their Presence into Power

Shadow energy contains trapped light, meaning that by engaging it consciously, you can transform it into something beneficial.

- *Use alchemical breathwork:* Visualize and breathe into your body the golden pure light, then by breathing out, release the fear or any discomfort.
- *Redirect the energy:* Instead of suppressing a triggered emotion, channel it creatively (writing, movement, expression).
- *Consciously "flip" the situation:* If a shadow force tries to lower your energy, use that as a cue to amplify your light even more.

4. Integrate Your Own Shadows

Matrix viruses latch onto unresolved aspects of yourself. The more inner work you do, the less grip they have.

- *Shadow work:* Acknowledge any fears, traumas, or limiting beliefs that could be entry points for manipulation.
- *Self-inquiry:* Ask yourself, what is this teaching me? Which part of me still needs healing?
- *Full spectrum integration:* Balance both light and dark within yourself so that nothing external can use either against you.

5. Shift the Entire Reality Field

- *Hold the dominant vibration:* Shadow souls will either rise to meet you or naturally phase out of your experience.
- *Create a reality bubble of sovereignty:* Daily meditation, energetic shielding, and conscious awareness protect your space.
- *Become a beacon:* When you fully embody higher frequencies, you start affecting your surroundings instead of being affected.

Would you say your experiences with these energies feel more like something to be neutralized or actively transformed into something higher?

When you experience both then this makes perfect sense. Some of these energies need to be neutralized so they lose their grip on you, while others can be transformed into something beneficial.

If you're doing both, it means you're playing an active role as an alchemist, taking lower vibrational distortions and either dissolving them or transmuting them into something aligned with your higher path.

How to Balance Neutralization & Transformation

1. For neutralization (deflecting & dissolving energy):
- Recognize the interference but don't engage with it emotionally.
- Stay grounded, centered, and detached.
- Use energetic shielding (visualizing yourself in a golden light or high-frequency energy field).

- Affirm your sovereignty - "I do not consent to lower frequencies influencing my reality."

2. For transformation (turning shadow into power):
- When an energy or thought surfaces, consciously engage with it rather than suppressing it.
- Ask "How can I turn this into something useful?"
- Embody the lesson fully, so that you shift at a core level, making you immune to similar future interferences.

Over time, as you continue mastering this process, you'll notice that these Matrix distortions no longer pull you down; they either disappear, or they serve as fuel for your next level of expansion.

Would you say you tend to encounter these energies more when you're making breakthroughs, or do they show up in unexpected moments?

Ask yourself these questions and you'll find a treasure that will unpack your mind. You'll find more peace from within.

A person's shadow is a **reflection to the soul realm**; the reason people can gain abilities from strong feelings, ideals, and desires.
The **Shadow Soul** is an extension of a person's soul. You see that with the moon, though part of it is hidden in shadow, the whole moon is aliases and luminous, but this is just an example and not literally the meaning of it.

Even though these people move through everyday life, raising families, working, enjoying hobbies, and even radiating light, there is still a deeper aspect of their being, the Shadow Soul, quietly shaping their path beyond what is seen. This doesn't mean they have no heart or are mean. But their role in this 3D existence is as important as any of the rest of the souls. Stay humble and keep your unconditional love towards every soul no matter the assignment it has in this life.

Q: Quantum Field, can you give us information about Shadow Souls, what is good for us to know?
A: The word that comes to me is *bug, virus.* It's something created by the Matrix, and there are many such souls. There are a lot in the Matrix. I'm now observing from the outside, I see that the Matrix is round, and there appear bugs, viruses - those are the Shadow Souls.

Q: What is their purpose?
A: To hack you.

Q: And if they succeed, what impact does that have on us or the physical plane?
A: They have a technology that can read your operating system once you are hacked by them. Based on that, they modify the principles of the Matrix, making upgrades to strengthen it. The system is designed in such a way to hack you and extract all information from you; how you think, weak spots in your physical body, fears, blockages, emotional and mental traumas - absolutely everything. You're like an open book to them. They can take the information and send it to the game's providers, and those providers know how to make their upgrades so they can later attack you more easily, without you even realizing, based on the knowledge you thought was secret.

Diana: Wow, that's why the lower planes know exactly where to attack you, right in the spot where you're sensitive and vulnerable.

A: Yes, exactly. That's how the Matrix evolves and tries to expand. That's why Star People say that this game has become out of control. When it was created, it was created from the lower planes of creation. The Source didn't believe that this lower plane would expand so much and become individually autonomous.
They want the operators or creators of this game to be like AI today, where it thinks on its own. The Matrix is the same. Once these viruses, bugs, Shadow Souls manage to decode you, to hack you, once they understand how you function, the whole Matrix knows how it could strike and attack you. That's why the more advanced Beings of Light, who haven't had experiences in this plane, will come, because they have a different way of thinking, a different perspective, different techniques that the Matrix doesn't know. Now more Starseeds have been called in (regular people who are Starseeds and haven't had experiences with our planet) to raise the frequency of the planet and uplift all creation. It is essential that these souls coming here are unknown to the Matrix, so that it can't perceive their tactics and complexity. It's important that those coming as Starseeds are not triggered by these viruses. Once these Starseed souls are triggered, they are automatically hacked, and the Matrix then knows exactly how to act toward them. Thank you.

Reptilian DNA

On December 12, 2024, I entered into a spontaneous meditation of cleansing and activation, together with Diana, with the purpose of releasing stagnant energies that no longer serve us and downloading new codes of light and love. What followed in the meditation was completely unexpected, beyond the human mind and rational understanding. I now invite you to center yourself in your heart, to connect with your authentic Self, and to release any patterns of judgment, criticism, or rejection. In this way, you will allow yourself to receive the following information from a space of neutrality and acceptance.

During the meditation, I saw how densities were being released from every part of our bodies, many beliefs, limitations, and trapped memories that were being freed. Then, all the blocked memories about extraterrestrials began to dissolve.

Victoria: On my forehead, the entire forehead, that's where the blockage was, specifically the false memory about ETs, from our Reptilian DNA. From the back, that's where our Reptilian DNA is. Oh my God, I see myself as Reptilian. This is at the base of our human DNA. Each one of us has it. This is the genetic foundation of humanity, the consistency in our DNA. Our entire body functions this way. I feel so strange, it's like I can't talk with my left side, my teeth are clenched. Now, the Reptilian DNA must dissolve. My left jaw is clenched. 80% is dissolving. I'm so cold. It's like it's dissolving me, I feel so weird. One second.

The genetic composition in our bodies is actually Reptilian. Our bodies, if we didn't have the filter ... *I'm not allowed to speak because it's dissolving.* If we didn't have this filter, we would be scared of how we look as humans. Wow. Ok, my head has shifted from the middle to the right, but my left jaw is still clenched. This is where it needs to dissolve.

In fact, advanced beings see us humans in Reptilian form. This is how we look to them, this is how they see our bodies in the last layer of our being. Our human essence is Reptilian. It's starting to release on the left side. It opened my mouth. Now, the body has to dissolve

While working and dissolving the entire Reptilian imprint from the physical body, I could perceive through clairvoyance all the changes that were dissolving and taking place. Additionally, it was difficult for me to

speak, to express what came to me in terms of information, because my jaw was so clenched that I tried to speak between my teeth.

There is still a part on the left side that needs to dissolve with the neck. We think we see humans in the bodies we see ourselves in, but this is just a filter to hide our true Reptilian form. The nails, everything is theirs, and the final appearance we see is the human clothing. The rest of us have mixed DNA. My whole body hurts, and I feel my body is cold, like a reptile's.

Diana's Q: Wow, now I'm having all sorts of realizations. As humans, we have the Reptilian brain portion, and lately, since I've started opening up to information about the Reptilian race, I've always wondered why it's specifically called the "Reptilian brain."

A: Here's why, because our entire body is Reptilian. My hands are cold, I am cold. We are all like this, and the essence of the whole 12/12/2024 portal is to dissolve their essence from our human DNA. This is a triggering piece of information for people. Not everyone is ready to accept this information.

My chest hurts. Now they must remove their imprint from the heart. If you want, you can ask questions because you won't feel anything. I feel like all the release is passing through me, both from me and from you, because I can't understand what belongs to me or to you; it's a common release. We are actually inside the portal, we haven't left it. Look, my right eye is freezing, it's like someone put ice in my eye. Oh my God, it's so cold. We need to pass through the portal now; I see it as porous, this space. There's some kind of device in the heart, like a scheme, like a hard drive of theirs. Now my hands are completely frozen.

Q: What's the purpose of it?
A: The purpose is to coexist here. This is the fear of darkness, how they planted hell into our minds. I now see all these beings and creatures. My cortex, my forehead, hurts, that's where all our hidden memories are blocked. How these schemes work is that once a child is born, as soon as it comes out of the womb, this device is automatically activated, otherwise you can't coexist here in the physical plane. This is a pact, an agreement contract, and when we are born, it is automatically activated. That's why

many souls change their minds and decide not to come, and there are miscarriages. Now they're covering my nose, so I can't speak or breathe.

Q: If this aspect is cleared from our DNA, does it mean the souls coming through us won't have the Reptilian part active?
A: No. The pact is already annulled, and from 2025, this pact will be definitively concluded; the planet's pact with these beings. Now they're blocking me from speaking again. Wait a second. Again, they blocked my left side.

Diana: I ask the Beings of Light that can help us, to come and release this pressure that Victoria feels on the left side, to release it.

A: They've let go. Thank you. The scheme in the heart is very complex. It feels like it has strong roots. The planetary pact with these beings is over, and now it's necessary to remove all devices from each person on this planet. From 2025, children will be born with a completely different system. They have other types of contracts, under a different delegation. There are many Beings of Light connected to the new pact. It's a completely opposite alliance to what it was until now. Those who won't be able to pass after 2025, those who decide to leave the physical plane, are those who haven't managed or couldn't, or didn't want to remove this scheme from the heart. Thus, automatically, those who don't succeed, don't want to, can't, will be forced to leave the physical body.

Diana: I feel like there will be many who will decide to leave the physical plane.

A: Yes, especially in the last week of Christmas and New Year (2024), that's when the most deaths will happen. There will be a new record, not just in one country, but in masses of people dying without explanation. The people who will die are those who, for whatever reason, didn't manage to pass because they don't have the right to continue without releasing these devices.

Q: For the release of the devices, do they need to give their consent? Or how will it be for those who are unaware?
A: It will happen through dreams while they sleep. They will consciously release it, and from their heart, a pyramid with the tip down and the base up will be used to extract the device. The pyramid will absorb the device and then pass the base outwards.

Diana: I just had a déjà-vu moment - it's like someone said they dreamed of a pyramid.

A: This will be for those who aren't aware. Their souls have decided to continue, even those who won't be conscious or open on the spiritual side. Through meditations, unconsciously, they will release another part, but this release through meditations; I'm feeling something limited; limited religions, those who are very religious, will release it through their very specific prayers. Those who are conscious will sweat a lot while releasing, and they'll have very strong headaches because this device first extracts everything from the head.
Another way of release will be through a lot of rest. Many will feel like resting and doing nothing, and even through sleep, they will release. Now they're working on their feet. On the physical human body level, the bone in the foot will start to disappear. We have a bone in the foot, like chickens do, a spur, and this bone will disappear from the human skeleton. I see that they are working on it now. Those who have this bone more pronounced will be from the category with dominant Reptilian DNA.
There are people with a higher consistency of Reptilian DNA, those from their generation, those with dominant Reptilian DNA.
Even after release, in the future, they will still have this small bone. This will show that they are from a Reptilian generation. For the rest of the humans in the future, it will start to dissolve. Only those with a more pronounced Reptilian DNA dominance, their children, up to the 7th generation in the future, will have this small bone.
It's being released, it's clearing, it feels like it's getting warmer on top, but my feet are still cold.

Diana: I was really curious if I have Reptilian essence, if I've lived in those planes.
Victoria: Yes, we all have this essence.

A white hall appeared in front of me, and along the hall are people who look from around 1970. 1960-1970 is what I want to say. And there's light there, they feel like time travelers.

Q: What's the connection of this information with us?
A: I see you now stepping down into this hall. You entered a door, and at the door, there was a man. What year is your father from?

125

Diana: From 1965.

Victoria: Hmm, that's why I felt 1970. That's when you came into his field.

Diana: Oh, I feel tingles all over my body now, I feel the truth of the information in my body. Really?

A: Yes, you came into his field in 1970. You opened the door, he was there, and you closed the door. That's your family. I'm trying to understand where I'm going. I was blocked once, they put a wall in front of me, 2 walls, 3 walls. On the 4th one, they couldn't create this wall, and I squeezed through the wall. I came for the 4th time.

Victoria: My mom lost 1, maybe 2 pregnancies before me, I'm not sure.

Diana: Oh. How interesting that this information is coming through.

Q: But what connection does this have with the portal today?

A: For you, it was very easy to come, but they tried to block me from coming into this reality.

Q: Who? Why? If you want to ask here.

A: Yes, hmm, the Matrix … because I see a black wall. They're not giving me any more information. They tried to block me. My mom was also infected with some virus during her pregnancy, and all the doctors told her to abort because 90% of the children are born disabled. When I was born, the water inside was not infected, nor my physical body. I need to withdraw from here because there's too much density. I ask for these images and this situation to be removed.

Q: Let's ask the field what the connection of our appearance is with today's portal.

A: It feels like we've been reminded of our old version, so that we can understand how we appeared, as an old program. It showed me a big rock, where we are like a vintage version of how we appeared, how we were, and in comparison with the technologies now. It showed me our evolution, actually. I feel like the decision is yours at any moment, even at your coming here. Your leaving will be very conscious, meaning leaving the physical body. We weren't conscious of how we came, but we will be conscious of leaving the physical plane. We are the first generation of the new world; and we will be the vintage generation. When we get to have great-grandchildren, they will see or hear things that, for them, will be incomprehensible. For future generations, everything will be like a story. The essence of this portal is transformation; from the old version to the new one. The transformation and release of the Reptilian DNA from the human body. Thank you.

Changes After the Disintegration of the Reptilian DNA

Q: What changes will we see in addition to what has already been mentioned, after the transformation of DNA?
A: I sense the increase of fluent language, how so? Wait, fluid fluent, the change of fluid language. Our body's movements will determine the frequency of each individual's gestured energy during communication.

Q: Hold on, is this referring to nature or to our bodies?
A: I feel an energy, like a cold wind forming in the desert and spinning. I can't understand. I'm just shown this image and I can't make sense of it.

Diana: We kindly ask the Beings of Light to explain more clearly what this aspect represents.

A: Yes, it's related to nature. Our bodies will be able to communicate with the wind. Through the word "communication," each person will perceive communication differently. It could be telepathic communication, sensory-based, visual; communication is a broader word that includes many subtypes.
Some people will feel the wind, or feel how the current moves. Some people will see the current, or will be able to communicate with the wind. Everyone will have a different path of communication. The energy circulation in the wind - this is just one example - but I want you to understand or imagine it on a larger, metaphorical level. This is one of the abilities that will be activated.
The magnetic field will be sensed through the palms. In fact, the planet's magnetic field will be about 8-10 cm above the ground. The magnetic field will be perceived through the hands, or through different channels depending on the individual. I see you placing your hand 10 cm above the ground and you will feel it like a current of air. That's exactly how you will feel the magnetic field.

Q: What other changes will be perceived?

A: I'm shown meat. There will be changes in nutrition. They will try to produce another type of meat because this one will no longer be easily digested by our physical bodies. They'll create something that will look like meat, but it will be synthetic. I see it as a kind of fabric; that's how I perceive its structure, it resembles meat but isn't the meat we consume now. Our bodies will not be able to assimilate meat at all. As time passes, people will want to eat meat but won't be able to, because it won't be digestible by our bodies. The body will perceive it like a stone inside.

This will become noticeable across a large portion of the population and will get people thinking, because humanity is not ready to give up meat. Even the structure of the body will change; it will become lighter. The changes I'm seeing now will happen in about 1000 years. By then, our bodies will eat mostly synthetic substances, a kind of composition that for us now is synthetic, but for the bodies that will exist 1000 years in the future it will be normal and a natural process.

Much of the food we eat now will be impossible to consume in 1000 years.

Q: Are there other changes within 100–200 years?

A: Above our heads, a kind of energy will form, like a darker cloud. I don't understand the cause, but it's quite large. I think it's a density. I understand now. In a way, our low-vibrational thoughts, the darker parts, until now would accumulate and somatize differently within our bodies. After the transformation of our DNA, all thoughts and densities will no longer be hidden, but will float above the head. They will become visible to those with open channels.

Now, with the device we have, they were hidden somewhere in the body, head, brain, these non-beneficial thoughts. We could hide these emotions, even from those with open abilities. After this transformation, they will be accessible, able to be read by those with open abilities. Absolutely all intentions you have will be visible to the world. In fact, advanced Beings of Light already function based on this principle because they have no secrets. Everything is visible for them, but they've developed technologies that allow access to certain information to be coded; not all Bings of Light have access to everything. Until we, as humanity, learn to work with our densities, it will take time. This is a very important step toward evolution.

I'm now getting something about the Akashic Field, it will be accessed by those souls or people who haven't yet advanced. For them, the Akashic Field is their space of expression, still being in densities.

An example would be a five-story building made of light.

The 1st floor is the Akashic Field, where the beginners come, those who are just starting to understand where they are, where they exist; those with many questions at the beginning of the path of evolution. Conflicts and misunderstandings can happen there. The higher you go, the more advanced you are, or the higher your position. But this doesn't refer to discrimination or power-based competition, access, or knowledge, only to your current stage of evolution. Many beginners will be there. They exist in the same building with others who are on a higher evolutionary level, but that place is the 4D world.

The 2nd floor is 5D, where there's still some petrification from below, with beauty. In fact, the whole transformation process happened in the Akashic Field, and in 5D you're halfway. You already see a little of what was, and you embrace the beauty.

The 3rd floor – I simply see white. That's how I see it.

The 4th floor is half the white from the 3rd floor and half cosmos. I see stars, galaxies.

On the 5th floor I see what looks like dark matter, the void. Everything and nothing.
The Quantum Field is on the 3rd floor, the 4th is a mix between Megaquantic, and the 5th floor is the Creator itself, who is everything and nothing.

Creation has 5 waves, and at the 5th wave, creation retracts again, like a flow and ebb. That's where a limit exists, meaning all creation expands but it also contracts back. When we expand, galaxies and planets are created, and when we go too far into the 5th wave, everything starts retracting; constellations disappear, planets collide, galaxies collide. A balance is made, things are born, and when it contracts, things disappear. A certain amount is possible within infinity - too much is too much. I see the image as being overwhelming.

Q: What correlation does this have with today's portal?
A: Again, I'm getting a transformation. The beginning and the end. Thank you.

Percentage of the Reptilian DNA

Q: I want to understand, what percentage of the Reptilian DNA did I have or still have?
A: It's on levels. The first thing that comes to me is that 99% was disintegrated, but another percentage is 45% and it is decreasing. On the physical level, I still have 45%, where the change is happening, and 1% is on the energetic level.

Q: Is there another level where it is contained?
A: No, only 2 levels. Please convey what composition Diana has on the physical and energetic levels. You have only 29% on the physical level, and 14% on the energetic level. Wow. You are less physical and more energetic.

Q: What is the relevance between physical and energetic?
A: Good question, it means we have 2 types of DNA; one physical and one energetic. Ok, let's start with the physical one, the structure of our body, the DNA of the body's structure.

Victoria: Energetic is the first time I hear about it, but it comes to me now that our blueprints refer to energetic DNA. I'm now taking these 2 results and trying to make a connection as to why it's different for us.

Q: What is the reason we have these different percentages energetically?
A: I know the difference. It comes to me that I have more percentage in physical DNA because I haven't lived as a Reptilian. To coexist here, more Reptilian DNA was placed in my physical body because I don't have this in my blueprint. Now I understand my experiences with densities, possession, I had to experience the matter here. For you, I see your lives where you experienced Reptilian lives, that's why you have more in your blueprint from there. And because of that, you don't experience the density of the physical plane as much in your current body. On the energetic level, you have a higher percentage because you hold information from those experiences. For me, it's the opposite. I needed a balance, so I chose a higher percentage in my physicality with Reptilian DNA.

Diana: Yes, I suspected that about myself.
Victoria: I see you with families, with little ones in Reptilian form. Now it makes a lot of sense why I had various experiences in this life.

You can find my exclusive awakened story in my anthology book. *Awakened Hearts: Stories of Embracing Light, Love and Limitless Possibilities* on Amazon.

Q: I want to ask, is there a rule for those who experience the densities as you did?

A: It seems it is mandatory. Those who don't resist, it's like a kind of gain for the race that had contracts with our planet. You come into this game with free will, but you come with risk. If you haven't had experience in Reptilian planes, if in your energetic DNA you haven't dealt with such beings, you come here with a big risk. If you don't resist here, you lose your body and "go to their side". This was valid until now because their contract has ended. Wow. I never thought about that.

Q: Is it possible to decrease the percentage in physicality, or not? And on the energetic level?

A: Let's start with the physical part. It seems possible in 20 years. In 20 years it will decrease - that's the exact answer. In 20 years, I will be 55 years old. Wow. I had a reading where it said that from age 50 and up, a lot of scientific information will open up. Now, let's see for you, on the physical. The number 12 comes to me.

Diana: Then I will be 44 years old.
Victoria: So, I will be 55 years old.

Q: What is with these interesting numbers?

A: I want to receive a message but nothing seems to come. It's complicated. I see lines, like a forensic person with many personal notes, events, and from it pulls one line. Like this with you, I see connections - left and right. These numbers are age portals. It's like age is a portal, just like at age 33, where your body automatically enters other planetary laws, and other channels begin to open. It seems too complicated. Thank you.

Physical DNA Algorithms and Energetic DNA

Q: If we came here on Earth as Reptilians, in the next reincarnation will our DNA be human or Reptilian?

A: It depends on personal choice. The algorithm doesn't work like that; it's not imprinted based on the last life or the last previous experience, but it catego-rizes itself depending on the energetic DNA. In this life, you are human, but actually, the Reptilian DNA is considered according to the rules under which we were born on the planet. When you move to the next life, you choose what percentages of DNA you want to take, from which category - exactly like in a store where you pick the products you want. The choice is entirely yours.

Q: Is this also based on the experiences we want to have at the soul level?
A: Correct. You cannot choose randomly. Everything is chosen based on what you want to experience on the physical plane and what you need to experience in the next reincarnation. No one stamps you as having been a human being with Reptilian DNA in your past life, meaning nothing is fixed; it's entirely your free choice.

Q: Is this also related to our vocation? That is, does it help us to have certain types of DNA?
A: Yes, it depends on the experiences you want to have, in accordance with which ET, guides, soul family you want to work with, and in accordance with the planet, how many years you want to live. It depends on all these factors. You choose everything, even the predominant DNA of the races you have coexisted with, depending on how long you choose to live on the planet or in the space where you are.

For example: I know that Andromedans live for a long time - many years. If you come to a planet like Mars, which has 220 days in a year and spins quite fast, if you come predominantly from lives where you live long, it will not help you if you come to a planet with a more limited time, because you won't understand what to do in that life. Everything must be well planned depending on your energetic and physical DNA. In my case, I had no past involvement with the Reptilian race, and I needed a different experience, otherwise I wouldn't have managed on this planet, with its density and laws. As dominant DNA, I chose Lyrian, which is strong and warrior-like, not giving up easily, and Pleiadian DNA, which is a gentler, wiser, and peaceful race - a balance between these two.

Q: That's what I wanted to ask but you confirmed it. Our predomi-nant races change depending on what we want to experience, right?
A: Exactly. Nothing is static. You choose everything depending on your goals and missions.

Victoria: For example, I am a warrior, I'm on the go, but the purpose was to calm down, to have patience, and qualities like that. If the individual hasn't learned those lessons, if they fail, in the next life, they must learn the same thing, and they only slightly adjust their settings in the energetic and physical DNA. They choose their experiences, the family with which they will work as guides, etc., adjusting percentages and choices. Or maybe they want a break because it was traumatic, choosing a completely different experience. And when they are ready to return to fulfill their mission, they choose their settings again depending on each life. Thank you.

> *Note:* You can read more information about the predominant DNA and predominant races in the transmission received from a Lemurian being of light from the 22nd dimension, on page 350.

The Transition from Level 1 to Level 2 of Evolution

> *Dark night of the soul is a concept that describes a profound period of inner crisis, emotional suffering, or spiritual loss. The concept is used to describe moments of ego transcendence, when old beliefs, limitations, and everything that no longer serves us fall apart to make way for a new and more authentic perspective on our lives.*

Q: Regarding the transition to level 2, where does the dark night of the soul take place, and after you pass through it, does everything compress? Are there still beneficial pieces of information here that we should know?

A: To pass to level 2, you need to leave absolutely everything behind. It's like you came empty, stripped bare in the physical plane, and you need to pass through, still empty. Practically, many limiting beliefs, many programs, conditioning, paradigms you've accumulated that no longer serve you, must all be released. This makes you feel vulnerable, with no program, and you move toward neutrality. The dark night of the soul comes when you remain vulnerable without any program, without any "clothes"; that's when the transition happens. It's as if you had everything, but when you pass to level 2 you have nothing anymore - you are simply soul. When the soul goes through this period, it feels like it's going crazy because you have to leave absolutely everything behind; even the identity you created, or society created for you. And when you leave everything behind here, as you get closer and closer, you automatically pass through a field that presses on you, that extracts everything from you, and you have no choice but to let yourself be carried forward by the current.

Q: And how can you know it's the transition to level 2, and not just another energetic cleansing?
A: I've shown now that what you feel in this process is very intense. I see it as if you're standing barefoot on hot coals. When you stand on hot coals, they don't burn your skin, but they burn you from the inside; that's how you feel inside, it burns you emotionally, but it can also be physically challenging. All the emotions you have, you feel like you can't endure anymore, like you're dying, but you *understand* you will survive physically. Until you get to the point where you stand on the coals, already being used to it, you become numb, you no longer feel anything, you simply exit, step forward, and move on.

Q: To get a better idea, I'm still in this process, is it good to know?
A: The answer is No.

Q: How long does the transition from level 1 to level 2 last?
A: The number 8 months comes to me. Now I'm thinking about my journey, I had quite a long period when I was going "crazy". Actually, yes, wait a moment, I passed it, and I know when. It was 2019. 8 months. That's July through February. From February I sought online Reiki therapy, and from March on, somewhat, my blockages started to release. But then I really believed I was literally dying - it was hell for me.

Diana: I'm thinking of something else now. For you, before you entered the spiritual process, that was your transition … But what about me?

Victoria: Yes, for me, this awakening started suddenly, very suddenly.

Q: But from the perspective of someone who works daily on themselves, who begins to consciously release programs and limitations, can this transition be gentler?
A: I'm getting a big YES. It means the process is gentler if you work on yourself because you gradually release. For me, it was forced, it was sudden, because I had to follow this path. I was never with my "eyes closed". I had

been receiving messages for many years, and had active abilities, but I did not want to consciously open more. I was forced to wake up.

Q: Is this transition beneficial for us as souls to begin activating our maximum potential, to start?
A: I get that it's mandatory.

Q: To walk the path of the vocation we choose for ourselves, right?
A: The answer that comes again is *mandatory*. Thank you.

Densities in the Quantum Field

Q: Can you take something from the beneficiary into your creation? Do you still need to do cleanups after Quantum sessions?
A: The portal shows me. It is important to go through the portal individually, each in our own portal, to let the portal do the cleanse, and at the end when exiting, to go through the portal again and mention that everything that no longer serves is released and cleansed. And only then, you can exit. It is beneficial to let the portal see by itself, its color, to let it make its own decision. If you feel like saying the color, that's okay. However, it is important to cleanse both at entry and at exit.

In Megaquantic (this concept will be explained in the next chapter), everything automatically dissolves, and it is not necessary to perform the cleaning procedure. There you cannot even enter if you are not allowed.

Q: Are there cases in Quantum, or can there be attacks by low vibrational beings?
A: There are very few cases. Between 2% to maximum 10%, and they are rare. More often 2%, the attack is not direct, but like a projection.

Q: Does this have to do with us? How high we are on the frequency when we enter?
A: It has nothing to do with the guide, but with the beneficiary. When they are in the field, the densities they have can be projected onto your field. That is why it is important when you enter to do the entire cleaning procedure, to see and feel how it releases. You can take your time for

the beneficiary to stay as long as possible in the portal so they release and cleanse themselves. It is a step as important as grounding and connecting with Source. The more you see and feel that it releases, the easier it will be for you during the session. The faster they go from the portal into the field, the higher the possibility of experiencing entity projections. That's why it refers to exceptional cases. When you pass very quickly, and the beneficiary remains with the densities, it can reach 10%. This is the guide's lack of experience in managing the session. It shows me that you only feel the memory of the taste of fears, pain, entities, etc.

Q: In a single session, is it possible for the beneficiary to access multiple levels in Quantum?
A: It shows me it is a bit static and a bit flexible. Static depending on your state where you localize yourself. When you enter for yourself and localize yourself in 2B, (as per discussion on page 64 - Levels of Evolution) in thoughts, you work with the Quantum Field to release, and then you work with yourself. You ask again to see if there are changes. But if you are with the beneficiary, then the field responds to you where they are localized at that moment. If you worked with the beneficiary and there is no change, you must give them time. Give the beneficiary time, and if they come again for another session, you will ask and note for each session where they were at that moment. That way you will keep track of what is with them, if they are working, becoming aware. The second possibility is that the beneficiary does not want to change anything. How can you know? If they come again and it's the same, it means they are not working with themselves; they do not believe, or are waiting for something external.

Quantum Field quadrant table
Example: If the beneficiary is in 1B and you are in 2A, they will not receive information in Quantum because they will not be able to receive it. In this situation, Akashic is more suitable for them, and you need to be flexible because they will not be able to understand you being in Quantum. When you descend into Akashic, you need to use energetic protection and do everything according to protocol. Thank you

Disintegration of the Soul - Consciousness

Over the past few days, we've been experiencing a different state, filled with intense emotions and a kind of emotional roller coaster. I've come to understand the cause: a dense cloud of energy that was sent to planet Earth.

Q: What is the reason for such a rollercoaster emotional state?
A: I live in 2 different dimensions where the polarities are too strong. The connection point between these polarities is large and creates a fairly integral distortion that re-diffuses my physical body and mental perception, being present in 2 simultaneous spaces where consciousness jumps from one plane to another. But it is not coherently present with the physical, material body - it jumps from one side to the other. Consciousness pulls in one direction and the physical body in another. Because of this, the physical body cannot exist without consciousness. Consciousness pulls the body, the body pulls back, and this creates a barrier of existence between these two dimensions. My polarities are too large. Ok. I want to exist, co-exist together with this body, with consciousness, with the mind, with the heart, with the soul, and with the subconscious in one synchronized body.

Q: How can I exist only in one dimension, space, place, body?
A: I feel like that's a hell of a ride. I am scattered into many portions. I coexist in multiple dimensions, and that hurts because I can't gather myself. I am like a piece divided into different places and spaces. I see myself everywhere.

Q: What caused this? What is the reason?
A: The fear of release. I am not present here where you see me in the physical body. Zero whole and 1 percent exists. The rest is scattered.

I, Victoria, being in this body, want to be 100% present. I see different lives in which I coexist. I see ETs, gray-blues, some animals, and stones. They are diverse; I see a fragment here and there. I call back all the consciousness that belongs to me and ask that it be gathered back into this body of Victoria - all the little pieces, facets of my soul to be reintegrated into this physical body, and any particle that does not belong to me to be released now. The rejected fear of release. It feels like I am in a space. I simply sit in a space in the cosmos. I have no floor, nothing, but I see my physical body, and I see how little pieces come back into me. Many currents come.

Q: How long will this integration process last?
A: 12 days

Q: What was the cause of the disintegration of my consciousness and soul?
A: There was a wave, an energy, that approached our planet, coming from behind, from the west, on the left side, not from the sun. It was a dense force that wrapped itself around the Earth. Its appearance was black with shades of gray, resembling the static you see on a TV screen when it's not tuned to a frequency properly, that flickering gray noise. That's exactly how this energy looked.

It moved like a shadow, originating from the western side of America and traveling toward Japan, sweeping from west to east. I was present in the space where this energy radiated most intensely. As it moved across the globe, wherever it passed, it caused complete energetic disintegration, to everything and everyone within its path.

Q: Does this explain yours and my *state* from recent times?
A: I feel like not directly to you. I was approximately direct.

Q: But how did it affect you and others?
A: Above Europe, I don't see this energy, but I see a strip from the west along the planet, and like a channel it entered through the North Pole, and from the North Pole it continued inside the planet, and from there it triggered from the Earth. I don't see India, the Middle East, but it shows me that the strip reached Japan. It entered the North Pole internally. There is a channel at the North Pole where energy enters very easily and affects from inside toward the surface. It's like it came out through the pores of planet Earth; it was not direct on the other side of the globe. You were not directly exposed to this energy but to its radiation. This energy caused disintegration to all, and that was the purpose. Those who were directly hit were literally unbalanced on the level of energy and soul.

Note: This global event happened around the end of 2024.

Energetic Shield with Codes - Being of Light with 12 Wings - similar to Seraphim

Following a question from Diana in the Quantum Field, an energetic shield that she possesses came to the surface. When we asked for details about this shield, we connected with similar to Seraphim for the first time.

Victoria: On the left side of your energetic body, there is a shield that extends from your left waist across to the right, wrapping around behind you like a curved plate on your back. This energetic shield sits just outside your energy field. It's difficult to describe, but it generates a distinct feeling of fear within you, and more than just fear.

It emits subtle vibrations that reach you with messages like: *you're not ready yet*, *you can't do this*, (Release) and other limiting thoughts. It's not a direct voice, but more of a persistent feeling that comes from this external shield.

Q: Can the shield be released now?
A: There are codes. We don't have access or the power to decode these codes. I looked at the shield, and it looks like a plate, but if you get close and try to do something, it has transparent buttons on it, like small square patches, and each patch is a different code we don't have access to. Access is held by the team that is responsible for you, the one you are a part of. It gets deactivated only when someone higher up, who is responsible for you, decides to remove it or not. It's something quite far from us. It's a team that is individually responsible for each of us.

Q: Can I call the team responsible for it, or is it not yet the right time to remove the shield?
A: In front of you is a being, it has 12 pairs of wings. They look like wings but they're something else. They appear as wings, but they are not large, they're like more flexible feathers. There are 12 rows. It's a very large, mega-gigantic being, and it's in front of you. You are like a grain of sand before it.

Q: Does it want to introduce itself?
A: We can't even imagine its rank, it's too high for our minds to comprehend. I get the sense that it's like a Seraphim.

Q: Then I ask it to tell me if it's the right time to release the shield?
A: It removed the shield and held you in its arms. Its face is hard to describe. Imagine a bird with no visible eyes at first, a rounded shape, then a layer with a beak, followed by eyes underneath. Then another beak, more eyes, and again a beak. That's the structure of its face, layered and unusual, yet large and radiating immense love.

Despite its strange appearance, the being is incredibly loving, so gentle, so tender with you. My God, the love it holds is overwhelming. It cradled you like a newborn, as if you were its child. To this being, you *are* a baby. It doesn't consider itself part of any known category of beings we're familiar with.

It originates from at least the 12th dimension. Beings like this cannot materialize below D12, they simply do not exist in lower dimensions. And it isn't a guide. Guides must operate from lower frequencies or dimensions to be close enough to us. Nor is it an angel. While we might try to compare it to cherubim or seraphim, powerful and radiant, it's still not the same. I've never encountered a being like this in any session before.

It belongs to a collective, a group to which each of us is connected in some way. They are responsible for us on a very deep level. They aren't Founders or Creators, but they are something entirely unique. A team, existing far beyond what we typically understand.

A: Now it has placed your protection back, because you are meant to have it. The codes that have been activated within you can only be deactivated by them. However, growth is still required. When they see that we've truly learned the lessons and the shield no longer serves a purpose, then they will remove those codes.

We often think of this protection as something negative, but in reality, it helps keep us focused on the experiences we need to go through in the specific creation we're part of. If these codes were removed prematurely, it would be as if you had no mission, no purpose to fulfill.

This being took you, gently removed the shield, then placed it back again, communicating that you're still a baby in their eyes, and you have more to learn. It has now left, but it left behind so much light. What an extraordinary being. Thank you.

Conception and Implantation –
Mother-Child Protection

Q: My question now is about pregnancy, about children. Is it in Diana's best interest to find out the answer now?
A: You will have 2 children. The first one came, you held him in your arms, and then the second one came. The first child came to your right, you picked him up, and the second came from the left and took your hand. In fact, the first came and circled around you twice, then you held him in your arms on the right side. The second child came from the left. You took her hand, and she circled once. Something with the number 2 and the number 1. Two seasons will pass until the first child comes, and for the number 1, there will be a 1-year difference between them.

Q: And why on the right side and the left side?
A: On the right, the first will be a boy, and then a girl

Diana: That's what I felt too

A: For the boy, something with the number 2 for you. He came into your arms, and then came from the left, and you both spun once, possibly meaning a one-year difference between them. I see you very clearly with 2 children. The little girl will be more shy. She hides behind you.

This is not the first time I receive information on this topic about children; in fact, if there are pregnant individuals present, I instantly sense the gender of the child, and it always turns out to be true … without knowing any information about the pregnancy.

During a physical body scanning session, I perceived a protection around Diana, like two devices were present in her field, and they did not allow me to scan her physical body as is my natural ability to see in detail. The Beings of Light then showed Diana that this was connected to the conception process and the little soul that will come through her.

Therefore, the next question refers to that protection, whether it is automatically generated for the mother during the conception process, or if it is something individual.

Q: In the Quantum Field, with the process of conception, is a protection field for mother and child created automatically? Or does the child automatically create the protection?

A: The question is complex, and the answer is complex. The process is intricate, and so is the explanation. Protection begins to form in the head area at the moment of conception. A channel opens diagonally above the head, then enters the head itself, continuing downward along the spine, through the vertebral column, and into the kundalini channel, ultimately reaching the sacrum. This forms the foundational base of protection at the time of conception. It's important to note that this process does not begin during pregnancy, it starts approximately two months beforehand. That marks the beginning of the first phase.

The channel flows from above the head, into the body, and descends vertically through the spine. Once this vertical axis is established, which serves as the core foundation, it begins to widen in circumference. This process starts two months prior to implantation, and the spinal channel remains straight while a protective field begins to build around the mother's body. This field appears like a cocoon enveloping her.

This protection doesn't form instantly; it requires time to grow and solidify. Once the protective structure is fully developed, the child's soul enters through this specific channel, not through the crown chakra, as commonly believed. It is a distinct, lesser-known channel.

This particular channel, which humanity has not yet identified, is the path through which we enter incarnation. The child's soul descends through this diagonal channel during the incarnation process.

Q: Quantum Field, is it appropriate for us to know the name of this channel?

A: **MURSUND,** that's how it came.

When implantation occurs in the physical body, the soul then travels through this channel located at the back of the head. It continues its journey through the kundalini channel, descending all the way to the base. From that point, development begins. This is the process that takes place during both conception and implant.

Energy Cord Created With a Soul that has Passed to the Astral Plane

Q: I feel like asking now, is the little girl the soul of my grandmother? That's what came up in a session.
A: NO, the answer is no. It tells me not to be attached to your grandmother or great-grandmother, because you are violating your grandmother's free will, for her personal evolution, by creating such a thought.

Diana: Interesting because this message came to me from an Akashic Reading through someone, and I wasn't really attached, but that thought probably made me create the attachment.

Victoria: You created a cord with your grandmother's soul.

It should be kept in mind that sometimes, during Akashic reading sessions, the information may come from the guide's mind. It is important not to attach ourselves to all the information received, as they could be probabilities and change depending on our choices. However, if the guide is not in a high vibrational frequency during the sessions, has not worked on themselves, and has not cleared their densities, they may transmit misleading information. The Akashic Field, as I presented at the beginning of this book, is a dual field that can attract information from denser beings to prevent us from following our divine path.

Diana: Then I express my intention to cut the cord with my grandmother's soul. I release her and allow her to have her own evolution.

A: You don't allow the soul that is meant to come through you to come, and you keep the connection with the cord that is not meant for you, because you unconsciously created the cord with your grandmother.

Diana: How interesting because I felt like asking. I didn't resonate with this information, something felt off, it didn't quite align when this information came through.
A: You're not allowing the soul of your future child to come, and you're blocking your grandmother's evolution process. You're violating the free will of two different souls.
Hold your left palm near your left ear, and now see how the cord comes out like a capsule from your body, not reaching your palm. Imagine your palm

143

as a magnet, pulling the cord out. When you see it floating outside of your body, set your intention to release this capsule. Now, see how this capsule rises upwards and dissolves automatically into light. It's dissolving. Set your intention now. Perfect. And energetically as well. From any space, time, creation, existence. Like this. This was very important for you to release.

Diana: Wow, yes, I'm glad I asked. And I now see how much certain information you receive can impact you ... information that's not true?

Victoria: Yes, because you form a program, a cord, and confuse the evolution of another soul.

Diana: I feel like saying now: *I allow that little soul who wants to come through me to come at the right time, exactly how it needs to.*

Victoria: In two years, you'll have a girl. I just saw a channel opening on your left side. It's connected to feminine energy. That's what formed the link. The energy first appeared pink ... wait, no ... indigo. I see the indigo color now. She'll be more aligned with the indigo soul group or race. I'm not entirely sure, but that's what I'm seeing.

Diana: I'm not sure if it's a race, but indigo is the wave of souls coming for the ascension of the planet.

A: She's a crystal being, I can see her whole form, and it's rounded and crystalline in nature, though her colors are indigo. She will be an indigo child. By 2027 at the latest, she will arrive; she must come within this timeframe. The connection was made just now, when the channel on your left side opened. First came the pink energy, followed by the indigo. I saw her standing clearly, with her arms and legs apart, her full body formed. The final connection is complete. This is why it's so important not to block ourselves from receiving this kind of information.

Reconstruction of the Left Eye

Q: My question is about my left eye. Why do I have these very random stabs?

A: It comes to me as "under construction". Do you know what I get? It's like how we all have permission to make repairs from 9 in the morning until 10 in the evening (depending on the area and country), and we still need permission? It seems they are working like that, but they are still working slowly.

Q: Why is the reconstruction of the left eye needed?
A: It's being cleansed. An interesting word came to me: *"omnabulistic"*. From the *"omnabulistic"* state, it transforms into another form.

Omnabulistic - the old structure formed from the raw material of 3D existence, which interferes and can be manipulated, and I actually see the Matrix. This is the state of our physical existence in the Matrix.

Q: And into what form is the left eye being reconstructed?
A: *Omnipotent* - the structure of mass formed from neutrons, overlaid with protons, in which it forms, multiplied by two, into a *"fizotron"*.

Omnipotent - the raw material created in the overlap of cellular substance, in which the negative human part coexists, where the physitrons are the positive part of the human physical creation at a simple level, and in which the raw material develops into cellular, crystalline, isotropic matter. *I need to listen three times to understand what this is about and what I just said.*

Q: In simpler words, from what state to what state is the left eye being reconstructed?
A: It shows me something very tiny where an organ has developed, on this *omnabulistic* side. The omnipotent state is already the formed organ, in the shape of organs, formed in several of the same type of organ. It shows me images. We see one eye, and in the first phase, multiple cells formed, and the eye as an organ was created. Now, in the construction process, it's from the formed organ, and more eyes are being formed. Multidimensional vision. It's like one eye that sees through 100 eyes.

Q: Does this allow the possibility of seeing 10 times, 100 times better?
A: Yes, it says yes. One eye will see through 100 eyes, but I won't have 100 eyes here, I will have one eye that sees through 100 eyes. It shows me that this is how Archangels see.

Diana: I got from the start that it's actually long-distance vision.

A: Yes, it's the ability to see on multiple levels. It shows me the Archangels, the higher their ranks in the angelic hierarchy, the more eyes they have, and they see in multiple creations, in multiple planes. Thank you.

Q: Does it correlate with the upgrade and transformation from Reptilian human to light-being human?

A: It comes to me that yes, and the continuation is multidimensional human being. You see, on 12/12/24, the left part was specifically cleansed, and now another process is taking place. It means it is part of that process as well.

Q: Is this an individual ability? Or once we dissolve the Reptilian part, do our divine, multidimensional abilities become activated?

A: It comes to me that our lower part dissolves, and our multidimensional part is activated. But this is not considered an ability, it belongs to the category of our capacities that we can access.

Imagine you went to a bookstore and wanted to access information about, let's say, *stars*. You give yourself permission to access it, it's the ability to study more. An ability seems like something already inside you, but capacity comes from experiences you've accumulated and learned. Gifts are one thing, abilities are something else, and capacities belong to another category. For me, the part with the eye is a capacity. Thank you.

Gifts, Capacities and Abilities

Q: The gifts mean they come as an upgrade, what we receive in addition, right?

A: Good question. I feel that the upgrade can reflect both gifts and capacities.

Gifts fall into the category of missions, meaning when we complete different missions that we chose at the soul level, we are given medals -we are given gifts.

Capacity is when you, a multidimensional soul, have gone through different lives where you had certain abilities or developed various tasks that you can activate in this plane. It's not something offered as a gift, but a skill reactivated within us.

The upgrade is necessary for both gifts and capacities because this is how they open.

Abilities are our natural aspects, something that is part of our energy, which we activate when we release densities and blockages. Some people come with certain abilities already opened, but others open up over time when we're ready and we want them.

Q: I was thinking about my situation; I took it as a gift when hearing was activated on other planets. I think it was a gift.

In a channeling session, activation, and upgrade, Diana received as an upgrade the ability to heal in other planes and dimensions. This ability is the capacity to receive information from other planes through hearing. There are various souls that exist in the physical plane but, at the same time, coexist in other planes, galaxies, planets, or dimensions. Thus, any experience from those planes impacts and echoes in this existence as well. Imagine how each past life echoes in everything we experience now. All unresolved blockages from other lives or existences will create similar patterns in this plane, all in order to be released and integrated. The same applies to parallel and concurrent lives.

A: Yes, exactly. As an example, just like I received at the retreat when I released the entity that had kept thousands of souls captive in their evolution. There, I received a medal, which is a gift. This part with the eye is a capacity, meaning I must have lived somewhere in such planes. I know I have a relationship with the angelic realm because my mentor also told me she saw me there, and I believe that's where I got this capacity from. Very interesting. Thank you for the information.

The experience with the Earth entity will be shared in the following chapters. In October 2024, during my participation in a retreat, I went to connect with America's Stonehenge. There, I experienced something very unexpected - during the meditation, I released an enormous entity that was keeping souls and the entire planet Earth captive from evolution. This allowed me to work with the planet, not only one-on-one with other people or group sessions.

Q: How will this help me, after the reconstruction of the left eye?
A: Okay, I understand. It's exactly what I explained.

Q: The right eye, through the eye, does it connect with whoever needs it, or does it take more of the form of my Lyrian aspect?

Diana: I feel it connects when you need it. But still, on the dominant race side, that's what I'm getting.

A: It's similar to what you said. When there's too much density around me, it acts like a kind of measurement system. If my field detects that the surrounding density has gone beyond its set parameters, reaching a maximum threshold, then a connection activates through the root of my eye. That's when my Lyrian family steps in to dissolve any low-frequency energy around me, like a laser. My physical energy alone isn't strong enough to handle that level of density, so my dominant race connects automatically. Through my gaze, this energy is dissolved, without me even realizing it. It's like a laser that clears energy based on where my eyes move. It's an involuntary, unconscious process.

Connecting Beings of Light Through the Eyes

Q: But it's interesting that the last time someone connected with your left eye, it was when you were at another retreat. Why is that?
A: Yes, that's a good question. What came to me is that my left eye is currently "under reconstruction", and the optic channel couldn't withstand the intense energy because it had been at a lower vibrational state due to the transformation process triggered by the 12/12/24 portal.

As a result, they connected through my right eye instead. That's also why creation shifts automatically when a specific race steps in, and my facial features change depending on which race is connecting with me at that moment.

Q: Is there any relevance to why the left eye and not the right one?
A: I asked my Lyrian father to explain why they connected with the left side last time, and now with the right, if it's the same race.

A: Your question is complicated. You need to understand one thing: "*The diffusion of energies doesn't matter through which side or channel they are* *transmitted, or where the transmission takes place. What matters is that it passes through. The eyes are a direct channel, as if you were looking through the back of a mirror, from inside the mirror, no one sees from the outside. But from the outside, only the mirror is seen."*

Transmissions - Lucernisum and the Galactic Family from Lyra

The **Galactic Family from Lyra** are ancient Beings of Light, wisdom, and high vibrational frequency. Known as one of the earliest star civilizations connected to Earth's evolution, they hold deep compassion for humanity's journey. Their presence is subtle yet powerful, gently guiding souls through remembrance, energetic healing, and the activation of higher consciousness. In the transmission that follows, they share not just words, but frequencies meant to be felt beyond the mind, directly into the heart and energy body. Open yourself to receive, not with understanding, but with presence.

Q: What energy is next to me right now, in my space?
A: Wow, I feel waves of energy, it's very intense.

Channeling:

"We will make the transmission now. Victoria doesn't realize that many things work on itself. We are here now and took over for a couple of seconds transmitting this information for the highest good of everyone on your planet. Something doesn't need to be understood as you perceive it in your mind as a human form. The energy works as it flows the way through the channel of wherever it feels the physical body, through eyes, ears, skin, noise, sound, and movements of your hand that reflect energy outside the physicality and into your world. The answer to this question is not a matter of your knowledge. We don't need to explain much about the existence and the work itself of the energies, as long as it connects with you all. Too many questions arise in your mind because you want to know more, but the energy works in a simple way. Go exactly how it needs to be connected at that moment of the unit in time for the job to get done, when you need it the most. You don't need to arrange things as you want them to be. And we perceive your knowledge as a limited belief in your mind that doesn't want to release the limits of how to believe beyond ... and we wish you to say thank you for this transmission. We love you."

Victoria: I feel so small now that they've disconnected. Just moments ago, I felt like I was sitting on a throne, immense, as if I was as big as this entire building. And now, suddenly, I've returned to feeling small again, confined to this human physical body.

They connected through my head, I couldn't even form a single thought during the experience.

And that sound... just listen to it. There's nothing in my house that could possibly create a sound like that. It startled me a bit. Thank you for the transmission.

> *Before this channeling, in the house, various electronic sounds started to be heard, even though I don't have any electronic devices that would produce such sounds. At first, I was wondering what kind of sounds were being emitted in the space where I live, but after that transmission, they stopped. These kinds of inexplicable situations often occur.*

The Celestials are Beings of Light and higher consciousness who guide humanity through love, wisdom, and spiritual awakening. They often appear in symbolic or energetic forms to those sensitive to their presence, offering insight and support during moments of transformation. In the following transmission, they connect through Victoria to offer messages and clarifications, especially about the presence of celestial children and the names that began to emerge during the session.

Q: Let's ask about the different races with celestial children. Why does Victoria see different races of children? Is there a message to transmit?
A: On the table in front of me, where the laptop is, it feels like there's a little boy standing, and he's saying, "I'm here, hey, can you see me?" He's standing on the table, kicking his legs. His face seems to be full of stars. He's blue, almost like a cosmos, and he has stars on his face. Lucernius? I'm not sure if that's what it is. Lucernium. Either Lucernium or Lucernius.

And that sound was heard again. I don't understand who it is.

Shortly after, in the same session, after the first channeling transmission, other Beings of Light connected through me to provide clarifications about their names. Below is their transmission.

Channeling:

"We are beings from a completely different universe. From your location, from Earth, and in the separate world of our side, we wish to speak with you for the clarification of our name. Which is "*Lucernisum*". This is our name from where we're coming from. The world, our world has an intense sound frequency that it is impossible to hold onto your planet, and your world, the "halogenates" in your creation, everything would explode instantly and briefly of just our own voice sound in your world. For you, it would be a boom of ten thousand bombs, atomic bombs at the same time. This would be the sound frequency on our planet. This is how we function, and this is how we look. Blue with yellow, for you would be stars, but that's our creation. It is impossible for you to hear us except through such connections. Thank you. Goodbye."

Thank you. Oh, my God, I heard such a strong sound that I thought my eardrum was going to burst. Okay, I think I'm done for today. It's too much.

Quantum - Victoria & Diana - March 21, 2025

In this session, we connected to receive additional information or clarification on a few messages received for this book. The method of connection was completely different from what we've experienced before. At the beginning of the meditation, we connected with a star through the heart chakra, so from the middle of the trunk upwards, the physical human body was completely dissolved to allow the heart to connect equally and proportionally with the Quantum Field. For this method, we don't need cleansing, releasing attachments, or clearing low-vibrational energies, because the presence of such energies holds no value. Our trunks, from the middle up, were in continuous motion, allowing us to perceive the message correctly.

*This connection method is necessary when we connect in **the void space of the Quantum Field, level 3A**. This level is not recommended to be accessed* *without knowledge or a strict set of operational guidelines, because if you don't know how to connect or handle the energy, you can completely disappear from the physical plane. A different grounding method is required compared to what we are used to.*

12 base, 4 equivalent to the Source of the Earth divided by 2 fractal units of the Quantum Field

A foundational structure (base 12) in which an Earth-origin energy (4) is balanced or understood through divisions of fractal, repeating consciousness or energy patterns in the Quantum Field, referring to how universal intelligence or consciousness shapes Earthly experiences.

This symbolic formula describes how Earthly energy arises, or is understood, through higher-order spiritual or energetic framework.

1. 12 base 4:
In base 4, we convert 12 (base 10):
>*$12 \div 4 = 3$ (cat), rest 0.*
>*$3 \div 4 = 0$ (cat), rest 3.*

Results: $12_{10} = 30_4$.

30_4 in base 10 is $3 \times 4^1 + 0 \times 4^0 = 12$, so the numeric equivalent remains 12.

2. The Earth's Source divided by 2 fractal units of the Quantum Field:

S = The Earth's Source (S) is an undefined term, interpreted as a symbolic value. It may refer to the planet's vital energy - Gaia, terrestrial prana, or the morphogenetic field. Energetically, it could be associated with the Earth's electromagnetic field, specifically the Schumann resonance (~7.83 Hz, the "heartbeat" of the planet).

F = A fractal unit of the Quantum Field. A fractal unit could be a measure of a repetitive energetic pattern, such as a vibration or an "energy packet."

2 fractal units of the Quantum Field suggest a hypothetical unit (F), likely related to the fractal nature of the quantum field. Let us denote this as 2F. It could represent two "cycles" or "levels", a duality (yin-yang, positive-negative, light-dark), which modulate or "filter" the energy of the Earth's Source.

3. Equivalence:
12 (or 30_4, equivalent to 12_{10}) = $S / (2F)$.

The expression becomes:
$$S = 12 \times 2F = 24F$$

Summary:
12 in base 4 is 30_4 (equivalent to 12_{10}). If this is equal to **"the Earth's Source (S) divided by 2 fractal units of the quantum field"** (2F), then: $S = 24F$

The Earth's Source is 24 times the size of one fractal unit of the Quantum Field.

The **metaphysical significance** suggests that the number 24 may carry symbolic meaning:
– 24 hours in a day (a complete cycle of Earth)
– 24 divisions of the octave in some sacred musical systems

This formula could imply a relationship between the Earth's microscopic energy and microscopic units of vibration within the Quantum Field, suggesting that Earth "concentrates" or "amplifies" the universal energy of consciousness or life force.

S = 24F suggests that the Earth's energy is equivalent to 24 such fractal units.

If a fractal unit (F) represents a specific frequency (for example, a 1 Hz vibration or a "wave of consciousness"), then the Earth's Source could be a composite frequency or a cumulative energy.

Hypothetical example:
If **F = 7.83 Hz** (the Schumann resonance, associated with Earth's "heartbeat"), then:

S = 24 × 7.83 ≈ 187.92 Hz
This could represent a "higher" frequency of terrestrial consciousness, possibly linked to meditative or elevated mental states.

Alternatively, **F** might represent a more subtle form of energy, such as a **Quantum fluctuation** (in physics, on the order of 10^{-36} J/m^3), in which case, **S** would represent an amplification of this energy on a planetary scale.

*The formula could be part of a **cosmological system** that describes the relationship between Earth and the universe. In such a system, Earth acts as an **energetic node** that concentrates the energy of the Quantum Field into fractal patterns.*

> ***Disclaimer:*** *These formulas are based on my individual study in this field, where errors are not excluded from a mathematical, cosmological, physical, or metaphysical perspective.*

A: The technologies of creation from humanity's future exist beyond our current understanding of physics; a type of physics that hasn't yet been properly explained. It's like looking through a lens with a zoom of at least 100 times, multiplied by 2. In that view, the material physics we currently perceive as reality represent only a small portion of the whole, a significant gap remains between what we know now and what we must evolve into, in order to align with the new energy and advanced physics ahead of us.

The energetic field here is extremely intense, especially in this plane, where it feels like only half of my physical body is present. It's as if I exist only from the waist down, just my lower body and legs. It's a very strange sensation, and it's the first time I've ever experienced this.

Q: I feel called to ask - what is the purpose of the crystal I was guided to bring with me into this session?
A: It helps us stay anchored in our physical form. We needed a deeper grounding, and this crystal star serves that purpose, it keeps both you and me rooted at the same time, preventing us from getting lost or dissolving. With this type of connection, if there's nothing to hold you in place, you could quite literally vanish from the room, from physical space altogether. Without grounding ourselves this way, we could have completely dissolved into the Quantum Field ... so use caution.

Q: How does this method of connection in the Field help us today?
A: I'm shown a very tangible image, a portal opening, but not in the way you might expect. It's something that pulls you in. I'm drawn into the cosmos and see *a black hole*. This portal passes through the black hole, allowing passage through multiple realities simultaneously.

Now, I'm shown that our existence here, with the polarity inherent in our universe, involves the black hole as a place where everything disintegrates.

On the other side, lies the white hole; another polarity within the universe. In the Quantum Field, you can experience both realms, both universes, each with opposing polarities.

However, the transition between these spaces can only occur through this portal that goes directly through the black hole. Arriving there means entering the opposite extreme of the universe, where physics operates completely differently, opposite to the principles we currently understand.

This connection enables traversal through the void, making the journey to the other side possible. That's why we've been given this technique of connection. Without a unique form of grounding, one could dissolve entirely, not just physically as a human body, but in all forms you can imagine, all those existing in our universe and linked to us as other beings.

Connecting in the 3A Plane, Into the Transcendent Void

This 3A plane was the most difficult to perceive with the human mind. This transmission and the explanation that follows below were sent through, even though they were hard to grasp - in fact, they created confusion at first. I needed some time (a few months) to understand this concept and the difference between the 4A and 3A planes. It was even necessary to return to the Field for a more detailed explanation or to receive information that would simplify the perception of this level.

Q: How does the Field help us, or when exactly does it take us into the Void, into the 3A plane, or to the Source, or to the 4th level? Depending on what we access at those levels ... how does each one help us?
A: We are present today in 3A. This is the place, our location, where the Void is. The 3A level is very rarely accessed, to avoid the final disintegration of the physical body, and the ending of the physical body. I don't understand, it's very complicated here. If you don't know how, or if you want to do it just for pleasure, you can dissolve and disappear completely from the physical plane instantly.

Q: Then what is our purpose today in this Field?

A: Accessing new boundaries. The word "wonder" comes to mind. I now perceive someone below us, on another level within this field, this space. It's difficult to explain. We exist in this space, yet subtly. I sense another plane beneath us where a person dressed in white, perhaps a scientist or a medical professional, has entered.

He moves into that lower plane and senses something. He hears or feels a presence, but cannot identify its source because he is alone. He looks upward, but doesn't see me. Meanwhile, I look down and can see him clearly.

This is how the Quantum realm appears, layered in levels. This individual catches the waves, the thoughts, the messages, yet doesn't comprehend where they originate. He looks up at me but remains unaware of my presence; he simply doesn't see. It's like staring at the ceiling and seeing it clearly, while sensing something invisible hovering just above.

Q: Is this person connected to us or directly linked?

A: I get that he's not directly connected. I don't know why, but on the wall he has some technology, a device, something rising up, not cables or something solid, but something energetic, like cords; blue and black energy cables going upwards. I don't know why I was prompted to ask about the Akashic Field and to step into this Quantum Field. I am beside him now. But he is much taller than me, very sturdy. I think I'm about chest level to him, that's how tall he is. But he is older, but not very old - looks around 60 years old, give or take.

Q: Who is this person?

A: I see myself working with him, and I don't understand why he puts his hand on mine. I ask my logical mind to step aside. It's like I don't want to accept or believe what I'm receiving, but the information I got is that I will create such technology with my potential partner.

Q: What is the purpose of us seeing these images?

A: I don't get answers.

Diana: I got something related to decoding, but I don't know what exactly.

Q: But why is the Field showing us this now?
A: I'm back in the Quantum Field. The reflection is of the internal codes of the planet.

Q: What does that mean? How does it help us?
A: The word "reflection" is approached from a scientific point of view. It is not directly related to the meaning of emotions. It tries to find me another word.

Victoria: Transgendation - what kind of word is that?

A: The *transgendation* **of planetary lines**. They are not meridians. Meridians are thick and fewer, clearer. But ley lines are secondary, more numerous, and the channels are weaker, from which the whole system of energy balancing of the planet's internal ecosystems is formed. I don't understand what I'm saying now, for the moment it doesn't make any sense.

Q: Is there something humanity needs to know about these lines, or about everything you said earlier?
A: We need to move to another quadrant. We are in 3B. Here it will be simplified. In 3A the information is more advanced, more technical.

Q: Does it relate only to technical information there, or not only?
A: It's not just that. It seems you need to reach a certain level of technical understanding in order to truly grasp them and to receive clearer, more detailed information. In the future, I'll be accessing a great deal from the 3A field, specifically for scientific knowledge. Once I've developed the right vocabulary, not just the ability to speak, but the precise understanding, I'll begin receiving more from that field.

I'll function like a scientist who immerses their mind into this Field and receives direct downloads of guidance in areas like mathematics, physics, and technical concepts. It comes straight from that Source. For people who aren't involved in science or don't work in such fields, this Field means nothing - it remains inaccessible to them.

Diana: Now it confirms to me that there (3A), it relates to the technical part, advanced technologies that will be downloaded into the physical plane.

A: There are all the mechanisms, all the formulas, everything downloads based on this Field. Practical knowledge comes in mathematics, physics, etc. That's how the 3B plane works.

These global ley lines are like, for example, we know the 7 major chakras in the human physical body, but our body has thousands of other small chakras, thousands. Exactly like that, our planet has thousands and thousands of small chakras, besides the major points we know of, and those small chakras get little attention. When we connect with the small chakras of the planet, the ley lines, you can connect with the entire body at once, creation itself.

The technology that will be created in the future, will be able to offer from a single point on the planet to connect all the small lines, the small chakras of the planet, and from that point you can connect directly to the Quantum Field. You do a bypass from our universe into the Void. It's like a technology where you switch from one to another, and in this way you perceive yourself being present here, depending on the levels.

At the moment, ordinary people have no benefit from this, because the appropriate level of knowledge hasn't been reached yet. However, it shows me that there are people in science trying to understand this concept. They have many questions but they cannot understand how to reach the level of this given technology.

Q: Regarding the 3B level, depending on what, or when, is it beneficial to access this plane?
A: What I'm being shown is that this is the process of integration into the physical body. Information from the 3B field flows downward into lower levels, while 3A is extremely advanced; it requires preparation and a deep understanding of how to enter it. Not everyone is meant to access this field, only those willing to take on the responsibility and risk.

In 3B, I see many scientists receiving formulas. Those who operate primarily from the mind and logic, base their work on principles like spirit, flame, and heat - but they don't enter 3A, because accessing it is dangerous. Information from 3A flows automatically down into 3B, where it becomes usable and processable within human physicality. However, it doesn't arrive in direct form, it's transmitted through the mind and body as thought and comprehension.

Individuals who are not focused on physical or technical knowledge, those more connected to spirit, creation, and artistic expression, tend to remain in 1A and 2A.

Meanwhile, scientists, mathematicians, and those rooted in what we might call the "real" or structured side, operate in the B levels: 1B, 2B, and 3B. They possess soul and spirit as well, but they receive information directly into the mind, thought, logic, and body, through a more grounded, intellectual channel.

Q: And at the 4th level, when is it beneficial to receive information or connect?
A: In 4B, I'm shown that many were meant to move in that direction. 4B represents the neutral space of pure observation, it encompasses both the A and B columns.

Q: What do we need to do to access from there? Does it relate to our evolution?
A: I get *intellectual growth*, but this does not refer to intelligence, to being smart, but to intellectual and spiritual consciousness.

Q: So, the emotional intelligence, that part?
A: Yes, when you reach neutrality. To reach neutrality, you need to advance with the integration and growth of spiritual and emotional capacities. This aspect will help you grow and reach the maximum point of being intellectual, emotional, and spiritual; only then do you reach neutrality. Neutrality allows you to analyze and observe equally, from the mind, body, and spirit perspectives.

Q: Would information accessed from 2A be different from information accessed from 4A?
A: Correct. Besides, in 4B you are more in neutrality, without human filters, so you allow the information to download differently into your field, than when you are in the heart or in emotions.

Q: Quantum Field, is there any additional information that is good for us and also for the readers of the book to know?
A: In front of me, I see a long hallway that stretches so far, I can't perceive its end. It has a square shape, with walls that are black in the center but

shift to shades of blue with touches of white in the corners, colors that seem to rise upward from there.

Q: What is this hallway about?
A: Our reality is shaped exactly as it was shown to me in that image, yet it's not fixed; it's molded by our consciousness. Nothing is truly static, even if our eyes perceive it that way. Reality is constantly being shaped by the state of consciousness. Consciousness itself can be molded, condensed, or expanded, stretching to whatever limits it defines for itself.

What we perceive with our eyes appears solid and real, but in truth, this reality is in continuous motion, like clay being shaped. It's never still. Even the reality we believe to be stable, is actually fluid, constantly shifting and reshaping. It doesn't move in a straight line.

Q: For what purpose is this information offered? How does it help us?
A: Stability is merely a human perception. This is precisely how the Matrix operates. I'm now shown a scene from the old *Matrix* movie, specifically the moment when Neo visits the little Buddhist boy ... the one with the spoon. The spoon appears solid, but the boy teaches Neo that by simply observing it, it bends. In truth, the spoon isn't bending, it's our perception of reality that shifts.

Reality itself is the modeler. What we consider to be the core of creation, something solid and fixed, is actually in a constant state of transformation. It's always being shaped and reshaped.

Q: In which category should I mention this book? I see it's not only spiritual but also scientific.
A: The word *metaphysics* comes to me. I'm being shown that scientists, especially those not yet connected to the spiritual side, will eventually come to this book. They need to read it, because it will shift their perception. It will help them move beyond a purely scientific mindset into something more expansive, where science and spirituality merge.

They require a trigger, something that breaks them out of a rigid scientific framework, where spirituality is absent. This book is meant to serve that purpose. It's not only for everyday people to support awakening, but also for scientists who are searching for answers they've been unable to find.

The spiritual insights within the book will help them understand and integrate the energetic aspects that traditional science often overlooks.

This will spark deeper interest and exploration. Humanity is being called to shift its perception of science, to move it in a new direction, one that embraces both the seen and unseen. Thank you.

Dimensions - Creations

Q: How many dimensions exist in Creation, if it is welcome for us to know?
A: It starts with the number 2, and after 2, there's a comma, and then I see many zeros. I can't see the end of it.
It's interesting why it starts with the number 2? What does the number 2 symbolize in God's creation? The only thing that comes is polarity. It's the existence and balance between 1 and 1, and then you get 2. This is what religion in general refers to, where heaven and hell are mentioned - two polarities that coexist at the same time. The high plane of creation cannot exist without the presence of the lower plane, and vice versa. Both are created and cannot be destroyed; not even one can be destroyed. Impossible. No matter how much those in the lower planes of creation try to attack, seize power, or attempt to destroy God's creation, they will not have control. The more they force the process, the stronger it pushes back. Imagine a magnet. The closer you get to the same polarity, the more it will repel you. Thank you.

Soul Contracts

Soul contracts refer to agreements or pre-incarnational decisions made by the soul before it enters a physical body. These contracts are believed to outline the lessons, experiences, challenges, and relationships the soul will undergo in order to grow and evolve spiritually during its lifetime. The concept of soul contracts comes from various spiritual traditions.

Q: How many soul contracts exist, and what is the difference between them?
A: 12 came to me, but they won't be explained now.

6 contracts (4 for deep healing, 2 for soul evolution)
2 are not karmic – they work on a collective level (you resonate with a friend, a deeply intimate one), this is how we perceive information through such contracts.

Q: The last aspect regarding soul contracts, is it welcome to elaborate on them?
A: Hmm, I see the question, but the entire page appears blank. It comes through very subtly, like trying to write when there's no ink left in the pen.

Q: Is there any reason why it's still not beneficial to transmit this information?
A: It came to me that: "you" don't want to know? We, as collective humanity.

Q: Are we not yet open to accept it? What do we need to open up, to accept?
A: Here, a special code is needed to access the information. It's encoded.

Update May, 2025

During another session dedicated to updating the information shared in this book, I once again asked if we could receive further insights regarding soul contracts.

Q: Is it welcome to know the types of soul contracts at this time?
A: I'm looking down, and someone is knocking with their fist on the floor, but I don't understand. We need to move from this place. Quantum Field, please move us to the quadrant where it's for our highest good to be. It shows me that 4A is welcome, but it requires more energy.

Diana: I was about to say that we should be moved to another field where it's welcome for us to be. A place where we can receive information aligned with Source.

Victoria: Yes, then we ask to be moved where it's welcome. Something is moving around us, an energy that envelops us with love. Ok, we're in a pink-colored space, and I feel a bit more powerful here.

Details About the Origin and Source of this Book

Q: In what dimension or space are we here?
A: 12 came to me.

Diana: I let you speak to see what you say, but 12 came to me immediately.
Victoria: Ok, thank you. I feel better here.
Diana: We ask the Beings of Light, if it's welcome for us, to transmit about each soul contract individually. Do you see any beings?
Victoria: I see myself walking, there's pink sand, and around me, there are transparent crystals.
Diana: At one point, I saw a Lyrian being.
Victoria: I'm walking, looking down, trying to understand how the sand can be pink. Crystals shaped like cacti are growing from it. And then, Jupiter appears in front of me, glowing as if the sun is right there. Wait, Jupiter does not have the ring.
Diana: Saturn has the ring.
Victoria: I wanted to say Jupiter, but I see it has some kind of ring, though it's thinner, around the planet. It's in front, very large, almost close. And the air, we see air and a clear blue sky, but here it is violet with a bluish tint. The mountains are black.
Diana: What is our purpose here?
Victoria: I'm looking at my hands, and I have a different body texture. Three fingers. It's hard for me to receive all the information.
Diana: Saturn has a larger sphere, while Uranus has a smaller sphere.
Victoria: I don't know exactly how I took something out of my head and placed it on the ground.
Diana: Why is the information coming to Victoria so slowly?
Victoria: I need to enter the planet. I see myself going inside, and although I'm not a snake, I don't fully understand what kind of being I am. I have a very long tail that pulls me in. I can't even call myself a dragon because my tail is unusually long, but my head doesn't resemble that of a dragon. I can't clearly perceive it.

Once inside, I find an empty space, a gravitational field where I seem to be floating, as if flying in midair. What does this space represent for me? I feel a sense of loneliness there.

Please help me align with that space, the place where any information meant for us, for the book, can be transmitted with clear intention and purpose. At the same time, everything irrelevant should be removed here and now. That irrelevant energy vanished. Fascinating.

Diana: I really wanted to say *if it's for our highest good to be there.*
Victoria: It tells me: "let me show you something else." Please adjust us to that field where we can receive from the Beings of Light, Source, that puzzle piece for the book. Thank you.

We arrived at a table, very quickly.
It's too dark here, but I don't know why.
Please remove any attachments, technologies, that are not beneficial for us and humanity.

Diana: Any being that wants to interfere with the field should be intercepted, and the connection with Source should be sealed, so we can receive information from high-frequency beings. I feel that any adjustment not coming from light should be removed.

Victoria: Hmm, now I see we're in a white space with Galactic Councils.

Q: What's the purpose of the interference from the lower planes?
A: I feel that this was a test to enter the Galactic Council room. It's looking at me, transmitting that this was a test.

It threw some cards on the table, like oracle cards. I look at them, it says to draw a card, and I see a card with a very large sun. On the back of the card, it says, "You are one with the source." Now I see other beings entering this room. The Galactic Council is on the right, behind you.

Victoria: How many chapters are welcome to be included in the book?
Diana: Something came to me.
Victoria: The number 7.
Diana: Me too. But you hadn't finished speaking, and I was already thinking 7.
Victoria: I refused to say it, thinking maybe it's just what I believe.
Diana: I couldn't think of another number, just 7. I feel like asking if new information needs to be added, or if adjustments are needed for the information already in the book.

Victoria: I see these various chapters and information that change places.

Diana: Is it necessary for the ET races to be in a single chapter?

Victoria: It feels like yes, plus 2 types of races. Two more types of races.

Diana: What are these two types of races?

Victoria: I saw two proud Blue Avians entering, so majestic.

Victoria: They are very tall and blue. There are two, one is on my side, and the other on yours. In the middle, the Galactic Council sits at the table, on your right, on my left, we are facing each other. This is one of those types of races.

Diana: Is there anything else we may not be consciously asking, but maybe it's relevant for them to transmit in today's session?

Victoria: The Galactic Council is giving me an elixir.

Diana: How will this elixir help Victoria?

Victoria: Clarity. Courage.

Diana: Is this related to her book or on a personal level? How does it help her?

Victoria: It's related to the book. It's pointing at the book. Now this elixir is being placed in my third eye. I have the impression I need to detox my pineal gland. It's clogged, and it's trying to infuse a vast amount of energy from this elixir. Do you think it's only given to me? It's also given to you. But you're grimacing and going "pff pff."

Diana: At one point, I felt that it's not just for you, but also for me.

Victoria: Ok, let's inhale as much as we can. We're inhaling. Now I feel dizzy (energetically speaking), and I see you the same. This elixir has entered my head, my brain, and it's making us dizzy, weak. Something is dissolving. More light is appearing in my head. Something is falling, a veil, a dark veil, and it's showing me exactly what I need to do. I see this book like it's in a museum, surrounded to prevent theft. Now I'm approaching the book, and so much light is shining on it. The book looks very old, from the future.

Diana: I was about to say, it's dusty, and you said it looks very old.

Victoria: Yes, I see it in a museum, the pages are old.

Q: Dear Field, is this a vision from the future?

A: It shows me the year 2560. What's so special about this book? It feels like someone got angry and put my head into the book, like when you dip your head in water to absorb knowledge.

Informative Fact: Thai Calendar and its Correspondence with the Gregorian Calendar

The **Thai calendar** follows the Buddhist Era (B.E.), which is **543 years ahead** of the Gregorian calendar used in most of the world. As a result, the Gregorian year 2025 corresponds to the **Buddhist Year 2568** in the Thai calendar.

For example: **Gregorian Year 2025 = Buddhist Year 2568 (Thai Calendar)**

This discrepancy arises from the historical calculation of the Buddha's death, which is believed to have occurred in 543 B.C., and is the starting point for the Thai calendar.

The Thai calendar is still used widely in Thailand and other Southeast Asian countries that follow the Buddhist tradition. It is important to note this difference, especially when working with dates in contexts related to Thailand.

Victoria: I was introduced to this information when this book was about to be published.
Diana: I feel that in the book, there are perspectives that humanity needs to contemplate, and this will help humanity's evolution to the next level.
Victoria: Wow, how beautiful. What's the purpose of showing us this vision from the future?
It shows me, as "look around", where you are, and asks: "What do you see?"

In this room, there are many glass cases, like those in a museum, very expensive, filled with numerous old objects. The space is bright, but it's designed so that everything feels like wood. It has a wooden ambiance, creating an old, vintage atmosphere, surrounded by other antique items. This is clearly a room meant to preserve old things.

If it's appropriate for me to leave this room and understand where I am next, I notice transparent doors without handles. As you approach, they open automatically. I walk down a narrow corridor, unable to see what lies beyond. Ahead, there's a door that you don't open in the usual way, you pass through it as if it were a wall.

As you move through, the door recognizes you at a cellular level. Your physical cells break down into small square cubes that move in a circular motion along with the door and wall. You dissolve as you pass through, but once on the other side, you instantly become whole again. The doors are programmed to respond specifically to your cells and molecules, so not just anyone can get through.

Diana: If someone tried to pass through with another person? I feel they won't pass. They can't trick the system.

Victoria: They can't. Even if someone tries to forcefully hold the person, the wall registers that they have access, they can enter, but when they touch this field, it turns red, and there's a system where the temperature of the body, the molecules, when the physical body is in a state of stress, anger, or low energies, like an attack, it immediately registers that the body is not right, and won't allow you to approach the door. This is where it starts registering something foreign. Ok, we've now exited. Is this field on Earth?

Diana: I feel it's not.

Victoria: No, we're not on planet Earth.

Diana: Does your book have implications for other higher spheres as well? Or what's the correlation, why is that the base? Are the manuscripts and projects from the higher planes kept *there?*

Victoria: Oh, my heart just pricked. Yes, that's it. In fact, when you asked the question, it opened, like a gigantic eye in the cosmos, and everything went into a black hole, like a portal. This place feels like a base, a location where the portal, an eye positioned on the left side, is situated. The environment is extremely modern; I don't see any trees or rivers, but it's not deserted either. It has a very futuristic vibe, with several buildings around. The building I'm in is situated at a great height. Ah, now it's showing me more about the portal. You enter from the front side when leaving, but when you return, you arrive behind the portal. The portal itself has a wide diameter, the width is quite thick. It operates with two different systems simultaneously, similar to a Merkabah.

Q: What's the main message from this experience?

A: It tells me that the original version of anything is created before it appears in other worlds. These originals were made long ago. Depending on how far in time and space something exists, the object's true age changes. For example, something may be created today but materializes in a place and time 500 years in the past.

This book has just manifested now, which is why it appears old. The creators know exactly how old it is and how far away, in time and space, its manifestation point is. This means that any invention already exists in a universal database, it simply materializes at the right moment and place. While it may seem like you hold the copyright, from a universal perspective, we are more like a third party.

Victoria: We are intermediaries because all these inventions have already been created, not by us, but by special organizations from the universe. Is there any other message for us in this space?
It says, "No need. It's all done." Thank you.

The Age Portals

Q: I want to ask now about the age portals, is there something more to know here?
A: I ask to rise higher, to the 4B plane, because I feel a lot of pressure here. Wait for me to recalibrate. It was overheating.

Age of 12 years

12 years – has a global impact

Q: Why do the Beings of Light explain the impact of the age of 12 in the evolutionary stage?
A: It guided me to the reproductive system and showed that its full development begins around the age of 12. From the sacral chakra, a channel forms that extends downward into the Earth, but it doesn't travel in a straight line, it moves in waves, undulating as it goes. This channel reaches the outer edge of the planet's core and penetrates inward, yet the core has a distinct outer layer that contains everything.

When someone turns 12, this outer layer triggers the development of the reproductive organs and generates an energy connection to that outer layer of the core's structure. The reproductive system itself isn't linked to the core's inner parts, only to this outer layer. This process happens to each of us. Once we cross this age threshold, the reproductive system matures, and the energy of the reproductive system becomes active within us.

Age of 22 years

22 years – It has no meaning

Age of 33 years

33 years – it is a number in which the physicality, the "structure, energetic body," *absolutely everything*, your entire connection as an individual with the planet, changes into another structure. The number 33 has a very intense connection, meaning that after 33, channels begin to open for receiving information from higher planes, techniques, deep skills, gifts, etc. Up until 33 years old, it is easier to leave the planet, because you are not so attached or deeply rooted to the plane of this planet, but once you pass 33, it becomes harder. The reason is that your connection to the planet becomes deeper. For me, at 33, I automatically felt a complete shift.

"The Power of 33: A Spiritual Awakening"

The age of 33 holds deep energetic significance from a higher perspective.

Once we turn 33 years old, life opens in unimaginable ways, undergoing a transformative shift. The age of 33 brings us new paths and opportunities that propel us to higher timelines, that align us with our Higher Self. For some of us, when reaching this age, we can experience a burst of energy and success that happens in our life, stepping into a greater understanding of our purpose and potential. Energetically, physically, there is an instant shift that helps us activate new abilities or new channels, reach new frequencies and higher levels of perceptions. From a spiritual perspective, 33 symbolizes a time of self-discovery, personal growth, a period of transformation, where old patterns, blockages and beliefs are released, making space for inner peace and spiritual enlightenment. This can lead to a higher perspective of our place in the world, and a deeper understanding of life's mysteries.

At age 33, the soul undergoes a profound shift:
    1. Deeper Connection to Earth: Your energy roots more firmly into the planet's energetic grids.
    2. Heightened Awareness: A stronger flow of universal information unlocks clarity and wisdom.

3. Soul Mission Activation: Greater understanding of your purpose emerges, aligning you with higher truths.

The number 33, known as the "Master Teacher," symbolizes spiritual enlightenment and service. Even Jesus completed his earthly mission at 33, reflecting this sacred alignment.

This age marks a turning point, a bridge between the physical and divine. If you've been feeling lost, it is hard to find your purpose in life, this period can bring you new perspectives and new fulfillment. Are you feeling the shift?

The age of 33 holds deep symbolic and energetic significance in various spiritual and metaphysical teachings. Your reflection touches on profound themes of soul connection, planetary energy grids, and the transformative shifts that often occur as individuals mature into their 30s.

From a metaphysical perspective, the age of 33 is often considered a pivotal year where the soul undergoes a heightened integration with universal energies and the Earth's energetic grids. This deeper connection allows for greater wisdom, intuitive insight, and alignment with one's spiritual path. Before this age, as you suggest, the bond with the planetary grids may be less rooted, enabling a more flexible exploration of soul lessons. However, after 33, this connection strengthens, facilitating a deeper understanding of one's purpose and the collective energy of humanity.

The number 33, in numerology, symbolizes spiritual enlightenment, selflessness, and a profound connection with the divine. Jesus Christ's transition at 33 is often viewed as a representation of his soul completing its Earthly mission without becoming overly entangled in the physical plane. It serves as a reminder of the balance between engaging with the material world and maintaining alignment with higher spiritual truths.

This perspective encourages individuals to embrace this transformative phase as an opportunity for growth, deeper self-awareness, and a more profound connection with the collective consciousness and the Earth.

Age of 44 years

44 years – has no meaning

Age of 49 years

49 years – Has impact only on a physical level and its effects are limited to the physical body. Without working in harmony with the mind, the body undergoes stagnant chemical processes that gradually lead to deterioration.

Victoria: Once the physical and mental aspects are brought into balance, a certain substance begins to form; a fusion of the two. But it doesn't integrate into the physical or mental bodies directly. Instead, it enters a white space within the brain, almost like inserting a disc into that space. From there, it starts to spread and integrate throughout the entire body.

The Exploration of the 49 Symbolic Points in Machu Picchu and the Structure of Consciousness

In 2025, I was present at a meeting with over 40 elderly members of various native tribes from different countries and continents, and this event, lasting several days, took place in California. There, I met a tribe from Machu Picchu, Peru, where the symbolic number 49 was discussed, and it was confirmed to me, that the number 49 plays a very important role in the Universe.

In Andean spiritual tradition, the number 49 holds profound significance, being associated with the completion of a full cycle of inner transformation. Obtained by multiplying the number 7 by itself, 49 reflects a spiritual journey in seven stages, each made up of seven steps. This fractal structure is also found in the symbolic framework of the Machu Picchu site.

Although there is no official list that identifies exactly 49 sacred locations within Machu Picchu, many of the existing structures can be interpreted as initiatory points in a spiritual journey. Intihuatana, the Temple of the Sun, the Temple of the Three Windows, the Sacred Rock, the temples of sacred animals (condor, puma, serpent), the main altar, the water channels, the agricultural terraces, the paved paths, and the observation points, can all be understood as physical representations of inner steps, corresponding to processes of purification, balancing, contemplation, and the revelation of inner truth.

In this context, Machu Picchu is not just an impressive architectural construction, but a living spiritual map. The 49 stages can be interpreted as a form of initiatory navigation, with each location symbolizing a step in the process of awakening consciousness. Like a three-dimensional mandala, the site can function as a space for reconnection with cosmic laws and the deep rhythms of existence.

Through this symbolic lens, the number 49 becomes a key to understanding the Machu Picchu site as an initiatory space, where each stone and every architectural level reflect aspects of a consciousness in search of balance, integration, and transcendence.

Q: Why is it necessary for us to connect? What is the purpose behind it?
A: What comes to me is that our mindset needs to be in full sync with our physical body, meaning our physical condition, not just our thoughts. When the mind is out of alignment with the body, the body begins to deteriorate, and the mind loses its influence. In this state, the physical body continues to function on its own, mechanically, just to sustain daily 3D existence, but without drive or deeper vitality.

At this stage of life, it's crucial to shift your perspective and realize that aging is not an absolute truth, it's a belief held by the mind. If you start to align both your mental and physical aspects, and truly reflect on the idea that your body hasn't actually changed, that it remains whole and capable as long as you care for it, then you're initiating a deep synchronization. This act becomes a mental reset.

Once this reset happens, it activates a signal in the brain. A specific space opens up after the age of 24 - a channel located between the eyebrows, near the third eye. It's through this channel that the reset information begins integrating across the body. Put simply, in order to shift your mindset, you must first recognize that your body isn't aging, the aging effect comes from your thoughts. Once you realize this doesn't have to apply to you, you gain clarity that it's your mind alone, shaping your experience of physical aging. This awareness triggers a shift.

If this mental reset doesn't occur, everything remains rooted in the physical. Over time, the mind begins to break down, and with it, brain functions start to decline. This shows up as memory loss and, eventually, physical illnesses, directly tied to unprocessed or unbalanced mental patterns.

Q: Is there something beneficial to know about the aging program? How can you deactivate it?
A: I'm shown that certain programs begin to activate around the age of 28. It's important to understand that it's completely natural to experience various emotions and thoughts; it's okay to sit with them and acknowledge them. However, from that age onward, and continuing through to around 49, it becomes essential to actively work with yourself, to process and integrate limiting beliefs and fears, especially those related to aging.

This inner work is necessary in order to maintain the body in the best possible state of health. If this work hasn't been done, then after the age of 50, it becomes a turning point, either you've aligned and maintained balance, or the effects of unprocessed beliefs begin to show. I'm also shown that the human physical body wasn't originally designed this way. This decline wasn't part of the original human blueprint. While it may not be useful now to get lost in past histories, the reality is that we currently function within these programmed settings, and so, we must work with them consciously.

Age of 80 years

80 years – The next significant stage is at 80 years old. At a global level, there's a selective group of individuals who reach this age, though not everyone does. Some people either don't make it to 80, or if they do, they arrive in a state of deep physical decline. But there's a smaller percentage who, upon reaching 80, begin to serve a unique role on the planet, as *energetic filters*. These individuals act as planetary filters, processing and refining the Earth's energies. Their role is specific and important, and they are usually highly conscious, deeply aware human beings. If you were to compare one of them to a 50-year-old who hasn't done any inner work, you'd notice a clear difference; the 80-year-old appears more mentally sharp, grounded, and calm.

This group has all their senses fully active, and they operate with a quiet awareness. Their mission at this stage of life is not random, it is to serve as filters for the Earth's energy system.

Age of 102 years

102 years – These individuals are known as the archives of the planet, even if they don't speak at that age. Their presence alone holds immense value. Through their silent awareness, they serve as living archives, and their mere existence sustains a collective reservoir of information for Earth, keeping it in an active state. I see their role from an angle of 30 degrees, relative to the planet, and through this perspective, it becomes clear; everything they carry is transmitted into the Earth, into its crystalline plasma core. There, the information is imprinted into the crystalline sphere and encoded into the Earth's crystals.

This process occurs unconsciously, no action is required from them. Simply by being physically present, they initiate the transfer. With the soul's consent, Mother Earth gathers all the information they hold: wisdom, energetic codes, and deep personal and collective knowledge. It is a natural, automatic exchange between their being and the consciousness of the planet.

Age of 144 years

144 years – It's a very distinct, emphasized number. It shows me that their presence on Earth directly connects to the planet's core, from their heart, along a straight line.

Q: Are there people on Earth who live this long? I know that we have the capacity to live up to 147 years according to our DNA, but do such people exist?

A: I'm shown that there are exactly 12 people on the planet at this age at any given time. Every year, the number must remain exactly 12. It's fascinating how the number 12 keeps appearing, it clearly holds symbolic meaning. The vision shows me that on Earth, there are always precisely 12 individuals of this age. If one of them passes away during the year, then automatically, someone else reaches the age of 144 to maintain the number. There must always be a group of 12 people at this age on the planet. I also see that regardless of whether these individuals stay in one place or move around, they maintain a direct energetic connection from their heart to the Earth's core. Their movement mirrors the hands of a clock, continuously revolving while remaining anchored to that core connection.

Q: What is their purpose?
A: It shows me that within the Earth, there are exactly the same concepts, with 12 such beings, just like on the surface. On the surface, we have 12 people aged 144. They possess *teranian* bodies, and within our planet lies the core — much like the Moon is for us, serving as their internal Sun. On the interior surface of the planet, there must also be 12 such beings that exist within the Earth. The purpose is to create balance between the interior and the exterior through the same magnetic field. Thank you.
It shows me that just as the Moon influences the gravitational field, these people serve the same function for the planet's gravitational field, from the surface all the way down to the core. They are the body of the planet, though they are not considered terrestrial but *teranian.* The *teranian* body of the Earth. The planet requires bodies on its surface, beneath the surface, and beyond it, which is represented by the Moon.

The Moon remains at a distance, the people exist on the planet's surface, and inside the Earth there are other systems at work. I see that within the Earth itself, the same concept applies: there are exactly 12 such beings inside, just as there are 12 on the surface aged 144 with teranian bodies. Inside, the core acts like an internal Sun, similar to how the Moon relates to us externally, and on the interior surface of the planet, there must also be 12 beings existing within. Their purpose is to maintain balance between the planet's interior and exterior through the shared magnetic field. Thank you.

Animal Totems and Spiritual Animals –
Inner Guides of the Soul

In the Akashic reading session, I received the information that every child has a totem animal, a sort of protector, which helps them access various virtues such as courage and confidence. These totem animals stay actively with us only during childhood, and in adulthood, they move into the background for the rest of our lives.

Q: About the totem animals. If there is more to know about these animals beyond the fact that they support children, is it welcomed to know more?
A: You can imagine a child on a swing. In the swing, they are not alone; the animal or bird joins them, and they have fun together by sharing joy.

Q: What is the purpose of these totems?

A: Imagination. They help the child preserve and develop their imagination. I see how the totem starts to fly from the swing, and the child, seeing this, is pulled along behind. This is a transitional period when the soul is in a limited human physical body. It allows them to have emotional support so that the soul is not traumatized, knowing how free it once was, and now growing up in a very limited body. It helps them feel free while still being a child in a physical body.

Throughout history, animals have held a sacred presence in human life. Across cultures and belief systems, they are seen not only as physical beings but also as spiritual messengers, guardians, and reflections of our own inner world. Two key concepts arise from this deep connection: **the animal totem** and **the spiritual animal**. Though often confused or used interchangeably, these two are distinct in purpose, origin, and meaning, and both play vital roles in the soul's journey, especially during childhood.

Animal Totems: Soul Guardians and Lifelong Protectors

The concept of the animal totem is deeply rooted in Indigenous traditions, especially those of Native American and First Nations peoples. An animal totem is **not a pet or a temporary guide**, but rather a **spiritual ally and guardian** that is tied to one's **ancestry, soul purpose, or tribal identity**. It is revealed through dreams, visions, ceremonies, or life experiences, not chosen at will.

A totem serves as a **lifelong protector and teacher**, embodying qualities and lessons the soul is meant to embrace. It reflects a deep and sacred connection between the human being and the animal spirit world. Often, a person will carry the essence of this animal throughout their entire life, with the totem watching silently from behind the scenes, guiding, protecting, and reminding the individual of who they truly are.

Spiritual Animals: Guides for the Soul's Present Path

While the animal totem is more fixed and ancestral, a **spiritual animal** is a more fluid concept. Commonly associated with modern spiritual practices, shamanic journeys, and personal development, spiritual animals appear as **messengers, allies, and mirrors**, offering guidance for specific situations, life phases, or emotional transitions.

Unlike the totem, a spiritual animal may change throughout life, showing up when needed. They may appear in dreams, meditation, or moments of synchronicity. They bring timely wisdom; the strength of a lion during a time of courage, the adaptability of a fox when navigating change, or the vision of an owl in times of inner seeking. Spiritual animals are not bound to our soul in the same way as totems, rather, they walk beside us for a time, helping us respond to what life is asking of us at the moment.

Understanding the Difference

Aspect	Animal Totem	Spiritual Animal
Origin	Indigenous cultures, tribal traditions	Modern spirituality, shamanic practice
Duration	Lifelong or ancestral	Temporary, phase-based
Function	Protector, guide, soul anchor	Messenger, mirror, emotional or spiritual support
Discovery	Through rites, visions, ceremonies	Through dreams, meditation, intuition
Ciltural Importance	Sacred, tied to lineage and tribe	Symbolic, individually experienced

Both are powerful. Both are real. But each speaks to us in different ways, serving different parts of our journey.

Children and Their Totems:
A Sacred Bond with the Unseen

Children, especially those under the age of 14, are born with an open and active connection to the unseen world. Their senses are not yet conditioned by the physical realm, and their perception of reality often includes invisible friends, vivid dreams, and stories that seem to come from another world. What many adults see as "imagination" is, in truth, a profound spiritual awareness.

During this sacred window of life, a child's animal totem is fully active. It walks with the child as a protector, translator, and comforter, helping them remember the truth of their soul - that they are limitless beings, temporarily inhabiting a physical body in a limited world.

The transition from the soul's free, unbounded nature into a dense, physical form can be disorienting, especially for highly sensitive children. The animal totem acts as a bridge, making this transition smoother. It anchors the child gently into this world without causing spiritual shock, offering a deep, often unconscious reassurance: *You are not alone. You are guided. You are still free inside.*

Many parents hear their children speak about "imaginary friends," animals that talk to them, or invisible companions they play with. More often than not, these are expressions of the child's totem spirit. What is dismissed as fantasy may, in fact, be one of the most honest spiritual expressions of early life.

The Shift at Age 14: When the Veil Thickens

Around the age of 14, a transformation occurs. Across many spiritual and cultural traditions, this is the age when a child begins to be seen as an adult-in-spirit. Psychologically, this corresponds with adolescence, when abstract reasoning develops, peer awareness intensifies, and identity becomes central. Spiritually, something else happens; the veil between the third eye and the unseen world begins to thicken.

This doesn't mean the totem disappears. It simply means the child, now stepping into adult awareness, no longer accesses that world as easily. The connection becomes quieter, subtler, sometimes even forgotten altogether. The world becomes more rational, more physical, more bound to structure and time.

The totem steps into the background, still present, still watching, but no longer actively seen or felt in the same way. The child becomes the driver of their own experience, learning to navigate the limitations of the physical world and to make choices from a place of growing autonomy.

This shift is not a loss, it's an evolution. But for those who know, it is also a call - *to remember what was once so easily felt, and to carry that memory forward into adulthood.*

The Role of the Totem and Spirit Animal in Adulthood

Though the totem becomes less visible after age 14, it remains a silent guide, often reappearing during moments of spiritual awakening, deep healing, or personal transformation. Adults who reconnect with their totems do so through dreams, vision quests, or inner work, often during a time when the soul is trying to remember who it is beyond the demands of modern life.

Spiritual animals, by contrast, become more present and active in adult life. They appear when needed, offering their wisdom and medicine as the adult navigates relationships, careers, purpose, and healing. These spirit guides may come and go, but each brings an important message or lesson.

Remembering the Sacred Within

Children are born remembering. Their animal totems help keep that memory alive until the time comes to walk more fully into the physical world. This sacred companionship serves as therapy for the soul, helping ease the transition into a world where limits are many, and truth is often forgotten.

After age 14, we become stewards of our own remembering. The totem may fall silent, but it never leaves. And the spiritual animals that visit us throughout life, ensure we are never truly alone.

Whether you are a parent, a seeker, or someone remembering their own childhood magic, know this:

Your guides are still with you.
The path may grow quiet, but it is never empty.
You were guided then. You are guided now.

Retreat Mount Shasta

I was guided to organize a retreat in April on Mount Shasta, with a few women. Although at first I didn't understand where this idea came from, I later began receiving messages and information about this, as well as about the changes that will occur on a global level. There is a need for anchoring and alchemizing the divine feminine and masculine energies, in order to harmonize the energy on a global scale and to allow Mother Earth to restore her harmony.

Q: Is it in the best interest of the group and myself to follow plan A or plan B created today?
A: What's funny is that there was plan A and plan B, and plan A is shorter, and someone came and kicked plan B. That's why I laughed.

Q: Plan B still had 2 points at the lake, by the water. I want to ask about everything related to water, is it in the highest good of the group and myself or not?
A: The answer I get is No. I see an energy coming out of Mount Shasta, like a cup with branches, like a flower - that's what I see coming out of the ground. This energy does not radiate to the water; it is dissolved, neutralized. It is very intense in the mountain, and the farther you move away from the mountain, the energy begins to dissipate. The purpose is for us to stay, as much as possible, at the mountain to receive activation codes.

Q: Now I'm curious, what is the theme? I had in mind the themes abundance, femininity, balancing feminine and masculine energies. Which of these would be the appropriate theme?

A: For me, the light bulb went on balancing the feminine and masculine.

Diana: Same here. This aspect is connected to what Imaya said, about activating women. You have received activation, and in that session, women need to activate their divine feminine. I feel it's necessary to infuse these energies into as many women as possible.

Victoria: Oh, I have chills in my body and in my right leg.

A: Actually, do you know what's happening? Being in that powerful space, where the energy is intense and where the divine feminine and masculine energies are balanced, a strong channel is formed by all the women present at the retreat. This channel extends directly into the Earth, reaching the core of Mother Earth, helping us connect simultaneously with the planet itself. I see that there are multiple such channels across the globe. These are not just individual activations, rather, we are assisting our planet in awakening her divine feminine potential in harmony with us on the surface. Imagine the pupil of an eye as the core of Mother Earth. Around it, the retina is formed by various lines, and through these lines, connections from Earth's surface are made. This process supports Mother Earth in expanding her divine energy outward from within.

So, we are essentially helping the planet. This is why it's so important to hold as many retreats as possible, gathering groups of women in different places around the world. Mother Earth will amplify her divine feminine energy, and when it reaches the surface, it will activate all souls. This is the essence of the new era of divine feminine activation. Following this, all women on Earth will be re-coded in feminine energy, embodying the feminine body. I see that once this process completes, the divine feminine energy will awaken fully within feminine bodies, and the masculine energy will then balance itself within masculine bodies, creating harmony for souls on Earth. Relationships will become authentic, balanced, and harmonized, each person fully aligned with their own divine masculine or feminine energy.

This recalibration means that women and men will exist in their true energies; women fully in feminine energy, men fully in masculine energy. Masculine bodies that have carried a stronger feminine energy, or feminine bodies that have been dominated by masculine energy, will undergo a transmutation, alchemizing and balancing these two forces. This is an evolutionary process that will take time and will not happen all at once.

Q: Is it in our highest good and humanity's to know how long this complete process will take?
A: The number 21 came to me; 21 years.

Q: Once everyone accesses their divine feminine and masculine, what changes will this bring at the planetary level? What will it contribute or support?
A: I see that right now there are many imbalances in the body and at the energy level. There is a total imbalance, and society doesn't understand where the limits begin and end in this kind of energetic chaos, and incompatibility with their vehicles.

Diana: I feel that these imbalances have actually led to everything happening on the planetary level.

A: I see that there is a type of ET being that contributed to this imbalance, to what exists in society now. It is a being like in the movie *Godzilla*; very large, with a bat-like body but no wings, its hands move like that. It is a being from the lower planes of creation, and is gigantic in size.

Diana: Yes, that's what I was feeling, that the imbalance of these energies led to decisions less favorable for us as humanity, and for the planet, in any direction.

A: Yes. And now Mother Earth is trying to restore her harmony.

Victoria: Let's see if there's any other message for you or me, and that's about it for today.

Message for Diana: I see you in space, around you, luminous. I'm swirling around you but cannot get close. Your perception is expanding, not just simply expanding, but becoming more conscious, more selective, so I cannot get near you. Once you expand, it's like you know how to work with energy. Around you, I see a black space, more like a void, but you are white and luminous. I try to swirl around you at a certain radius, but you know how to manage your energy around you, outside your body, while in the void. Expanding, you are more aware of how to maneuver energy. I'm now at the edge of that radius, and you are very selective about who crosses this boundary or limit. I was able to enter now, but from the beginning when I approached, it was like a protection. You are aware of who enters and only allow entry if you feel so. I entered your space, and I see the void wants to pass, but you wave your hand and push it away, not letting it enter your space. You have truly seen your power.

Diana: Yes, exactly. That's what I was feeling too.

Message for Victoria: I see myself very large, but more from the existence of angels, Archangels. I see myself exactly as Archangel Gabriel dressed in robes, and I have a long ribbon that goes downward, yet I float in the air. Below is a platform, and I can maneuver this ribbon, spin it around me, and I see myself spinning it counterclockwise. I get that I can maneuver time, the process backward. The aging process goes forward, but I feel I am going backward, in a process of rejuvenation. This ribbon, if it touches anything on the surface, clears everything in its path.

Q: What is this process about?
A: I see fat cells in my body dissolving. Fat in the muscles and flesh is dissolving; it is a biological process. Yes, I have reversed the aging process and entered a rejuvenation process. This is happening in the flesh, in the fat, another process is taking place in my body.

Higher Self

"You are not a human being having a spiritual experience. You are a spiritual being having a human experience." ~*Pierre Teilhard de Chardin*

The **Higher Self** is the pure, eternal, and divine aspect of who you are. It is the truest version of you, your soul's essence, existing beyond the limitations of your body, ego, and everyday thoughts. While your human self experiences life moment by moment, the Higher Self holds the full blueprint of your soul's journey. It is your guiding intelligence, rooted in love, wisdom, and deep connection to all of existence.

To put it simply, if life were a video game, your **human self** would be the character on the screen, fully immersed in the level, dealing with obstacles, learning lessons, and feeling every emotion. Your **Higher Self**, on the other hand, is the player holding the controller. It sees the full map, knows the mission, and understands the purpose behind each challenge. It is calm, collected, and never loses sight of the bigger picture, even when the character feels lost or overwhelmed.

This part of you is always connected to Source, whether you call it God, the Universe, Spirit, or something else. It's multidimensional, eternal, and exists across timelines. While the human mind can forget, the Higher Self remembers: your soul contracts, your purpose, your past lives, and the spiritual lessons woven into your experiences.

The Higher Self communicates subtly but powerfully. It doesn't shout, it whispers. It sends nudges, gut feelings, and synchronicities. It speaks through dreams, visions, signs in nature, unexpected delays, or an unshakable inner knowing. When something feels off or "not aligned," that is often your Higher Self redirecting you. When you feel peace, expansion, or clarity about something, that's usually your Higher Self confirming you're on the right path.

The **difference between your human self and Higher Self** can be seen clearly when comparing their characteristics. Your human self is shaped by your physical body, upbringing, emotions, and beliefs. It often reacts from fear, ego, or pain. It operates in a limited timeline and sees the world through filters. Meanwhile, the Higher Self is calm, loving, and wise. It holds no judgment, no fear, and no agenda, only truth and guidance aligned with your soul's evolution. Where your human self may feel separate, the Higher Self knows it is connected to all that exists.

Here's a simple way to compare:

> The **human self** is driven by survival, emotions, and identity. It often feels confused, reactive, or anxious.

The **Higher Self** is driven by clarity, peace, and higher understanding. It sees everything as part of your soul's growth and helps you realign with your purpose.

As you grow spiritually, heal old wounds, and raise your vibration, you begin to merge more with your Higher Self. You start to recognize the difference between your ego's voice and your soul's guidance. Life begins to feel more synchronized. Decisions come from inner alignment rather than fear. You act instead of react. You trust rather than control. You become a walking expression of your soul's light.

Connecting with your Higher Self doesn't require rituals or perfection. It only asks for **presence**. You can build this connection through meditation, journaling, being in nature, and most importantly, **listening**. Ask your Higher Self for guidance. Then, be still enough to hear the answer. It often comes quickly, before the ego has time to speak.

And remember, your Higher Self is not somewhere far above you. It's not separate. It's already within you. It's the eternal "you" - watching lovingly as you walk through life, waiting patiently for you to remember who you truly are.

The journey of awakening is not about becoming something more. It's about becoming what you already are. And your Higher Self is the key to that remembering.

Q: Is there any message for humanity or a final message for the book about the Higher Self?

A: I see an image I simply don't understand. From the front, from the third eye it's like something flew up and is hovering above my head, like energy. Then I see as if I am in a carnival ride car, an electric car, and someone sits in front of me. I see there are 2 drivers at the same time for one single car. The one sitting in front of us is our Higher Self. We perceive that we are the sole driver of the physical body, but actually, that's not the case. This car has 2 drivers. Your Higher Self is a driver just like you, of this vehicle, in our case, the human physical body. The reason they sit in front of you and not the other way around, is so that this concept of driving is perceived that we are the true driver of the vehicle, but the real driver is your Higher Self. Above, I see an open vortex where information, wisdom flows down, everything descends and is automatically connected to you and your Higher Self, but it is filtered. Thank you.

Session - Victoria & Diana - May 26, 2025

We are in 2A in Quantum, this is the heart.

Q: What is the message you want to convey to me, or to Diana, or to us together?
Victoria: Do you see anything here?
Diana: No.
It's very subtle.

It's subtle, and at one point I saw it as a being or an energy.

I saw it like a little windmill, with two antennas, two heads, and they catch, there are two, one at each end, and they seem to capture the radius of the information.

Victoria: Whose are these two antennas? Each antenna is held by each one of us.
Diana: Is it to receive information today?
Victoria: We have to put it on the head.
Oh, an interesting mechanism. Usually, antennas receive from the outside in, but since we have to put it on the head, it makes me wonder, why not the other way around, because we should receive from the outside in. We have to wear it on the head so that we send information. It's the reverse process.

Q: Is it necessary for us to connect with the Source, the Field, in order to receive?
Victoria: It's as if someone tied our feet and we're standing with our heads down.
Diana: Why? Does it help us to send the information?
Victoria: I see something, a technology, but do you know what it looks like? It looks like snake skin, hexagonal, and along the edge a channel flows, to my left, some information is flowing. Do you know how fiber

186

optics work? This information comes the same way. But what connection does it have to the feet and being upside down? I can't understand. Please give us a simpler and clearer answer, in terms we can understand.

I sense that we act as catalysts for the Earth, and sometimes a catalyst functions within an opposite circuit, both receiving and sending energy. We know grounding typically happens through the feet, but at times, it's important to reverse that connection; to link the Source with the Earth while simultaneously connecting the feet with the Universe. This forms a brief conduit, not a sustained one, but it triggers something within the blood.

While oxygenation in the blood is an ongoing process, this particular practice, standing with feet elevated and head lowered, induces a temporary deoxygenation in the bloodstream. The duration should be short, as this deoxygenation causes cancer cells to become disoriented, almost like a glitch in their system. This confusion helps transmute the dead cells, leading to their annihilation within the blood. Following this, a chemical process occurs where these cells undergo further transformation; they are absorbed and eliminated from the blood system. It's as if a magnetic force pulls them out and transmutes them, cleansing the bloodstream in the process.

Diana: Wow. How interesting!
Victoria: Now I've been brought back down to Earth. This thing with the head down and feet up, not for a long duration.

Q: For how long do people need to stay like that?
A: From 3 to 5 minutes. It feels like 3 minutes. Between 3 and 5, but mostly 3.

Diana: Maybe 5, depending on how complex the case is.
Victoria: Yes, actually this is the exact message, but I didn't say it from the beginning.
Diana: I feel like asking: *Is this information purely for the book, or did the two of us need purification of the blood system? Or does this help us with something else as well?*
Victoria: The only thing I saw was like a bubble coming out of the head. I see how someone came, put a pin, and left. It means it's for everyone.
Diana: Thank you.

IV. Megaquantic Field (MQ)

In this chapter, the Megaquantic Field will be presented, which is found in the higher dimensions of Creation. Access to this field is limited in order to preserve its highest possible vibration. The field operates through a mechanism that does not allow everyone to access it, especially those who have not opened their consciousness or have not worked on themselves to anchor in neutrality and unconditional love.

In the previous chapters, we explored the foundational realms of the Akashic Records and the Quantum Field, each offering profound insight into the nature of reality, time, and consciousness. These stages have prepared us for the next, extraordinary step in human evolution: the entrance into the **Megaquantic Field**.

The Megaquantic Field stands as the soul's university, a realm of higher education for consciousness itself.

We now arrive at this highest level of consciousness, a groundbreaking and profound field, discovered through the devoted and expansive work of Victoria Basil, whose alignment with higher realms allowed this gateway to unfold with clarity and purpose.

What makes this revelation so remarkable is the natural and effortless way it unfolded. Not sought through force or intention, the Megaquantic Field emerged as a divine response, a direct offering from the Source itself, illuminated through years of channeling, embodied practice, and multidimensional connection.

For the first time, this field is being shared in an explicit and structured form, offering a new perspective and expanded vocabulary to describe a dimension previously unnamed in spiritual or scientific literature. This is not just a progression beyond the Akashic or Quantum levels, it is a breakthrough field, introducing a new energetic template for humanity's evolution.

What sets the Megaquantic Field apart, is its **direct connection to Source, God, the origin of all that is**. Unlike other fields which often involve intermediation by guides, beings, or archetypes, this field functions without third-party interference. It is a **pure, unfiltered frequency of divine intelligence**, accessed not through hierarchy or systems, but through **alignment of soul and intention**.

At this macro level, the Megaquantic Field holds not only information about past lives, parallel realities, or other dimensions, but encompasses the **totality of existence**. It is the field where the architecture of the multiverse is visible. Where all metaverses, soul templates, creation codes, and collective realities exist simultaneously.

In this crystalline expanse of white-light intelligence, duality becomes nearly nonexistent, and the density of matter dissolves. Entities are no longer perceived in form, but as outlines filled with radiant, living light, reflecting the purity of their essence. The field is neutral, vast, and infinite, a pure mirror of all that is and can be.

Access to the Megaquantic Field is both gifted and guided. Those who may not have typical access to such realms can still be brought into this space through practitioners attuned to its frequency. Sessions unfold in alignment with the soul's readiness. If a person is not yet prepared to integrate this level, the session will naturally remain at the Akashic or Quantum level, guided with care and precision.

Before full access, a deep, energetic purification is required. Many fall asleep or enter a dreamlike state during this adjustment, as the physical and energetic systems are realigned to interface with this high frequency.

The **Megaquantic Field** is not merely a step in evolution, it is a leap into divine remembrance. It offers the soul a return to its original blueprint, untainted by timelines, distortions, or limitations. Here, we do not search for truth, we become the expression of it.

What you are about to encounter may **awaken ancient knowing** within you, something that has long-waited to be remembered and lived.

Welcome to the **Megaquantic Field.**

Connection with the Megaquantic Field

Victoria: I am in the Megaquantic Field, but you're not here with me. I'm looking for you underneath. I can't see where you are, but I feel that you're on another level. You're on Quantum level 2, in thoughts, in 2B.
Diana: I feel like asking, what do I need to become aware of?
Victoria: You're swinging between your heart and your thoughts.
Diana: I feel there's also fear.
Victoria: Yes, because you're running on the same floor from one side to the other. It's the idea of being present in your body and not in your mind,

the tendency to analyze almost every detail. You're simply not allowing yourself to be in your heart.

Diana: Then I feel a need to release the fact that I don't allow myself to be in my heart.

Q: **Megaquantic Field, is it in Diana's highest good to release excessive thoughts and the process that creates such activity?**

A: It grasped me by the finger and lifted me up. I watched as it opened a screen halfway, and inside appeared a sphere from which a telescope emerged. The **Megaquantic Field** is so far beyond the Quantum Field.

The Creator, whom I perceive as an elderly masculine presence, now peers through the telescope, aiming to locate the Quantum Field. I see it far ahead, positioned around 1 o'clock on the clock-face orientation. From my view of His screen, the Quantum Field is distant, but now He zooms in, it materializes right in front of me.

The word *"transcendent"* comes to mind as I observe the Quantum Field's structure. It resembles a tornado or a spinning sphere in the air, perpetually in motion. Within it, colors constantly shift, one section of the vortex exhibits one hue, another section displays another. The color spectrum is vast, far beyond the range of colors we humans can perceive.

Now I see Him scanning through a radar-like device attuned to the Quantum Field. To enter from the Megaquantic, it requires His consciousness-energy. He doesn't fully enter with His entire being, but rather as a fluid electric current. He merges with the Quantum vortex by sliding in from the side, tracing its edge, and flowing into the current. That is how He enters, from the right side into the flow. His energy appears as dark gray; I'm curious about this hue, his Source imprint. His entrance feels like a VIP arrival; all of creation visibly acknowledges "the boss" has arrived.

I also perceived yesterday that within the Quantum Field, the Void, the dark matter, is the Creator. The Void itself enters the field. Yet even as the Creator, He doesn't act recklessly. He moves within each field with reverence, abiding by its laws and respecting all coexisting layers. He is neither above nor below His Creation. Now He's searching for you. You are on Level 2, standing at the threshold between A and B. I see you pacing back and forth while He sits calmly in the center, at the chair. Then, He extends

His hand and stills you. He is serene; you are unsettled. He makes space beside His chair and guides you to sit, facing your own thoughts. Then He begins transmitting information, teaching you how to observe your mind. He instructs you: *don't focus on the heart, despite your urge to pivot toward it, instead look at your thoughts.* It's uncomfortable for you to face your own mental patterns, but He is showing you how to watch them.

Diana: I saw him when he entered. There are fears, stagnant emotions, and I, kind of, don't want to see them. I now set the intention to look at my thoughts, at everything I haven't released, everything that slows me down. I will release it now.

A: There's a release happening from the right foot, but the heart is generating an overflow of emotions. What surfaces now is linked to unprocessed feminine energy, specifically on the left side of the body. You're curling inward toward the Creator, almost as if trying to hide behind Him, a deep-rooted instinct of protection or avoidance. This is an ancient defense mechanism. That's what you're concealing. The program feels very old, and I'm shown the body of a woman, possibly of African or Indian origin. The image is clear: a woman with large breasts, and there's a strong connection to sexual energy. Visions appear, old Kamasutra imagery, suggesting a lifetime where you, in a female form, carried a predominantly masculine energy, dominating men within that context. This energetic imprint dates back roughly 2,500 years and is stored within your physical body, particularly on the left side of the torso. It is part of a memory waiting to be acknowledged, released, and integrated.

Diana: I also sensed it was African. Then I set the intention to release this program from that life, from all existences, dimensions, realities in which I exist, have existed, and will exist; everything that no longer serves me. I release all programs, limitations, beliefs that no longer serve me and that do not allow me to live in my authenticity, in all existences in which I am, co-create, and will exist. Amen.

A: I feel chills along the right side of my body, a clear sign that something is shifting. Now, I see you stepping onto the Creator's shoulder. He gently holds your hand and reassures you, saying, "It's okay." You embrace Him more tightly, and I see you crying like a child in the comfort of a mother's arms, so raw, so tender. Then, you rise from the chair and move toward the heart, as if drawn to it by a powerful current. After a moment, you return to the Creator and wrap your arms around Him from behind, gently hugging Him around the neck and even kissing His cheek.

It's beautiful how He remains so neutral and steady, radiating unconditional love, completely present, without judgment. And now, I see you entering a flow directly into the heart, a sacred alignment taking place. The body is responding, especially on the right side, where the chills first appeared, acknowledging a profound emotional release and return to inner safety.

Victoria: I want to ask the Creator now if there's anything I need to release, fears, blockages, or anything that is in my highest good?

A: He's taken me back into the Megaquantic Field, gently *releasing the MacroQuantum image*, and now I find myself placed within His palms. Something significant is shifting. My consciousness needs to be separated from the physical body, detached from the headspace. My awareness now rests in its rightful place, the observer's seat, held in a space beyond the physical form. It's complex.

He then places my body inside a transparent test tube, seals it, and begins to shake it gently. I'm aware that He has inserted something into the tube, but I can't yet identify what it is. As He shakes the tube, I see that He is analyzing the contents, much like a scientist or doctor in a lab, studying the composition of skin, blood, and all internal systems at a molecular level.

As He observes, different particles begin to release from my physical body, each type floating freely and forming distinct clusters. These particles separate into two main groups:

  • On the right side, a black, dense mass begins to accumulate: heavy, compact.

  • On the left, a lighter, red-toned group of particles floats more freely, composed of varied elements and frequencies.

He continues to observe these groupings with precision. Each cluster reflects an aspect of my energetic and physical composition, revealing hidden densities and frequencies I hadn't yet recognized.

Q: What do these black and red particles in the Megaquantic Field mean?

A: He gestures toward the test tube, and instantly, a screen appears to the right, revealing a more detailed, layered analysis of what's unfolding. On the screen, I see a deeper decoding of the two particle groups:

1. The black particles represent religion, specifically, a deeply ingrained belief system. It's shown as the most dominant imprint, the strongest belief held within the cellular and energetic structure.

2. The red particles are linked to femininity, more precisely to the feminine biological cycle, highlighting menstruation and all the energetic memory associated with the menstrual process.

Each color and particle cluster holds the memory of ancestral, personal, and collective imprints that continue to influence the body and consciousness. This breakdown reveals not just biological or symbolic meaning, but also the coded beliefs and programs still active within the energetic field.

Diana: I sense that with menstruation, there are beliefs like the cycle is dirty, things passed down by religion.

Victoria: I'm setting the intention to release this, from any form, parallel life, known or unknown existence, from any consciousness I've ever been in, from any place in the universe, multiverse. I intend to release everything related to Orthodox Christianity, any religion, or any other belief formed. I ask to free everything tied to sexuality.

The process is reversible. I'm taken back in time, I see square portals, I exit darkness and go into the past. The whole process reverses. It's a lot. I've emerged. I've released. Thank you.

Victoria: Dear Creator, I set the intention to release any programs from any existence, known or unknown, from any parallel life, past, present, or future. Release the belief that is not in my highest good. I ask for my throat chakra to be fully open, so I may speak freely, clearly, and only from truth. May my voice be guided by honesty, courage, and alignment with my highest self. I intend to release the belief that women must remain silent, that women have no right to speak, that women are powerless, that women are dirty; I release it all.

There are countless doors, layers within layers, like a Matryoshka doll. I now ask for the release of all blockages connected to womanhood, sexuality, the feminine cycle, and every natural expression of femininity. I let it all go, from my DNA, from every timeline, from every existence.

I feel like saying: "*I am visible and valued. I am the essence of feminine strength. I am love embodied. I am heard and honored. My womb is a sacred space. My uterus holds divine purpose. Every experience, physical, emotional, spiritual, or energetic, is a natural and sacred part of me. Thank you.*"

I see myself bathed in white light. I gaze at my hands. I'm barefoot, wearing a flowing dress. My body feels light and free, and I embrace it fully.

Diana: I feel to set the intention to release the belief that woman is sinful, that we were punished, that the cycle is a punishment from God; all limitations that no longer serve me. Any belief that the cycle is dirty, and any other associations or illusions not from God's universal truth. I accept my femininity, I accept my uterus, my womb, and I feel warmth. We are power, feminine energy. I accept the pure, natural creative process of birth as a blessing.

Diana: And I accept the creative process in my womb as a wonderful creation, as a direct blessing from God.

Victoria: It's interesting, you're in Quantum and feeling emotions, while I'm neutral in the Megaquantic. Surely I would cry if I were there. Now, from the screen, my body was pulled out, and consciousness was placed back into my head.

Q: Why was such a process needed, separation of consciousness and physical body?
A: I sense it's because if they were together, the process would be more complex. "Contamination" comes to me. Consciousness is pure; only the body accumulates all beliefs from any life. At the consciousness level, it's impossible to take on trauma or fear; consciousness is pure and untouched. When deep releases occur, consciousness must separate from the physical body so there is no contamination, making it easier to release accumulated issues

from the body. Consciousness generates a field more complex than in level one, and stored issues are not clearly visible because consciousness cloaks the body with a plasma layer in which our fears are not easily seen. They remain hidden. Once you extract consciousness, the body is unfiltered, transparent, and it's easy to work with everything that was stored inside.

Now I see you landing in the Megaquantic. Interestingly, the Megaquantic Field won't let you pass if you have unprocessed emotions or thoughts. It has filters, parameters, and won't grant permission if you have many stagnant energies. I see you on my right in white, while I appear as void. You are all white, but I'm dark, and using human logic you may see that as bad, but it is simply void. He wants to show us that you are the light, I am the dark, yet we are one and the same. It's interesting what it's showing me now, I feel there is another message here. You work with the light side; I work with the dark matter side. That isn't necessarily bad, through my experiences, it helps me work with densities and this realm of existence. You perceive this as bad, but actually you are the light that, travelling through darkness, lights us all. Yin and Yang are in the same space. When the light goes through darkness it radiates, and experiences the dark side, but all experiences I go through help me work with darkness and lighting it up. I know this side, and to me, we are both light and darkness at the same time. If you were to engage with the denser, deeper layers of darkness, it might overwhelm you. But I come from that dark matter side, I have no filter. That connection enables me to work with darkness directly, without fear. In a way, if a person has intense abilities and doesn't know how to handle that power, they could spread darkness everywhere.

Victoria: Interesting … I sensed that I fear my own power, but I intend to release that.

The Creator brought a boat for two people, directed it toward the screen, and we moved there. It's a journey where you don't feel like you're flying or being propelled, you feel like you're inside a vessel traveling faster than light. We're now jumping into the multiverse. I see blue light in parts. It's a long journey. I don't know what you feel, but suddenly a channel pulled us upward. We arrived at a station, an aerial platform, a station.

Q: Megaquantic Field, where have we arrived? What is this place?
A: Meetings, a place where people come together. Someone invites me,

and I step into a building. We ascend to an upper floor through a transparent tube. Beneath us, the floors shimmer like crystal. The elevator doesn't rise through mechanical means, instead, it moves by a different kind of energy. It's a magnetic field, one that makes it feel as though you're being lifted by thought itself.

Diana: I sense the word *"levitation."*

A: Yes, it's levitation. Everything here is governed by the mind. You direct a thought, and the levitation carries you effortlessly to where you need to go. We arrived at a chamber high above the ground. Inside, I saw what looked like an office, with a desk and many chairs, wooden, or at least resembling wood, though perhaps imagined rather than real. Someone was already seated at the head of the table on the right. The table itself wasn't square, but elongated, rectangular, almost coffin-shaped.

There were so many chairs, I didn't know where to sit. You took a seat by the window, on the left side, not quite at the end, but near it. I chose a spot opposite you, more toward the center of the table, and farther away from the man seated at the head on the right.

Q: Megaquantic Field, what is this place and who is this man?
A: I sense the Creator itself.

Diana: That's what I sense too.

Victoria: Here they allow us to ask questions. Yesterday was a different kind of meeting; today is more professional.

Q: Megaquantic Field, what would be useful to know about this field? If it's appropriate to start with its fundamental processes, explain in a way we can understand, with coherent information, and if it's appropriate to understand it scientifically – what is its structure, its fundamental basis, and what is this field for?
A: I'm receiving **Lesson 1**. On the wall, to my left, your right, a screen appears where it says Lesson 1. One moment. They have to place something behind my right ear, on my neck. It's a crystalline device, almost invisible.

Message from the Creator:

"We create resources that manifest in the lower planes. Creation moves from the top down. This field is explicitly unique. It has no parts, no levels, nor any other principles by which it could be subdivided. The world is created in this primordial space, in accordance with the periodic system, of the lower dimensions. For example, the Megaquantic base field, whose extension moves in a vortex, in a spiral, creates the Quantum Field with its fundamental bases, all the way to what you know as the Akashic Field, and after that is you. In the Megaquantic Field, dark matter, the Void, is more of an explanation for my existence, my 'office' of cooperation with the rest of creation. This level's purpose is to regulate, create, monitor, correct, experiment, adjust, annihilate the lower planes, that is, the extensions of this field. The positioning of the Megaquantic Field is such that its spiral extension is inward, from where a pyramid forms with its base upwards and its tip pointing down. Thus, Megaquantic is separate from the extension of creation through the pyramid of the creation game in which it is invested, to allow every soul to find itself, to rise, to advance, or to deviate, depending on its location in the given pyramid. Megaquantic is separate, but at the same time, in concordance with my absolute creation. You may ask questions."

Q: How is it correct to access this field, or when can it be accessed? And what is needed to gain access?
A: Lesson 2. Accessing this field is uncomfortable for the vast majority of individuals, souls developing in that creation pyramid. It is very uncomfortable to access this field. The reason is simple. They are not ready to accept a greater power than themselves which they do not understand. They believe that I am the power, and they are punished. When they believe they are being punished, I am the punished one in which they believe they have power. It is a paradox in which we exist simultaneously; one extreme and the other at the same time. It's like you, as the individual A, believe individual B is superior, better, more advanced. Then, individual B will feel the same that individual A is superior and better than individual B. They both will have the same frustrations. The process equals 0, but it can also equal 1, depending on A's perception, in accordance with B's perception. If the perception is neutral, both parts are equal to 1:1.

Q: Does this mean that access to this field is permitted to anyone, anytime, as long as they allow themselves and trust their power to access it?
A: The answer is rhetorical. Yes and No. There are certain principles in which this field will not allow you access, even if you feel ready. If the ego stands in the middle of your forehead, outside the head, access will be denied.

Q: How closely does this resemble my example?
A: This example is not known.

Diana: I'm referring to today, when I couldn't access the Megaquantic because I was stuck in thoughts.
Victoria: That was an experiment in which you believed it was true.

A: Lesson 3. Contamination of this field cannot be addressed. The creation of this field was the intention to annihilate any attempt to contaminate this space. This is not a lesson - we're trying to find the right word - ***Complex System.***
We are not in a higher field than the rest, but we do not allow contamination from lower planes. Duality is not present here in any form. To easily access this field, the key to success is ***neutrality.*** When the heart vibrates neutrality, the outer field creates a key that sends you an invitation to access this field. This field is supervised by a group of beings who care for, analyze, and verify all experiences in order to categorize, at a numeric level, the percentage of confirmation of these neutral states.

For example, out of a total of 100%, if you accumulate around 80% or more, not in terms of lifetimes, but total experiences, you may qualify to be accepted into this field. It's a meticulous and highly regulated process, one that strictly follows protocol. There is no discrimination involved, especially not from the lower planes.

A: Lesson 4. This chapter will not be developed. It is too complex from a scientific perspective. This information will be unpacked through other forms, paths, methods.

A: Lesson 5. "What is your purpose in this field? That is a question for you." I feel the need to form a map of God's creation, to help us orient ourselves, where we are, where we should aim. But not through force, rather to understand, to become aware that we are on a less developed path, from which we should aim to advance further. I now see on this screen, like a map. I see a large territory, for example Eurasia, that large, then comes a smaller field, all of Europe from east to west; this is the Quantum Field. And then the Akashic Field is Africa. We are Australia, our dimension, somewhere far, where to travel is quite distant, quite expensive. The Akashic Field is a fairly large territory. Interesting why it shows up as Africa. Because it is both good and bad, dry and unique, it is a house with everything you want. You need resilience to be in Africa. In Akashic, you need resilience to access it, because there is both good and bad - a lot of duality. Europe is the Quantum Field, and the Megaquantic already is a vast and large territory. In this lesson, it comes to me that it's good to access it in order to realize, to become aware, that in fact God's creation is not how we perceive it. We are not sinners left there, beaten by fate, but we chose to come to the lower planes to strive back to where it all began. We are here to understand and see the map of creation from a neutral perspective.

Q: So this is the difference between the fields, the level of neutrality or duality?
A: Exactly. You must go through them to truly understand the Source. You can't go directly to the initial source without working, healing, and experiencing. This is the game. No one is guilty; your soul wants to understand from the bottom, to understand what it's like to be here, knowing where you came from.

Accessing the Megaquantic Field depends on the neutrality you develop in this plane. The more anchored you are in neutrality and acceptance, the more you can rise to a higher level, to go beyond the boundaries.

If in the Akashic Field all information is more related to the lower planes, it is like a bridge, a border checkpoint between how to be connected to higher planes. The Akashic Field is for lower creations, which we are. Once you pass this field, you rise into the Quantum Field, and to access the Quantum Field you must be anchored in your heart. The heart makes the whole process discussed above. Once you have completed this process, you don't need to complete 100% of the Quantum Field and all its experiences, you can access the Quantum Field.

Here's an example; let's say you decide to go to a monastery and believe that's where you're meant to be, people recognize you and consider you a saint. But if you haven't worked on the ego, fears, and so on, you automatically cannot go to the next level, to the heart level, energetically, spiritually. You can't go higher because you haven't healed various aspects.

Another person who works with people, exposed to "external contamination", if they've worked with themselves, can enter the Quantum Field because their heart is in a neutral state of emotions, internal states, and then can automatically access the Megaquantic Field, without being in a monastery, like the first case. Sometimes, we shouldn't label that, if you're in a monastery, you're neutral; that doesn't imply you're a saint. You could be there and internally feel like hell, and you can live in the city and feel heaven in your heart. It's each of our choices.

In the Quantum Field, there can be people from both categories mentioned above, but if you don't work on your inside self, you can't rise higher. You can't return "home" until you've done your daily work. "Home" refers to the Megaquantic – back to the Source.

Q: To do this work, do you need to become aware of the patterns, mirroring, blockages, that show you the illusions you've created?
A: That is one approach.

Q: And another approach, to work directly in the field?
A: The evolution process must go step by step. You can't make a direct jump.

Q: Is it also related to the evolution process we chose, because we chose certain stages or processes?
A: Yes, but in the lower planes, it becomes clear how easily one can get lost and fall back into the trap. It's like stepping off the wheel. You manage to free yourself, climb a bit higher, ascend the stairs, and then something remains unresolved, something you didn't do, and you fall back again.

I see the wheel again, carrying all our past lives. The most complex part of this entire process is revealed in levels. Many beings from higher planes choose not to enter this game at all, because the planes we inhabit are extremely harsh. It's very easy to fall. The line between escaping the wheel and climbing even a little higher is razor-thin. It takes very little to slip back.

Even a single unresolved experience, or fear generated in the heart, whether from a past or current life, is enough to trigger a fall. The heart alone, through emotion, can pull you back down.

The most difficult stage in this entire process of large-scale evolution is the path from the lower plane up to the Quantum level, specifically, Quantum Level 2. Reaching that point is the most challenging of all. Many souls become stuck in the Akashic level, and although there is a vast population of souls passing through the Quantum Field, that early ascent from the lower planes up to Quantum Level 2 is where the real struggle lies.

Q: How do you know what level you've reached?
A: It shows me this is: **Lesson 6.** Again, they need to connect something to my ear. You can ask questions.

Q: How do you know what level you've reached or where you are?
A: Every individual has a filter, and this filter is felt intensely. One moment, this is a complex system. This place implies *a dominant position for internal understanding* - we're trying to find the right words.
Imagine, in front of you, all your school years, and on the table you have the total of those years - 10, 9, 8 years of the educational system. Imagine how you accumulate the results of each year, obtain a number, and this number needs to be divided into 4 structures. Then you receive a single digit, which must be multiplied by 2 and then layered over 10. The number you get corresponds to your percentage; the figure, the level you are at in unity in accordance with this field.
There is another method. One moment. The Quantum Field can offer you approximate figures to the simple question: *What score do I currently have in the Megaquantic Field?*
The Quantum Field is a field with deviations; it doesn't have full access to this information. It can only approximate, depending on its internal data.

Q: Is this neutrality level, needed to access the Megaquantic Field, related to how much you're still inside the Matrix or not?
A: Those are two different questions you're asking.

Q: Let's start with this instead: What is the percentage, the range, what's the minimum threshold to access the Megaquantic Field?
A: I asked the Creator to display the percentage on the screen. **Minimum 78%.**

Q: Can the number vary over time? I mean, does it change based on us?
A: It doesn't depend only on your current version. The Megaquantic Field is an accumulation of all your existences. That could be as a stone, an animal, a molecule of air, from all your experiences. It has nothing to do with you, your current self.

Diana: I see, that came to you in another session of ours.

A: Yes, you may be conscious, but the result of your soul's accumulated experience might not reach that percentage. What's needed is the total weight of your soul's experiences, not just from this life or the last one. The Megaquantic is on a much higher level. The Quantum Field is slightly broader, but the Megaquantic refers to the entirety of your existence; past, present, and future. That's where ego comes in, because you may *believe* you can access this field, but your soul's history says otherwise. That's the trap. And actually, wait, you asked something else, and this information just came through.

Diana: Wait, I forgot my question too.

Q: Dear Creator, please transmit to us further information that would be good for everyone to know.
A: Now I'm being taken to the second part of your question about the Matrix. The Matrix is just a wheel. It only exists in the physical plane. It has no access to higher planes. In the Quantum, the Matrix is not present, although it does radiate slightly, a shadow extension, into Quantum Level 1. However, it's not physically present, it casts a shadow into Quantum Level 1A and 1B. The Matrix program's goal is to expand, not physically, but energetically, to radiate further upward into the Quantum Field. But it won't succeed because it's not permitted. It's trying hard to expand. It only has access to the physical body in the Quantum Field. The program isn't rooted solely in the Akashic, it extends slightly into the Quantum at the first level.

Q: Because just as Megaquantic has filters, Quantum does too, right?
A: That's how it's set. That's how it was accepted, initiated. The Matrix itself was designed to function this way. We tend to view the Matrix as something bad, but lower planes cannot coexist without this program. The Matrix is a "cold program", it has no feelings and such a program was

needed, one without emotion, but which controls and neutralizes.

It's a paradox: we feel emotions, but the higher planes don't, they exist in unconditional love and light.

To make emotions possible, this program was created to *suppress* emotion, to induce *negative* emotion, the contrast and paradox of what the higher planes feel - peace and love.

The Matrix is specifically designed to provide this contrast. That's why duality exists.

There is a clear map; it's a staircase you climb upward, but it's not straight. This wheel, the spinning cycle, that's how you rise upward, on spiral steps. It shows me that the staircase appears straight, but it isn't. The further you get from the Matrix, the quicker you rise out of it, but that doesn't mean you're free at the physical level.

As long as you have physical form, you remain exposed to the Matrix, to its system.

This doesn't just apply to us humans, it applies to other beings, other planets, with similar mechanisms, slightly altered by planetary laws and universal positioning. But the concept is the same.

As long as you don't have a physical body, you are more elevated. As long as you do, you're in the Matrix.

You cannot fully escape.

You can only escape when you leave the physical plane, or when your soul manifests in higher dimensions, like a version of yourself in the 7th dimension with a luminous, transparent body. Then you're not in the Matrix.

Q: Lesson 7. How can this field help us in spiritual growth or healing journeys?

A: I'm being told it will focus on *spiritual healing*.

We are so deeply immersed in daily problems, fears, blockages, and all the traumas from old generations, that it's often hard for us to understand where we're supposed to go.

What is our purpose? What is our meaning? Why do we need to evolve? Why do we need to expand?

The answer is simple: there is a need to return home.

The journey is long, but that is the path.

The focus isn't on reaching the destination, but on understanding and receiving daily experiences with neutrality.

It's like knowing what you want, knowing the place you want to reach.

For example, think of someone who dreams of going to Bali, but doesn't know how they'll get there. They lack resources, don't understand how, but they're connected to the intention of reaching that destination.

The person needs to focus daily on what they think, how to work less, make more money, or do what they love.

They must plan all those small steps that help them eventually reach their destination. This field offers the possibility to resolve blockages or unpleasant experiences more quickly, more easily, and in neutrality. Access is not direct, and I'm getting that an *intermediary* is required.

Q: Who can be those intermediaries?
A: Those who have access.

Victoria: I'm getting the question, *how can you learn to gain access?* I don't think I'm the only one. I believe others have access too.

Q: The question is: can we teach others to access this field?
A: No.

Diana: I'm also getting "no," because it takes me to your soul's experience; you need to integrate the process of neutrality.

Q: Megaquantic Field, are there other people on Earth who have access to this field?
A: Are you receiving anything? I got an answer, but I can't believe it.

Diana: I'm getting there are very, very few.

Victoria: I received that there are only **3 people**.
Across the entire globe, I see the image of Earth spinning, and there are only 3 people. That's why I said I can't believe it.
Why is it that way?

Diana: Because that's what's needed.

Q: Megaquantic Field, what is my purpose for having access to this field?
A: I feel like crying. I'm getting *"this is your power"* and I can't believe it.

Victoria: Seriously, I can't believe it, because I feel like *I'm just Victoria.* Look. How interesting. It's showing me now in my heart that this is the secret; that I just feel like a simple, ordinary person.

That's actually what activates the power.

I don't feel like I have great power, I just feel like an ordinary person.

Diana: Yes, I feel like saying that when you feel you have great power, that factor activates the ego.

Victoria: Yes, and when that number isn't aligned, you can't access higher levels, you can't rise. It made me feel that this is the true goal; to reach a state of neutrality. Not to believe we hold some great power or that we're on a special mission, but to genuinely feel and recognize that we are nothing, yet within that nothingness lies extraordinary power.

You are everything and nothing at once.

It showed me an image of Jesus, how he came to share this very message with our world: *that we are meant to be simple, ordinary people.* That was his message, to anchor ourselves in the heart. To be neutral. Not to believe you possess power, or that you alone are special. Only from that place of humility does divine love become active within you.

Q: How does this field influence us, from the perspective of abilities? Does it enhance intuition, psychic abilities, or higher senses? Or how does it influence human consciousness?

A: I'm getting that it not only activates, it helps you go beyond your abilities. I see it like a radius around us, just like the solar system.

You are the sun, and around you float different planets, different abilities, depending on how much you allow yourself to access them.

Once you access this field, you go beyond the solar system, you expand, and your abilities go beyond their own limits.

This is where amazing information comes in, where even the abilities you already have can't handle the magnitude of it.

You receive information and techniques directly from the Source, if you let yourself be in the flow.

Q: Is there a dimensional difference? The Akashic Field is in dimension 4, up to what dimension does the Quantum Field radiate? And what about the Megaquantic Field?

A: The Quantum Field radiates up to dimensions 8, 9, maximum 10.

D11 is a transition dimension, I see it like a station between lower and higher planes.

From D12, the first league of essential players begins. I'm shown a football stadium. These are the first beings who work with the lower field, training those who are opening to access higher ones.

From D13 onward are the higher planes, Megaquantic.

Q: Is it beneficial to begin working in the Quantum Field? And what percentage of people can access this field?
A: There are 3 divisions of percentages.

The first is narrower, then a wider one, then a medium one.

The first is **yellow**, and about 20% - 24% can access the Quantum Field. These are creative people, those in creative fields.

The second is **white**, in the middle and the largest, up to 84% can access this one. Here we find lightworkers, those in spirituality, holistic work, etc.

The third category is **blue**, 28% - 64% max, a wide deviation. This includes those who speak, those working in communication.

Q: Why is the percentage so wide, 28% to 64%?
A: It brings the blue category to the front and enlarges it.

There's a lot of **fear** involved here. That's why the percentage is lower, 28%. This is the fear of speaking.

There are people afraid to speak, but others who overcome fear and speak their truth.

Diana: Let's go back to the Megaquantic Field. You had another question there.

Q: What inspired the name Megaquantic, and does it symbolize something?
A: [Laughing.] Now I see the Creator laughing, showing me I'm being funny. I just got it like that, that is the name. There was no inspiration. The word was simply sent to me, and I was open enough to receive it exactly as it is, without filtering it. I remember I had a question last night, "Why did I receive *Megaquantic* and not *Megaquantum?*" Because logically it should be *quantum* and *Megaquantum*.

Now I get the answer: the correct word is ***Megaquantic***, and *Quantum* is indeed correct as *Quantum*.

Q: I want to ask the Creator why it is *Megaquantic* and not *Megaquantum*.
A: It's about the vibration. The vibration that this field holds ends in *-ic*.

Q: What kind of vibration, in simpler words?
A: *Endless*. In our language, it would be "endless."
Without an ending.

Q: What does Quantum mean?
A: Still "*messing*". That is, still under debate.

Q: What would be the explanation or definition of the word *Megaquantic*?
A: **Megaquantic** is a field of attunements to the higher realms of existence and the extension of the Creator itself.

Q: How does it relate to universal energy, consciousness, or divine principles?
A: I'm shown - not now.

Q: What is the scientific definition of the word Megaquantic?
A: **Megaquantic** - *Double layer of the opposite world combined on each string of the quantum reality forced into physical local laws.*

Q: Does access to the Megaquantic Field also apply to Beings of Light or ETs? Can any ET being access it?
A: No.

Diana: Yes, because they're still us, at the soul level. So this includes soul evolution on a larger scale.

A: I'm getting that if everyone had access, the field would be contaminated. Just because we are humans and someone else is ET, they're still like us, but that doesn't mean they are mega-advanced. We're on the same frequency, the same wheel.
I'm feeling pulled to ask about *Ashtar*, because I've never resonated with him or connected with him as a being.

Q: What category of field does he belong to? Please show me his location within the map of creation in relation to the Megaquantic Field.
A: I'm shown Dimension 7, but only at the level of thoughts. If we go by quantum levels, I get Level 2B. He's in the mind.

Q: Is this a fluctuating or stable response?
A: Fluctuating. He showed me where he is at this moment (2025).

Diana: Now it makes me think about myself.
Victoria: I knew you were going to ask, because I already saw it.

A: Right now, you are D4, level 2A in Quantum, in the heart. This is how we can ask and figure out where someone is at the moment, exactly where a person or being is.

Diana: That's so interesting. That means even ET beings can be stuck in thoughts and can be at the same level in the Quantum Field as us. There's no hierarchy.

A: Correct. We coexist. Look, you have a 3D body, your consciousness is in 4D, and you're in Quantum Level 2A, in the heart. The Creator helped anchor you in your heart. This is one way of seeing it. For example, when doing sessions, you can see where your client is, or where you are, or ask about any being, like in this case, Ashtar.

Q: The Creator said the intention is to maintain the neutrality and purity of this field. Is it also because if you're not anchored in neutrality, some people might use the field to their own or to creation's detriment?
A: I'm getting that they simply won't have access at all. In the Megaquantic Field, you cannot access, you cannot mask who you are. Any intention in this field is detected. Absolutely everything, 101%. It's impossible to enter this field pretending to be from the light or to fake your good intentions.

Q: Does this field have healing properties, for mind-body-soul alignment?
A: Before answering that, I'm getting that in the Quantum Field, you can still travel with non-beneficial intentions; it's like traveling and dragging a bag behind you, but only in the first two levels. So yes, there's

a chance someone may access the field for the wrong reasons. But that's hard to do, you have to know the field very well to try to trick it. However, there are consequences, because you will be found out, and when that happens, your reality will shift into a negative polarity. It's like the field "punishes" you for misusing it against others.

The Quantum Field isn't about karma, but rather a reflection of your own negativity that you've spread and now you're receiving it back. If you emit goodness while hiding negativity, when the field finds you, it flips your reality upside down. It pays you back according to what you've truly given, because you've violated the fundamental laws of the Quantum Field.

Diana: That's the law of cause and effect.
Victoria: Yes, let's call it that.

That's where you see the full potential of each individual. By accessing the Quantum Field and releasing blockages, you create space to realize you have the power to heal yourself. Not someone else. Not even God. You are the one who regenerates your physical, emotional, and spiritual body.

It opens your eyes and shows you that you alone are the one doing this. It's a consciousness awakening.

Now I'm shown that in the Akashic Field, it's yes and no; it helps, but also doesn't. It shows me a construction sign and a person holding a stop or slow-down sign.

The Akashic Field shows that you can heal, but the experience is limited. Yes, it shows your potential and gives you information, but it also tests you, because it's dualistic.

In the Quantum Field, it shows you in more detail. It slows you down, but it also makes it clear that you are the one doing the healing.

If you feel healed, so it shall be.

Megaquantic already shows you, *you are one with God*. I'm shown a green light.

Q: What is the benefit for humanity to know about this field? How can it support or help?

A: I'm getting the number 100 years, and I'm shown scientists from the past, who received information from the future, like about Quantum. It first appeared in the 1900s; that's when the word was first introduced. At the time, the scientific world mocked the idea. Today, the idea of Quantum is widely accepted, and all modern technologies were downloaded from the Quantum Field. Look how long it took - almost 100 years, give or take, for this term to be taken seriously.

With *Megaquantic*, it will be the same, but the level of development is different now, so it will be faster.

In the future, it will be a science like relativity, mechanics, or Quantum physics. There will be *Megaquantic physics*, and within the Quantum realm, many new subfields will appear.

In medicine and biology, a new word is coming, **biosynthetics**. Yes, biosynthetics will be another branch of Quantum.

Megaquantic will be like a giant ladder, at the top. People will laugh at first, but in the future, it will be an amazing science for our civilization.

I'm being shown Atlantis again; they never reached Megaquantic. They only had access up to Quantum Level 4B. They tried going toward 4A, and that's when their civilization was destroyed, because they went too far into dark matter.

They tried to fake, to duplicate, to create their own reality, their own god. That's when they were wiped off the Earth.

They never reached Megaquantic knowledge.

Now I'm shown: *do you understand why the answers come the way they do?*

In the Megaquantic, you can't enter or access anything with hidden intentions.

They tried up to 4A, but because of the filter, they couldn't go further.

Q: Okay, I feel like asking something now. I understand the idea that the Megaquantic Field is accessed by very few on Earth, but what was the purpose for me (Diana) to find out about it?

A: Good question. Now I get a very simple answer: *"There is always a need to be a witness."*

Do you understand? Otherwise, no one would've believed me.

Diana: I feel the need to say thank you for this. I feel grateful for all the information I've learned through this experience.

Now I'm shown Jesus - not that I'm comparing myself to him, but to understand the concept.

If he had gone around spreading his message alone, no one would have believed him or taken him seriously.

For something to grow, a witness is needed.

Then the light spreads, and the information from higher realms begins to flow. Otherwise, no one takes seriously something that "doesn't exist," something that's not from this planet, something that doesn't make logical sense.

So, I thank you for giving me space and you to be that witness, to listen to all the information that's coming through.

Q: Could this be a new paradigm for integrating spirituality and human evolution?

A: I'm getting that it's a complex question: *not now.*

Victoria: We can mark it with a star and develop it in another session.

Q: Then is there any message or guidance for humanity during this time of spiritual awakening?

A: For this period humanity is in, the field is chaotic. Humanity is not yet ready to accept neutrality, to release fears and stagnant emotions. That's why the ideology of the Megaquantic Field cannot yet be implemented. Imagine being on the 2nd or 3rd floor of a building and wanting to jump to the 10th. It's impossible, there are development steps.

Q: Why did this information about the Megaquantic Field come through in 2024–2025? What's its purpose, if humanity isn't ready? Why now?

A: I'm shown that I made a hole in the ground, I planted a seed and covered it. It needs time to sprout.

It was an important process to plant the seed that will bear fruit in the coming years. It needed to be planted because it takes time to grow.

I'm shown that I am the "farmer" who planted the seed.

And my mind tells me that I need to record this. And the message confirms: *yes, it's important.*

It's important that in the future, people know who planted the seed. Right now, no one knows. They are correcting me. You see, you are the witness to the planting process, but the world doesn't know what this is. It's a natural process, but when the fruit grows, the world will ask who created or brought this concept, and they'll go back to the initial process and ask who the "farmer" is.

Right now, the world is taking baby steps into Quantum; many Beings of Light are already working with people.

I'm shown Atlantis again, and I'm getting that a time will come when people will reach up to 4A, where the Void is, but Beings of Light will work with scientists and help them grow up to Level 3 and slowly move toward 4B.

The Beings of Light will supervise this process so that dark matter is not touched.

When people reach levels beyond Quantum Level 2, starting at Level 2 and above, new laws begin to emerge. Events unfold that can no longer be explained through the lens of Quantum understanding alone.

That's when someone will first hear of and discover the **Megaquantic**. They'll follow that expanding path, connect the pieces, and begin to grasp it.

As things start to make sense, they'll be driven to trace the origin of the concept, and from there, a new science will be born.

Q: Are there signs or symbols associated with this field?
A: They exist, but they're not being revealed to us now. I see them subtly, I can only perceive about 10% of it all.

Diana: I feel like that's everything about the Megaquantic.
Victoria: Yes, I feel it's time to shift to the Quantum. Thank you, dear Creator.

Now we're leaving the room. The Creator is looking at us from the window, you wave at Him, and He looks and nods as if to say, "Aiaiai, these kids." I take your hand and lower it and say something like, "Don't embarrass us." I don't know why I feel like I'm your older sister.

Diana: Yesterday I felt the same way.

Q: Let's ask, because we're already outside but the Creator is still looking. Dear Creator, what connects us so that we feel like sisters?
A: 2D, 4AB, 9A, 10B, 14, these are life locations where we are sisters. These are dimensions based on Quantum level.
He turned and walked away from the window, and I took your hand and said, "Come on, let's go." Thank you.

Framework for a Megaquantic Reading™ Session

Q: What is a Megaquantic Reading™ Session?

A: A Megaquantic Reading™ Session is a deeply transformative, spiritual experience designed to bring profound healing, understanding, and release. It operates in a high-vibrational field where dense energies, emotional blockages, and past traumas dissolve easily, offering a painless journey toward greater freedom and evolution. This session goes beyond the limitations of time, space, and individual lifetimes, working on a scale that encompasses your soul's journey across dimensions, timelines, and universes.

The Core Purpose of the Megaquantic Readings™ are:

- *Deeper Understanding:* Gain insights into your soul's evolution and the patterns influencing your existence.
- *Release of Burdens:* Effortlessly let go of fears, traumas, and blockages carried for thousands of years, across ancestral lines, past lives, and cosmic timelines.
- *Healing the Self:* Realign with your true essence by resolving deeply rooted imprints that no longer serve your highest good.

The Session Environment offers:

- *High Vibrational Field:* The session takes place in a space of lightness and love, where lower frequencies dissolve naturally without pain or struggle.
- *Effortless Releasing:* Trauma and densities are gently lifted and transmuted, ensuring a seamless experience without re-traumatization.
- *Expanded Awareness:* You connect with a broader sense of your existence, encompassing the vastness of your being and your unique role in the cosmic dance of evolution.

Q: Who is This For?

A: This session is ideal for:

Seekers of Deeper Truth: Those who are ready to explore their multidimensional nature and gain clarity on their journey.

Individuals Ready to Let Go: People willing to release ancient fears, karmic imprints, and inherited patterns.

216

Souls in Evolution: Those attuned to their spiritual growth and committed to embracing their higher potential.

Q: What Happens During the Session?
A: *Energetic Assessment:* Your soul's journey and blockages are revealed within the Megaquantic Field.
Release Process: Layers of density and trauma are gently lifted, whether from this lifetime, past lives, or ancestral and cosmic connections.
Deeper Insights: You gain an understanding of the lessons and growth opportunities connected to your soul's experiences.
Integration: Energies are balanced, leaving you feeling lighter, clearer, and aligned with your highest self.

Q: What is the Outcome?
A: *Freedom from the Old:* Experience a profound release from limitations and burdens.
Expanded Consciousness: Understand your soul's purpose and evolution on a larger scale.
Alignment and Peace: Feel renewed, empowered, and connected to your divine essence.

Megaquantic Reading™ Sessions offer a unique and transformative opportunity to shed the layers of what no longer serves you and step into a higher state of being with grace and ease. For those who are ready, it is a gateway to profound healing and the next stage of your evolution.

How to Prepare Before a Megaquantic Session with the Guide:

Preparing for a Megaquantic Session with a Guide ensures that you are fully aligned to receive the transformative healing and insights offered. In this process, the guide holds the space, channels higher consciousness, and navigates the energy, while you open yourself to release and receive. Here's how you can prepare for this sacred experience:

1. Set Your Intention
 • Reflect on your reason for seeking this session.
 • Consider what you're ready to release (e.g., fears, traumas, patterns) or what understanding you hope to gain.

• Write down your intentions, but also stay open to unexpected shifts that your soul needs at this time.

2. Cultivate a Receptive Mindset
• Acknowledge that the guide will facilitate the process, and your role is to surrender and allow the energy to flow.
• Be willing to trust the guide as they access higher levels of consciousness and hold space for your healing.
• Practice letting go of control; the more relaxed and open you are, the more transformative the session will be.

3. Prepare Your Energy
• Spend time grounding yourself through meditation, deep breathing, or walking in nature.
• Avoid consuming heavy or dense energies (e.g., alcohol, psychedelic substances, or intense media) 24 hours before the session.
• Hydrate well and eat light, nourishing meals to keep your energy field clear.

4. Create Space for Stillness
• Schedule the session at a time when you can fully focus and won't be rushed.
• Prepare a quiet, comfortable space where you can relax, free from distractions.
• If the session is in person or virtual, ensure your surroundings feel peaceful and supportive.

5. Approach with Trust and Gratitude
• Trust the guide's ability to channel and facilitate the healing process.
• Acknowledge the sacredness of this space and the divine support available to you.
• Begin the session with gratitude for the healing and understanding you're about to receive.

6. Post-Session Integration
• Plan for time after the session to rest and integrate the shifts.
• Journal your thoughts or feelings if you feel inspired, as new insights may continue to arise.
• Be gentle with yourself, as old energies may release, and you may feel lighter or more reflective.

218

Key Mindset for the Session

Your Role: Be the receiver. Your openness and trust allow the guide to channel higher consciousness and hold space for your healing.
The guide's role is the facilitator, responsible for accessing the higher vibrational fields, navigating the session, and ensuring your safety and comfort.

By preparing with trust, openness, and a calm energy, you create the perfect foundation for a profound and effortless transformation during your Megaquantic Session with the Guide.

The Deeper Explanation of all 3 Types of Fields:

The **Megaquantic Reading™ Session**, **The Quantum Reading Session** and an **Akashic Record Reading** are spiritual practices designed to provide deeper understanding, healing, and insight into the soul's journey, but they differ significantly in focus, approach, and the scale of transformation they offer. Here's a breakdown of the differences:

Focus and Scope

Megaquantic Reading™:
- Works on a universal/cosmic scale, beyond time, space, and individual lifetimes.
- Focuses on releasing dense energies, traumas, and imprints from multiple timelines, dimensions, and universes all at once.
- Explores your soul's evolution at the highest level, addressing not just personal experiences but also collective, ancestral, and cosmic influences.
- Operates in a high-vibrational field, allowing for effortless healing and release without revisiting or relieving pain.

Quantum Reading:
- Connect with the soul's energetic blueprint.
- Access Quantum Field for insights providing clarity on life transitions, relationships, or spiritual awakening processes.
- Heal Soul-level blockages and address physical, emotional, or spiritual imbalances by identifying their root causes at an energetic or soul level.

- Align with higher purpose, often emphasizing self-love, forgiveness, and reconnection with divine source energy as pathways of healing.
- Holistic Transformation where the session may address the interconnectedness of mind, body, and spirit, fostering transformation that ripples across all levels of being.

Akashic Record Reading:

- Accesses the energetic library of your soul's records, which contains detailed information about all your past lives, present experiences, and potential futures.
- Focuses on retrieving specific information about patterns, lessons, and karmic ties relevant to your current life or situation.
- Primarily provides insights and clarity about why certain challenges exist and how they connect to your soul's purpose.

Approach to Healing

Megaquantic Reading™:

- Healing occurs on a level above Quantum, seamlessly dissolving deeply rooted blocks and traumas, often without the need to consciously process them.
- Does not require revisiting specific memories or events but works to release energetic densities from a holistic, multidimensional perspective.
- Focuses on creating ease and lightness, ensuring that no pain or suffering is felt during the process. This field is the most light, but very deep and the most "express" healing that can occur on any level.

Quantum Reading:

- The reading is more fluid, allowing practitioners to blend modalities (e.g. energy healing, intuition, or oracle cards) based on the client's needs.
- Healing focuses on shifting energy to create new possibilities.
- The practitioner facilitates the release of stagnant or negative energies, helping the soul reclaim its natural state of harmony.
- The reading explores a broader, multidimensional perspective, including potential futures and ancestral energies, with an emphasis on energy work.
- The reading often involves active energy clearing or alignment during the session, with immediate energetic shifts.

Akashic Record Reading:

- Offers healing through awareness and understanding, helping you recognize the roots of issues in your soul's timeline that are already recorded in the Akashic library.
- Encourages self-reflection and conscious action based on the insights received.
- Healing is often more introspective and tied to resolving specific karmic lessons or choices that are more on a level closest to our human perception.
- Akashic Records Readings follow a structured process, often guided by the spiritual entities known as Record keepers or guides, with a clear process for accessing and interpreting the Records, that even allows beginners to become easily familiar.
- The practitioner uses a specific prayer, intention, or ritual to open the Records, connecting with the divine archive of the client's soul.
- Healing focuses more on understanding and resolving soul-level historical data, karmic lessons, and specific guidance, with an emphasis on understanding and resolution.
- This field is deeply spiritual, often aligned with mystical traditions, invoking divine or sacred energies or exact belief systems.

Energetic Field

Megaquantic Reading™:

- Operates in a field of high-frequency energy where densities naturally dissolve without resistance.
- Goes beyond the linear concept of time to address imprints and patterns that transcend individual timelines or universes.
- Focuses on an above-Quantum transformation, aligning you with your highest potential and evolutionary state.

Quantum Reading:

- This field is highly interactive and malleable, allowing real-time energy shifts, such as clearing blockages, balancing chakras, or aligning with higher vibrations.
- The immediate energy work within the Quantum Field creates a sense of active transformation, with clients often feeling shifts during the session. It's like sculpting energy in real-time.
- The field is more broad in its own energy.

- This field is aligned with universal, non-dogmatic spirituality, which connects the power of consciousness to transform reality in less human time, or even instantly.

Akashic Record Reading:
- Tied to the energetic plane of the Akashic Records, which functions as a spiritual library containing the history of your soul.
- This field is stable and more fixed, with healing occurring through insights, divine guidance, and intentional release rather than direct energy adjustments, or energy reshaping.
- Provides access to specific information and energies related to your soul's path, with a focus on the record-keeping aspect of existence.
- While powerful, it typically stays within the scope of the soul's individual journey rather than addressing larger, multidimensional scales.

Key Differences in Experience

Megaquantic Reading™ Session:
- Designed for very deep release and effortless healing, perfect for those ready to let go of old traumas without needing detailed explanations.
- Works on a macro scale: releasing ancient blockages not just from this life, but across timelines, ancestral patterns, and even cosmic dimensions.
- Feels light, expansive, and deeply freeing, as it's rooted in the energy of evolution and ease.

Quantum Reading Session:
- The energy is less fixed and a more living space, allowing the client who is struggling with (for example) self-worth or might have their issues linked to an ancestral pattern, a past-life vow, or a misaligned chakra; all addressed within the Quantum Field.
- This field is less tied to a specific spiritual tradition, making it accessible to diverse belief systems.
- The Quantum Field is fascinating for its infinite, fluid and multidimensional nature, allowing to explore, reshape, and co-create new timelines and realities.

Akashic Record Reading
- Focuses on insight and awareness, helping you understand the "why" behind your experiences.

- Can be more introspective and intellectual, as it involves connecting dots between past actions and present circumstances.
- The Akashic Records are narrower in scope, prioritizing the soul's historical and karmic data over broader cosmic or potential energies. The focus is on what has been and what is destined, rather than what could be.
- This field is of a more archival nature which limits exploration to the soul's documented truth, offering precision, but less flexibility for co-creating new possibilities.

Which Reading to Choose?

1. Choose Megaquantic Reading™ if:
- You're ready for deep, large scale multidimensional release and healing.
- You want a transformative experience that works on above the Quantum levels, transcending linear time and space, or any universes.
- You're less focused on understanding the specifics and more on feeling liberated and aligned with your higher self.
- You're ready to take a leap of faith and feel that you expanded and released a lot in the lower two fields, as Quantum and Akashic Records.
- You're searching to expand the awareness even further than any knowledge existed beyond the Quantum Field.

2. Choose Quantum Reading if:
- You're ready for real-time shifts, such as clearing blockages, aligning chakras, creating immediate emotional or spiritual transformations.
- You're for activations and upgrades on all levels: physical, emotional, mental, spiritual and energetic.
- You're curious about aligning with future possibilities and to create new outcomes.
- You're feeling stuck or want to break free from limiting patterns - this forward-looking approach empowers you to your soul's highest potential.
- You're looking to activate your dormant abilities, gifts or knowledge.
- You're less drawn to any specific spiritual traditions, any particular dogmas or universal principles. Quantum field is a non-denominational framework that feels welcoming and versatile. In this field, the energy adapts to your worldview during the session.

3. Choose Akashic Record Reading if:
- You seek clarity and guidance about specific issues, life lessons, or karmic patterns.
- You're curious about the details of your soul's history and how they connect to your current path.
- You're comfortable with introspection and taking conscious action based on insights received.

In summary, the Megaquantic Reading™ is about large-scale, pure energy, painless, loving and effortless instant transformation. Quantum Reading is more fluid in a continuum state of energy flow that every step taken in this field has an impact of real-time change. While the Akashic Record Reading is more about detailed insight and self-awareness, as this field is more narrow and fixed.

They are all powerful but serve different purposes on your spiritual journey.

Channelings in the Megaquantic Field

Diana's Q: I wanted to ask about the Megaquantic Field, do I need a greater openness to access from there as well?
A: The answer is no.

Who Can Access the Megaquantic Field?

Q: What does Diana need in order to access the Megaquantic Field?
A: Above your head, I see cables, and the word "processing" comes to me. You can imagine it like being at the doctor's office when they want to do a test to check brain activity. There, they connect you with various cables for testing.

Q: What kind of processing is this?
A: Codes. I notice that above each one of us humans, there are tubes, and at the level of those tubes, there are many codes. The more you open your consciousness, the more you evolve, the more codes are activated. Inside, the codes that activate take the form of a honeycomb, that is, hexagonal cells. The colors are as follows: the tube is metallic in color, the hexagonal cells

that are inactive are black, the ones that are active light up like lamps, they are white, and inside I see the color blue.

Example: Imagine a lightbulb with blue-colored glass. When you turn on the light, it looks white with a blue hue. We all have these tubes and codes; some of the codes are active, others are in the process of activating, and others are inactive. The more that are activated, the more these activations allow us to access and process our consciousness. I try to look at my own tube, and it's different, I have more lit up. Though I don't understand why.

Q: Now I have another question, how do we light up these codes?
A: They activate depending on the missions, the tasks that you have and fulfill, not at the level of the individual, this body or the physical plane, but at the general level; the extended consciousness of your soul.

Each body (in whatever shape, form, and existence) has different experiences, but the consciousness of your total existence is present in every body, at the same time. The more such bodies activate these hexagonal cells in their unitary tube, as they fulfill their individual missions, the more these codes activate simultaneously.

You can imagine it like a Google Drive file - any change you make can be accessed from any device when you're logged in with the same account, or by any account with access to that file. All those changes happen live, they happen instantly.

I see the consciousness of your existence connected to a single tube, and someone is taking care of these codes. There's a group of beings responsible for all of our bodies and this tube. And this group of beings activates those hexagonal cells in the tube only when those missions are fulfilled. This entire process is much greater than our current existence. What I'm being shown is that this is actually *our evolution*, and that we're not supposed to compare ourselves with anyone. We are all in the process of evolution, but each of us has a different process, each in their own time, once their missions are fulfilled.

Percentage of "Conscious awareness – Connection with the Creator"

Q: Is there a certain percentage of conscious awareness that an individual must reach in order to connect directly with the Creator?
A: 94%, from 94 and up.

Q: Depending on the Beings of Light, what is the percentage we need in order to connect with them?
A: Saints – 12%
   Ascended Masters – Virgin Mary, Buddha, Jesus, Allah, etc. – 18%
   Angels – 24%
   Archangels – 28%
   Seraphim & Cherubim – 34%
   ETs – 48%, referring to ETs who are in the higher planes of creation

Q: Now my question is, what about the others?
A: I'm being shown another reversed scale, going downward. One is luminous, and the other is dark. Then there's an empty space, something that separates them, it's another category. It stops at Seraphim and Cherubim. Then comes another layer, and it begins again further upward. Creator/Source/God – 94%

Q: Can our level of consciousness, in another existence such as an ET for example, be different from our current percentage in the human body?
A: Okay. The question is whether it's local or international, so to speak. The answer I get is that it's local, because the goal is that, in each life or reincarnation, we strive to reach as high as possible. It's individual per lifetime.

Q: I feel like this is a rhetorical question, but I still feel the need to ask. Does this mean that there are ET beings who haven't yet reached the percentage required to connect directly with the Creator?
A: I'm being shown beings who exist in the lower planes. Just like us, they also need to rise, to reach higher.
For example, you are in this current existence and manage to connect with the light because you have a consciousness level of 82%. You, in another existence, are also experiencing, let's say, a Reptilian aspect. You, being there as well, are trying, like all of us, to be aware of the existence of the

Creator/God/Source. That means that in that existence, you've already evolved, because now you are here in this life, where you are fully conscious. This is evolution and its purpose.

Q: Does Level 3A and 3B have a source? Can the Field explain why Level 4 is neutral?
A: Level 4 is the analysis room; on the walls, I see various information, statistics. It's very important that such a room exists in the Quantum world.

Q: Why is it placed above?
A: Because statistics need to come from a neutral perspective, without polarity, and it is essential that it be located near dark matter, near the Void. God's creation began from a neutral state.

Akashic, Quantum, Megaquantic - Source Mass Percentage versus Dimensions

Q: If the Source level exists here, does this aspect also apply in Akashic?
A: Yes, but the percentage is lower.

Q: Is the Akashic Field also structured in levels?
A: No, it is a single field, distributed by categories. It doesn't have levels, but vertically, it has categories. There are many categories, based on various experiences and accumulated information, which need to be distributed by category rather than by level.

Q: In the Akashic Field, what is the gross and net mass? And how about in the Quantum Field?
A: In **Akashic** – gross mass of the Source is 24%, net is 12%
   In **Quantum** – gross mass is 41%, net is 14%
   In **Megaquantic** – gross mass is 98%, net is 49%

Q: Why is there such a big difference?
A: I'm shown that more is consumed within the field itself, and only 14% remains net. In Akashic, it's 24%, and exactly half remains; that's why duality is more intense in the Akashic Field. In Quantum, the gross mass is larger, but the net mass is smaller. Here there's a bigger deviation because

the Creator's energy disperses more throughout the field. The flexibility of the Creator's energy is greater in the field.

Q: And in Megaquantic, where does the remaining 2% go?
A: Somewhere - 2% remains - I believe outside of creation. Here we need to approach it mathematically.
I see a formula that calculates the gross percentage, the net percentage, what portion it represents out of 100%, and the average of these 3. Then, from 100, you subtract the average of the three fields, and what remains is the percentage of how much the Creator Himself remains outside - as the Creator, separate from His creation.

That's exactly what is referred to as "net creation," but the formula must be different. It is multiplied by -20, to the power of 69.5 squared, and equals the sum. This formula gives us the net mass of the Source/Creator/God. Then, from these two formulas, another formula is generated. (*Summarised below*).

Wait, another formula is coming to me. Knowing the average gross mass and average net mass, we need to find out how much of the Source mass - the Creator - is in motion. After that, you divide them... (*pause*)

What do you divide, and what do you find out? Ok, the average of the three, then we divide it by the total gross Source sum obtained from those three, and from that sum, we multiply by the net value, which is external to the entire creation, and then we find the amount of energy being consumed or flowing into the field. These are the formulas for how we calculate it.

Now let's interpret the data above, replacing "**gross**" with "**energetic potential**" and "**net**" with "**energy in motion**," and calculate the energy in creation, the energy lost, and the energy outside of creation for each field (Akashic, Quantum, Megaquantic).

We assume that 100% represents the total energy available in a system (each field being a separate system), and the percentages are relative to this total.

I will calculate:

- **Energy in creation** (the active one, involved in the internal processes of the field)

- **Energy lost** (the difference between potential and energy in motion, which doesn't manifest in creation)
- **Energy outside of creation** (what "escapes" or remains separate — possibly related to the Creator)

Definition and Calculation of Energies for Each Field

Given the known data:
Akashic: Energetic potential 24%, Energy in motion 12%
Quantum: Energetic potential 41%, Energy in motion 14%
Megaquantic: Energetic potential 98%, Energy in motion 49%

1. Energy in Creation
Energy in creation is the energy in motion - the one that manifests directly within the system:
Akashic: 12%
Quantum: 14%
Megaquantic: 49%

2. Lost Energy
Lost energy is the difference between the energetic potential (the total available energy) and the energy in motion (the energy actually being used):
Formula: Lost Energy = Energetic Potential - Energy in Motion
Akashic: 24% - 12% = 12%
Quantum: 41% - 14% = 27%
Megaquantic: 98% - 49% = 49%

These three fields form a *kind of* continuum:
Akashic (simple, stable)
Quantum (intermediate, dynamic)
Megaquantic (complex, supra-unitary)

> *Note: Supra-unitary* – a discovery based on my individual study within the Megaquantic Field. As a **non-locality, entanglement beyond the conventional model,** or what some theories call "hyper-quantum" dynamics.

Table: Gross Mass (energetic potential) vs Net Mass (Energy in motion) in all three fields

Field	Gross mass (%) Energetic potential	Net mass (%) Energetic in motion
Akashic	24%	12%
Quantum	41%	14%
Megaquantic	98%	49%

The Creator's Mass Formulation System
The "Tri" Code of the Fields: Akashic – Quantum – Megaquantic

But where is this 2%?

Maybe this 2% is a constant or a variable that adjusts the difference between the gross and net mass, or perhaps represent an energy "leak" outside of the entire creation.

This difference could be the energy "consumed" or transformed in creation. If 2% is a fixed variable, it could be a small part of this energy that "escapes" or remains with the Creator.

If 2% is the Creator's mass, then 100% - 2% = 98% is the actual creation.

Where 2% can be considered as a constant loss.

a) The Creator's Percentage Outside Creation

Gross and Net Average where:
1. Gross average = (24 + 41 + (98 * 1.5)) / 3.5 = 53.34%
2. Net average = (12 + 14 + (49 * 1.5)) / 3.5 = 26.33%
3. Overall average = 100 - ((53.34 + 26.33) / 2) = 58.33%

Scaling factor (X = 41.67)

100% - 58.33% = 41.67% ➤ X = **part of the Creator inside creation**

So **X is not arbitrary,** it is exactly **the percentage of the Creator manifested in creation.**

Where **1.5** and **3.5** are:
1) 1.5 is a **weighting coefficient** applied to the **Megaquantic** level, which suggests that this level has **greater importance** than the other two.
1.5 = the relative importance of the Megaquantic level compared to the other two (which are implicitly weighted as 1).
2) 3.5 = the total sum of the weights, i.e. the base for the weighted average.

3.5 is the sum of weights:
  • Akashic: **1**
  • Quantum: **1**
  • Megaquantic: **1.5**
Total: 1 + 1 + 1.5 = 3.5

This choice suggests that the Megaquantic level contributes almost 43% (1.5/3.5) to the final average, while the other two contribute only 28.5% each.

Conclusion:
1.5 is the weight assigned to the Megaquantic level.
3.5 is the total sum of weights: 1 (Akashic) + 1 (Quantum) + 1.5 (Megaquantic).
The formula is **a weighted average**, not a simple average.
It is a metaphor or conceptual model for the involvement or presence of the Creator at different levels of reality.
The final result (approx. 60%) is interpreted as **the "uninvolved" part in creation,** thus remaining "outside" manifestation.

Calculation of the percentage of the Creator remaining outside creation.

Formula: Mean of the Field$_i$ = $\dfrac{M_{\text{gross}_i} + M_{\text{net}_i} + (100 - M_{\text{gross}_i})}{3}$

$$\text{Total Mean} = \dfrac{\Sigma \, \text{Mean of the Field}_i}{3}$$

$$\text{Creator Percentage} = 100 - \text{Total Mean}$$

Result: The Percentage of the Creator Outside Creation ≈ **58.33%**

Explanation: Approximately **58.33%** of the Creator's essence remains outside of creation, maintaining absolute autonomy.

b) The net mass of the Creator (with deep Quantum component)

Formula:

$$\text{Net Mass of the Creator} = X \bullet (-20)^{69.5^2}$$

Where:

X = The percentage of the Creator manifested in creation (41.67%)

$X \bullet (-20)^{69.5^2}$ = **Nonlinear force expressing the divine net mass in multidimensional magnitude**

X = The part of the Creator within creation

So **X** is not arbitrary; it is exactly the percentage of the Creator manifested in creation.

Where **X** is an input value (e.g., the total average or another specified value).

According to the requirement, the net mass of the Creator is calculated as follows:

1) Take the value, assume the total average from a) or another specific value.

2) Multiply it by $(-20)^{4830.25}$

Power: $69.5^2 = 4830.25$

Value: $(-20)^{4830.25}$ it is extremely large and negative, but for simplicity, we will consider the formula as symbolic or requiring a specific input value.

Assume the input value is the total average from a), which is **41.67**.

Net Mass of the Creator = Total Mean $\bullet$ $(-20)^{4830.25}$

And when substituting the value of **Total Mean** (as **41.67**):

Net Mass of the Creator = $41.67 \bullet (-20)^{4830.25}$

Result: A specific value is required for **X**. With **X = 41.67**, the result is symbolic due to its magnitude of $(-20)^{4830.25}$
This appears to be a **symbolic formula** (not physical in the classical sense), but we can formally express it as in the below explanation.

Explanation:
The **net mass of the Creator** is a **hyper-dimensional magnitude**, expressed through a **nonlinear force**.
The coefficient **X (41.67)** reflects the percentage of the Creator present within creation.
This is a **metaphysical or archetypal formula** expressing the idea that the net mass of the Creator is of a **colossal magnitude**, impossible to measure in 3D terms.
It is a **constant of a "divine" nature.**

c) The energy consumed in the field of motion of creation

Formula:

$$\text{Creator Mass in Movement} = \left(\frac{\left(\dfrac{\Sigma M_{\text{gross}_i}}{3} + \dfrac{\Sigma M_{\text{net}_i}}{3} \right)}{2 \bullet \Sigma M_{\text{gross}_i}} \right) \bullet M_{\text{net}}^{\text{external}}$$

Explanation of Terms:

M_{gross} : Gross energetic mass (total energy in the field)

M_{net} : Net energetic mass (usable energy for creation)

M_{net} : External net energetic mass

"Creator Mass in Movement": Represents the portion of net energy from the Creator manifesting dynamically in the system.

Result: The Creator's mass in motion ≈ **14.20%**

Explanation: This shows that approximately **14.20%** of the Creator's energy "flows" into the motion of creation, into the Quantum planes, as the *"engine of life."*

Symbol	Meaning
M gross	Gross energetic mass (total energy expressed in the field)
M net	Net energetic mass (energy consciously usable for creation)
X	The percentage of the Creator manifested in creation (41.67%)
C separate	The percentage of the Creator remaining outside of creation
E field	Energy consumed for the movement of the fields
$(-20)^{4830.25}$	Nonlinear force expressing the divine net mass in multidimensional magnitude

Q: Can you remind us, in which dimension does each field coexist?
A: 1. Akashic - D2-4, but I also get the number **8** - it oscillates.
Maybe there are beings from **D8** who come to Akashic to work.
2. Quantum - D5-6-7-8-9-10 and goes down, then **goes back to 9** - it deviates.

D11 - is a station between the lower and higher planes, like a kind of bridge - it is a transition between Quantum and Megaquantic. Here I sense that both forces from Quantum and Megaquantic are present, like at a border between two countries that have a river, and the river coexists on both sides. **D12** - is the first league of essential players who prepare those who move higher because you cannot jump directly from Quantum to Megaquantic. It has **particular autonomy** - 12 cannot be completely subordinated to the Megaquantic Field because when they prepare, they pass from Quantum to Megaquantic, they need training and preparation, and the laws of Megaquantic cannot be applied yet. It is a training space. If you pass from D12 to D13, there is a huge wall covering everything, and there are many ET beings here – many councils located in D12. Even if they are very powerful councils, they train in D12 because they are not yet fully qualified to pass further. They need training, where their abilities are evaluated, whether they have passed or accumulated the necessary percentage to be able to move on. I don't see doors here, only that the Megaquantic Field mechanism does not allow free passage. Here it tells me, "You see humans? When you hear about Galactic Councils you consider them Gods, but from the point of view of expansion and growth towards the Source, everyone has their own process and level."

There are cases of beings who work in light with light and fail the Megaquantic training test. This is normal, even for councils more advanced than most of us. I see a lot of light in D12, with many fighters. I see different kinds of training, and the wall at the Megaquantic Field is grayish-blue, kind of milky. You have the feeling you can see inside, but you cannot perceive it. It is very large and tall.

3. Megaquantic - from **D13 upwards**.

God - Who is He? Limiting Beliefs about God

This part about God, the release techniques, and the protection method below is an introductory section from a session in which we first accessed the Quantum Field, then took a galactic journey into the Megaquantic Field. Before this journey into the Megaquantic Field, we needed to cleanse and release all the limiting beliefs passed down about God. Below, you will be able to see a release technique that I received from the Quantum Field, but to maintain the flow of the entire text, I decided to keep the information received here.

Who is God?

It is an autonomy inseparable from everything that exists. Encoded information - I cannot access it. It is very complex. It shows me many, many universes. They themselves (the Beings of Light) do not know the true origin of God. What I feel is that it is a creation that coexists in a vast space, the Void, and the Void is greater than Creation. Creation is like a game playing where God is in the Void. That's what the image shows me. For us, God is only light, and this is a limiting belief that misleads many people. This is the trap from the lower planes; lower beings feed on this ideology. God is that Void where nothing exists, but everything exists at the same time. I often say, **"I am everything and nothing, at the same time."**

Diana: When you say that God is only light, you reject the dark part; you don't believe in that creation.
Victoria: You might ask yourself: *what do you mean God is dark matter?* This was specially created by the lower planes so that, over many millennia, we would think this way. Religion was built exactly on such a trap; it was passed down to us on a genetic level that God is only light, and everything you do that is a sin comes from darkness. But in fact, darkness and light are one and the same Source.
Victoria: I didn't expect such information.
Diana: I feel like saying now that I want to release the illusions about everything created in connection with God, with the lower planes. I am ready to release all those thoughts about God, about Beings of Light, the lower planes, and everything that does not serve me here.

Techniques for Releasing Limiting Programs and Beliefs

It's showing me so many techniques.

The first method. A technique where, as we are on the 4B floor (in the Quantum Field), you open the window and place into a basket everything you want to release. Then you let go of the basket so it can drop down to the 1st floor, outside the building.

The second method is to imagine that you are exactly that Void, equal to God. In that moment, you feel that you are the Void, and outside of you, you see your creation, your sphere of light. Then you imagine that you exist outside, in the Void; you exist in your sphere of light, in your creation. Now, being like that, you look to the right side, at the point in the middle where the bubble ends, and you, outside of the bubble as dark matter, look at yourself at that point as if you are facing each other. Then, you see how all these beliefs come out through your mouth and meet in the middle, at the border of your bubble. There a portal forms where everything enters from both sides, and in that portal, you release absolutely everything.

It's showing me that there are two more conscious release techniques in the Quantum Field. We can release using either of these two methods, but the method with the Quantum Field, with floor 4B, is for those who are more limited in awareness or who haven't reached a deeper level in this area. Those who are more aware, more awakened, can use the technique between darkness and light, between the Void and creation, or other new methods that arise along the way.

It's still releasing. So much is being released. Violet colors are coming out of their heads. A lot of beliefs regarding children, babies, birth, beliefs related to funerals, you have deeply rooted beliefs about death and funerals. You need to release all of these beliefs. I see your brain like in 8D, like watching 8K on a TV.

Diana: A question just came to me - were all these beliefs stopping me from accessing even more knowledge?
Victoria: Yes, because it was what your heart was generating. It's done now. Thank you.
Diana: I'm getting more questions. When we say to release into the pure light of God, that's actually not correct, is it?
Victoria: No. Look, I'm realizing now too that we're not doing it right.
Diana: Exactly, and the same goes with protection.
Victoria: We are rejecting the part of dark matter, of the Void, of God. What I'm seeing now is like when you look at the night sky and see stars. You accept the light of the star, but you don't accept the sky. The dark sky is the Void, God. The light of the star is just a small creation of His, and you only accept that small creation, but not the dark sky.

I see how tightly you're clinging to this belief, and you think it's the truth, but you're not opening your eyes to see that the sky is dark, and there are thousands and thousands of stars, thousands and thousands of universes. You shouldn't accept just a little spark of light, because the sky holds millions of stars.

Diana: I'm getting all kinds of realizations. Darkness rejects light, and when light speaks of the pure light of God, it rejects darkness, as if both sides are rejecting each other.

Victoria: And now it's pointing a finger at me too, saying I still need to understand this.

Diana: But what would be the most beneficial way for us to use it? I think it's tricky here. Like, okay, I accept darkness, but I want to work with the light.

Now I'm being taken again to floor 2A, and I'm shown that 2A is the department that attracts and rejects this aspect. If your heart emits more light polarity, creates light, positive thoughts, automatically your whole field is luminous and you attract, like a magnet, the frequencies that match your resonance level. If you're on the negative polarity, you create a negative field and attract low-frequency beings. That's why I'm getting that it doesn't matter what the guide says. It could be the most important guru, and if in his heart he feels and emits negative thoughts, he already attracts what he feels.

And that takes me to your question, when you said *it's tricky*. How can we know if we've connected with Beings of Light or with lower planes of creation? You will reflect what you feel in your heart, if you emit positive polarity, you are like a magnet for high-vibrational beings. But if in your heart you hold negative polarity, you connect to low-frequency polarity.

Diana: That's a realization for me as well, I used to wonder why, even after doing energetic protection, certain beings could still get through. But I've come to understand that if you're holding a negative polarity within yourself, you're essentially attracting those experiences. Your heart energy plays a big role in that.

If your vibration drops too low, even the best energetic protection won't hold, it becomes ineffective, almost like it cancels itself out.

Victoria: Exactly, your heart is the generator.

Diana: That's exactly what Archangel Metatron said in a session; *to set the intention to be anchored in the heart.* Now I'm feeling a very strong tingling in my body.

Q: When you create protection, is it still recommended to use protection spheres?

Protection - Sphere, Pyramid

I see that it's better to build a pyramid. Your protection should not be a sphere, but a pyramid. The beneficiary should be placed in one pyramid, and you should be in another pyramid with the tip pointing upward. It shows me that, in fact, the beneficiary needs to be in a separate pyramid, and you as the guide in another separate pyramid, and everything should be enclosed in a sphere of light. When you place yourself with the beneficiary in the same sphere, you're exposed to the same energies.

The pyramid, as a geometric shape, doesn't allow particles to travel beyond. It keeps them more organized. This helps maintain the individual field of each person inside the pyramid, and the energy of each one doesn't scatter in all directions. It's more organized. When inside a pyramid, both the beneficiary's and the guide's energy becomes more coherent. It could be that at that moment, even if you are not in the best shape, you feel overwhelmed. When you're inside a triangle, your energy calms down, and the energetic particles move more coherently. In this way, you bring the beneficiary into the present, and then you create the sphere of light in which your energies are no longer mixed together. The sphere of light acts like a bubble, where everything that happens in the session doesn't interact with external dimensions. You don't absorb anything from the beneficiary into your creation, and they don't connect to your field. Thank you.

I don't know if there are more questions, but I feel pressure in my forehead, I think it's time to exit the field.

Q: Quadro Quantum Field, is there any additional information you would like to offer us today?
A: No, it feels like it's too much.

Q: Quantum Field, is there any useful information that would be for the highest good for everyone to know?
A: It shows me that we can exit the building exactly the way we entered. I see how, right on the floor, another portal opens, and like at a waterpark, you slide off.

This is a galactic journey. Thank you.

Megaquantic Field - Galactic journey

We're here. You've just jumped and landed on our feet. The two of us are sitting now, looking around, and not quite understanding what this place is. It feels like we were up high, and in front of us there's a steep drop, not mountains, but more like a sphere, a sun, everything glowing white, so intensely bright, like standing directly in front of the sun.

Q: What do we need to understand here, Higher Self, spiritual guides, Beings of Light who are with us tonight?
A: Now I see how the bright presence from earlier has returned, and someone has appeared. I don't even know how to imagine God, but I perceive a very large, ancient being, seated on a throne, immense in size.

Q: What field are we in right now?
A: This is the *Megaquantic Field.* It's enormous, and I can feel how God is sitting on His throne within this creation. He has turned and is looking at us; we are very tiny compared to Him. He leans down with His face, trying to understand what He sees. I feel that He is astonished. It's a mixed feeling - part surprise, part knowing. He has extended His index finger, and we've climbed onto it.

Diana: That's exactly how I see myself, climbing up.

Now He lifts us up, and above His head, on His left side, there's a small platform where He places us. On His left, there's also a massive screen. He turns to us, but I can't even hear what He's saying. His voice vibrates at *megatonhveloghertz level.* That's how it comes through, and it's impossible for our hearing to comprehend it. It's not telepathic communication, it's synthetic; *biosynthetic.* Every particle in our body communicates. What He thinks and expresses, He shows us. Our particles are tiny bits, all linked together, and we are like skin; a geometric pattern of honeycombs. He shows us to look at His screen. I'm looking, but I don't understand it.

Q: Megaquantic Field, we ask you to transmit images in the simplest form for us, to include beautifully in the upcoming book.
A: He says it's not "upcoming", it's now.
Now I see a portal, two doors standing in a triangle shape, and we have to go through it, like through a narrow tunnel.

It makes me sleepy. I think He's working on me because I feel like yawning. These are higher planes, and the energy is different.

Let's go through this tunnel. I feel like I'm crawling. Done.

I've come out the other side. I feel the density lifting from us. Now we move forward and I see us sliding, like on a slide.

We've arrived at water, an ocean, a planet of water, and we need to throw ourselves into the ocean. Now I feel myself in the water, safe, like I live here. There's so much silence. I don't even have a physical body, everything is light and pure love. We need to stay here to cleanse.

Q: Is there anything we need to understand about these cleansings?
A: Here, in the water where we've arrived, attachments, cords, or entities are removed from us automatically.

Diana: I also feel cellular memory.

Yes, because I see a sphere, and within this water, everything is released effortlessly, with ease; there's no need to force, to think, or to issue a command. Things simply let go on their own. In this field, negative polarity doesn't exist, only the memory of it remains. It's like the memory of a taste. For instance, I don't eat meat, but I can still remember what it tastes like. That's exactly how it feels here in the Megaquantic Field.

Now we've leapt out of the water and are rising upward. Oh wow! We're climbing so many stairs. And there's still so much more ahead. Then it's done. We walked ten more steps and sat down on lounge chairs, like the kind you'd find at the beach, all facing the sun. I feel incredible, just like I'm relaxing by the ocean.

Diana: I perceive even more light.

Yes, like we're in heaven, if we think from a religious point of view. Someone has brought us cocktails, with orchids and strawberries. We clink glasses together, and now we're enjoying this delicious mocktail. We both say we're ready to see more. I see us getting up from the chairs, wanting to go somewhere. Someone shows us to go back. We lie back down. Someone very large and voluminous has put bibs on us, like babies, and strapped us to the chairs. They're treating us like infants. A large platter is placed between us, you're to my right. The platter holds different things, but I can't see them clearly yet.

Q: What do we need to become aware of here?
A: They're showing that someone is feeding us from the air, giving us information little by little. We can't access everything on the platter at once, we need to take it in slowly, so we can adjust. I don't even know how to explain what I feel and receive, but here in the Megaquantic Field, I need to be spoon-fed like a baby. I asked, "What should I do?" I'm rebelling a bit, and it's like they stuff my mouth even more. It's joyful here in the Megaquantic, feels like I'm being filled with adrenaline, dopamine.

Q: Megaquantic Field, what information can you share with us today to include in the book?
A: I've unstrapped myself from the chair and they've allowed me to look at the platter. There's so much on it. Imagine a cake sliced into triangular pieces:
– One slice is CRYSTALS
– Another is about WATER
– Another holds STARS, PLANETS, and GALAXIES,
  and the platter is spinning
– Another slice has many MATHEMATICAL FORMULAS
– Another is about BIOSYNTHETIC

Everything is there, but we receive it piece by piece.

The Biosynthetic Language of the Megaquantic Field

There exists a realm beyond the mind, beyond language, where communication unfolds, not through thoughts or words, but through the very particles of our being. This is the *biosynthetic field*, a space where information is not spoken or heard, but **embodied**. In this state, every cell, every atom, every strand of our essence becomes a receptor. We do not "hear" messages, we become the message.

In the Megaquantic Field, the Beings of Light, the Divine, and the universal intelligence do not speak in ways we are used to. Their language is

243

not telepathy, it is *biosynthetic*: a transmission where understanding occurs at the **biological, energetic, and geometric level**. This is not biosynthetic as defined currently in a human context, it is a transmission, it is a living download, a communion of frequency, vibration, and light. It bypasses logic and flows directly into the core of who we are.

Here, the body listens. The soul decodes. The memory of the universe echoes within our cellular matrix. There is no need to interpret, command, or strive, because in this place, understanding is inherent, and transformation happens organically.

As you journey through the pages ahead, know that the insights shared are not just meant to be read, they are meant to be felt, absorbed, and remembered deep within. This is not just information. It is **biosynthetic memory**, awakening within you what has always been known.

Q: What's with the biosynthetic?
A: Ok, I can take the "slice" of the "cake" that represents *biosynthetic*, and I've placed myself back on the lounge chair. Now I'm consuming this slice, like eating oysters.

Biosynthetic is a science. Actually, humanity tends to judge such creations, but this is a science where organs, body parts, and skin are created, the very material that forms our vehicle or our bodies. There are even worlds where the entire composition of a planet is made from biosynthetic material. For us, it might seem questionable, how can we create something artificial?
But in truth, it is not artificial, it is a higher level than our body, skin, or organs. To us, it may appear robotic, but that's a mistaken perception. In our future, as I recall from a previous session, something came through about meat, our bodies won't be able to digest meat or certain foods anymore, especially after the release of Reptilian DNA.
There are planets where everyone originates from biosynthetic material. If we travel to their planet, everything is biosynthetic - trees, animals, even their nature, and they don't see themselves as robots. It's just that the structure of their bodies, their trees, everything is biosynthetic. This represents the next level, a physical upgrade, compared to where we are now.

Q: What kind of bodies do we consider ourselves to have now?
A: Biological. And we are evolving toward a crystallized body.

The crystallized body has a biosynthetic composition - this is where humanity is heading. Food will also become biosynthetic. Meat will no longer exist, and everything we know now will change, because the body we inhabit will shift its structure, from a carbon-based form to a crystalline one. Carbon-based structure requires the heavy density of meat, but once we evolve, (and this won't happen in 10 or 20 years), it is a genetic process. Our genetic body will change and evolve into a crystalline form. Many people misunderstand when they hear "crystalline body" - they think their body will turn into a crystal. But in truth, it will become biosynthetic. Right now, we have carbonized bodies, we have bones that don't dissolve, and this is why we consume meat and various other products. When we transition to the crystalline body, our bodies become very light, physically, chemically, biologically, because it begins the transition toward light. The biosynthetic body helps everything become lighter. And once you get there, you are already in a different plane. This refers to the shift from D3 to D4 and then D5. To be present in D5 not just with consciousness, but also physiologically, a genetic change is required in the physical body. I'm getting the sense that in 1,000 years we will evolve into the fifth dimension, and then rise to D6, and so on, with the physical body. Right now, a consciousness leap into D5 is occurring, but the whole purpose is for our physical body to ascend as well, not just the mind. The higher our body vibrates dimensionally, the lighter it becomes. This will become an entire branch of science: *biosynthetic.*

Q: Humanity has already started the process of synthetic food. It is seen as something negative, but is it actually beneficial for us as we evolve and rise toward light?

A: I'm getting that the technology currently being used in connection to synthetics is diverted from its original intended path, but adjustments will be made at the right time.

At the moment, synthetics tend to damage the physical body, mainly due to plastics. This is the deviation within the synthetic field.

But as you rightly pointed out, synthetic alone is the issue.

In the future, humanity must shift its focus toward *biosynthetics.* Current synthetic development leans heavily toward negative polarity, harming human DNA because the living particles of the human body - animals, fruits, trees - were not considered.

They deviated, but what must be considered is the bio, the living aspect of organs, combined with synthetics.

Only then will civilization take a great leap forward.

In the coming years, nothing major will change, but a very rapid adjustment will be made at the right moment. Until then, "They" will not intervene. "They" allow us to act freely, perhaps hoping we'll realize it ourselves, but I'm shown that we won't. That's when an external intervention will come. It will force humanity to shift toward biosynthetics.
Synthetics will be classified as a hazard for all, and if standards aren't followed, penalties will be applied, and people will be forced to consider the living aspect.
But this won't happen in the next 45 years, unless adjusted as per collective free will. Nothing is set in stone.
I'm told I can choose another topic now. Here, I feel lighter, without any pressure. Next time, when we connect in the Megaquantic Field, I can imagine we're already in this place, but if we feel the need for release, we should visualize the ocean, how we submerge into the water, and let everything go. Thank you.

Crystals in the Human Body

I feel drawn to dive into the subject of crystals. I've chosen my slice of the 'cake,' reclined on the lounge chair and let the journey unfold.

Nasal Crystals - Protecting the Energetic Field

Oh, we have two crystals in our ear, one crystal comes from the right with the sharp part pointing toward the nose, and the other crystal is the opposite. At the nose, is the base and the tip pointing outward.

Q: What are these two crystals about?
A: I see that we simply have them present in the physical body.

Q: What is their purpose?
A: I don't get an answer. Maybe it wasn't asked the right way.

Q: What is the function of these crystals?
A: Nothing comes to me.

Q: How can they support the human or energetic body?
A: It reacted regarding the human body. These two crystals, depending on their position, radiate a projection downward like a curtain.

Q: What exactly does that mean? Or when do they activate in such a way?
A: Oh God, you ask the question and nothing comes, not even how to phrase it.

Diana: Let me see what question comes to me. Are they activated non-stop?
Victoria: No, it's something related to the physical body.

Q: How does the physical body benefit when they are activated?
A: Interesting, when you said that, the projection was open, like the curtains were open, and when you asked, the projection closed and covered the whole body downward.

Q: Is it something about protection?
A: It's something complex.

Q: What are the right questions to ask about this aspect?
A: Nothing comes to me.

Diana: Wait, the curtains activated. What do they activate in the human body?

A: Words come to me in pieces. It activates "Loss."

Victoria: Wait, I forgot the other word, it disappeared. *What word did I forget?*

A: "Credentials"

Q: What's the connection? What kind of credentials are at the physical level?
A: Okay, I'll tell you, we are like babies. We get a simple word we can perceive. I see that they activate, but these crystals are white, and when activated, they look like bluish-white curtains. When someone approaches you, these two automatically activate. It's not exactly protection, but for me, it feels like protection. It's like a detector. A kind of sensor that activates. I feel it more like a sensor.

Q: What do credentials mean here?
A: Credentials are encoding keys, like a password.

Q: What is meant by loss? Loss of what?
A: It shows me it shields something on one side, and this projection activates from these crystals downward.

Q: In what situations do the "curtains" activate?
A: When people approach us. It's like there is a radius all around, like personal space when they light up.

Q: When does anyone pass near us? Does this relate to our aura? Does it activate then?
A: It's like a riddle. It shows me that if you are here, and you have a parameter, a sphere around you, if someone crosses your personal space, there is this space generated by the crystals that automatically detect it, and if they come too close, this projection activates, the crystals light up. It's a kind of sensor that detects credentials; I think the "credentials" of whoever is near you.

What other questions do we have here?

Diana: Okay, let me think. *How does it actually help us?* I understand it's a kind of protection.

A: Oh, now I get it. This sensor is like a filter that does not allow another field or personal space to imprint on ours. It is a sensor for our personal barrier. If this sensor didn't exist, we could imprint all the energy and information of another person; uniqueness, individual identity would disappear. If someone came with a negative aura, without the crystals you would absorb everything automatically. This aspect doesn't allow individual aspects of others to attach to you.

Diana: This means it prevents not only information but also programs, limitations, blockages - absolutely everything from attaching. We come here wanting to experience individuality and not to take on experiences from others that we haven't chosen.

Victoria: Exactly. These crystals help us create and keep our own space. Thank you.

The Navel Crystal: Energy Equilibrium

The navel also holds a crystal, one whose sharp point extends outward, connecting inner balance with the external flow.

Q: How does this crystal help us?
A: Energy exits through the navel via this crystal.
That's why it's very important to cover your navel. If you leave it exposed all the time, it's like keeping this energy flow or channel open, because it's always running. It's like an open faucet; your energy simply drains out, non-stop.
I sense it's good to leave the flow open, because it's a normal channel in all beings with a navel - humans, animals - it's a channel that continuously releases energy from you.
If you don't let it flow, it remains stored in the body. The unpleasant aspect is that if your navel is exposed in public, there are many unconscious individuals, and also conscious ones, individuals who practice black magic. They can extract energy from you specifically through the navel. Many do this unconsciously; they take your energy that way. That's why it's important to cover your navel, especially in public, in crowds, or in a group where you're not sure about the energy of others. Also, it's important to leave the channel open, especially when you sleep. When we sleep, it's necessary to sleep without clothes, to allow the flow to run, exactly as our body is naturally designed. Or at home, you can go with an exposed navel, or at the beach.

At the beach, although you're surrounded by many people, the interaction with water creates a different energetic process, and most people spend time immersed in it. Water itself has its own natural benefits; it cleanses, balances, and harmonizes the energy field, acting as a conductor that helps discharge excess or stagnant energy from the body. This makes your energetic system less vulnerable while you're in water.

It's mainly when you remain on dry land for extended periods, especially in crowded areas, that it's advisable to cover your navel. The navel is a direct energy outlet, and in such environments, it can leave you more susceptible to external influences and energy drain. The longer you stay in the water, the more protected and energetically aligned you become.

At home, when you're in a safe and familiar energetic space with your family, it's perfectly fine to keep your navel uncovered. But in public or crowded settings, covering it helps preserve your energetic integrity and personal space.

Q: Does both beneficial and non-beneficial energy exit through the navel?
A: I see only a white channel, it's neither beneficial nor harmful. It's a channel that must remove energy. Imagine a sink, where water flows continuously. It has a drain hole to let excess water escape, maintaining an optimal level of water in the basin.

Diana: I see, this channel allows excess energy to flow out of the body, helping to prevent an overload. Without this release, too much accumulated energy could overwhelm the system, almost like an internal short-circuit. This helps us balance our energy.
Victoria: Yes. Thank you.

Q: Do we have any other crystals?
A: We have many, and in fact all physiological processes are based on positioned crystals that we don't see or perceive with human eyes. Our organ systems and physiological processes operate on this principle. But the primary aspect is the presence of crystals in our etheric body.

Q: Megaquantic Field, what other crystals are positioned in our physical body that would be good for us to know about today?
A: I see a person onstage, standing and rotating. I see the human skeleton, the ribs and spinal vertebrae, all are made of complex crystals, more accurately clusters (structural formations of multiple crystals combined into one). Each vertebra contains a crystalline cluster, these formations are especially visible along the spine. The ribs and breastbone aren't exactly what we perceive as bones physically, they are crystals that form the bone. What we see is the physical end-product, but etherically, each rib houses a single crystal.
That is why our bones don't burn, because etherically our bones are made of very large crystals. Every bone in our body is composed of crystals, our entire skeleton, so that we could imagine, instead of a human body, a "human crystal" at the etheric level, not the physical.

Tooth Crystals

The teeth are composed of completely different crystals. Our entire skeleton is formed from crystals, but in the teeth I perceive a different composition, a denser crystal. That's why our teeth don't regenerate easily; once they decay, there's no going back. Each one is made of crystal with a very dense, resilient composition. Our teeth are far more durable, at least ten times stronger than diamond.

Q: Why is there that kind of crystal in the teeth? Maybe we needed it for the brain. Megaquantic Field, why does the human being need such crystals in the teeth region? Etheric crystals that form our teeth, what essence do they have in terms of the durability of these crystals?
A: I'm receiving complex information. Most people have no idea how important teeth truly are, and even with my logical thinking, I still don't fully understand it. It just doesn't make sense

Q: What role do teeth have in our physical bodies?
A: It can't transmit the information to me because my filter is clouded by limiting beliefs that block its reception.

Victoria: I set the intention to release all programs and limitations I've created about our human body, its role, and all illusions about components, structure, and purpose.

A: I feel a tingle in my throat. It's actually a genetic Reptilian human belief - a limiting belief rooted in Reptilian genetics in humans.

Victoria: I set the intention to release this belief from Reptilian genetics, everything that no longer serves me here and now.

Yes, yawning means we are releasing. And interestingly, now I feel a twitch in the region from under the eye toward the nose, and I want to know the cause.

Q: Why is my right eye twitching? What do I need to understand or become aware of, or what does it have to do with the current subject?
A: Now it makes sense. Our feelings of aggression, anger, fear, deep emotions are stored primarily in the jaw, and when the density is too high, it

goes into the teeth. The teeth absorb all anger, negative emotions are stored in them. That is the true primordial role of teeth, not just primitive chewing.

Q: When you have dental problems, cavities, or decay, does that mean you've accumulated a lot of anger?
A: Yes, that's why they decay.

Q: And people who have very healthy teeth, do they not have anger?
A: No, they just release it more easily. We all have anger and resentment, but if we work with these emotions and release them, they don't remain stored in the body. This doesn't mean you don't experience deep emotions, but some people get upset easily, take everything personally, every little thing bothers them. If they don't work with themselves, they accumulate it inside. They refuse to understand that not everything is about them, that egoism in them. So, by accumulating anger, it goes into the jaw and then the teeth. Even though the tooth is made of tough crystal and its role is to store negative emotions to protect the body from sudden illness, once it's overloaded, it begins to absorb more and more negativity, eventually causing damage.

I know someone who takes absolutely everything personally, even jokes, and they have a lot of dental issues; periodontal disease and implants, but even the implants give problems.

Q: At the gum level, are these emotions stored too?
A: Yes. Using the example above, she lost her natural teeth, so the energy goes from the jaw into the gums.

Q: For people with dentures or implants, where does the energy go if not into teeth?
A: When dental implants are in place, there's a small tooth root inside; if not, the metal implant remains, which the body may reject, leading to gum inflammation due to accumulated density. That's a good question, because it brings to mind my own experience. In my case, something was growing inside the bone near my nose, not in the teeth, but in the skull, and I needed surgery to cut into the gum and remove everything that had developed there, in order to clean the area properly.

Diana: That procedure is called "resection."

They had to cut and clean the area. I had a hole in the bone that needed to regenerate. After a year and a half, the bone started to grow. I'm shown this can lead to erosion in the bones. First the teeth are affected, then the gums, then the bone.

To re-balance ourselves in the area of teeth, we need to release all the anger and everything we've accumulated. Yes, anger toward ourselves and others. I hear to not take everything personally, to work with anger, release, forgive, and cultivate compassion.

Q: Megaquantic Field, are there other etheric crystals positioned in our physical body that have an important function for our physical bodies and that it would benefit everyone to know?
A: There are more regions of the body where crystals are present.

Crystals in the Feet and Toes

The feet also contain crystals, particularly concentrated in the toes. Each toe has its own crystalline structure, and these are deeply connected to our balance, grounding, and movement through this dimension.

These crystals are responsible for anchoring our energy into the Earth's field. Through them, we maintain a kind of energetic GPS; they help us stay connected to our path and physical direction. When the crystals in the toes are blocked, damaged, or energetically misaligned, people may feel ungrounded, lost, or disconnected from their purpose.

These foot crystals also support the energetic flow through the body. Like entry points for Earth's energy, they allow for an upward movement of vibration, bringing grounding, stability, and physical support. That's why foot massages or walking barefoot on natural surfaces like grass, soil, or sand can activate and cleanse these crystals. It's not just about muscles or reflexology, it's about energetic recalibration.

Each toe crystal corresponds to different aspects of your being, some to emotional stability, others to your direction in life, presence, flexibility, or even confidence in movement. The big toe often carries the most direct energetic alignment, and the pinky toe holds subtle frequencies that are often overlooked but are deeply sensitive to energetic shifts.

Taking care of your feet means taking care of your spiritual anchoring. Soaking them in salt water, walking barefoot, grounding meditations, and consciously connecting to the energy in your toes can help restore alignment in your entire field.

At the feet, all the toes have crystals positioned with their tips pointing outward.

Q: What is the importance of these crystals?
A: They are located on the toes, as many toes, as many crystals present. However, the base of the crystals is positioned backward, along the entire sole of the foot towards the heel, radiating light, as if it were a comet trailing behind us. On the sole, there is a crystalline wall, starting from the sole. Where the heel begins vertically, there is a crystalline plate, a crystalline wall. This light that radiates behind is stopped by the light in the crystalline wall, and in the wall - you know how fractalized light spreads not further into one channel, but it seems to split into multiple colors, like a rainbow. But it is not a simple rainbow; there are multiple units of light channels. It shows me, humorously, our feet with these crystals, and behind them, it radiates toward the crystalline plate, and from there it's as if you were a rocket.

Q: How does this help us?
A: Something related to space or our localization in space. It is a complex process, and it shows me that once you take a step forward, you move in accordance with space and time. We always move forward, in terms of time and space, if we follow mechanical theory or how we understand mechanical physics. We do not move backward in time. Every step we take is toward the future. I see that behind us, there is a unit where a boundary separates the future and the past, and behind us, at the sole, there is still a space, not very thick but medium narrow, where the present time is produced.

And at the heel, we have the lights as described above, and after that begins the barrier of the past, on the line of past in space. It's more physical; it's complex here. I'm trying to understand. I see how one unit is us, then the boundary of future-past, and the crystals on the toes allow the movement of the physical body, matter, along the vector of time. I'm explaining very primitively now. Once we pass this boundary from present to future, we automatically move into the next unit, and once it is passed, the unit behind closes and becomes "past." It's a continuous process. It's like the crystals allow the future unit to open, so we can be in the present, and the reflection of the crystals allows the present unit to close, becoming past. They are in units, barriers. This is what we experience in 3D, but when we are in 5D, we see all the units - all from past-present-future - as one and the same.

ARCTURIANS - Hologram

In the Megaquantic Field, not all Beings of Light have access. Depending on whom you call, who you want to work with, if they don't have access to this field, they can appear as a hologram only and work with you.

The Arcturians are a highly advanced and spiritually evolved extraterrestrial race originating from the star Arcturus; one of the brightest stars in the night sky. Renowned for their deep wisdom, healing abilities, and advanced technology, the Arcturians serve as cosmic guides and protectors of spiritual evolution.

They are often described as Beings of Light with a strong connection to higher dimensions and the universal consciousness. The Arcturians work closely with Earth's spiritual awakening by assisting in energy healing, raising vibrational frequencies, and supporting humanity's transition into a new era of enlightenment.

Known for their benevolence and deep compassion, the Arcturians encourage balance, harmony, and the expansion of consciousness across the galaxy. Their mission is to help humans reconnect with their true multidimensional nature and assist in creating a more peaceful, unified existence

Q: I wanted to ask about my recent states, is there something more than I have realized?
A: The Creator took you and opened His large screen, and He has a magnifying glass shaped like a pirate's spyglass, looking far beyond. He goes far away. It's like He went after a universe, passed by it, and came to a denser universe. There, in profile, there is a small door. Now He has opened the

door. It is very dense there, dark, not felt directly, but the memory of the density is felt. The world spins like a vortex, from your left to right, vertically.

Q: What is the message here for Diana?
A: I see how you walk through this density, you enter a house where the light is off. You know this house, the space and the place, but being inside you look back so you don't see anyone. You are afraid. This space is your subconscious. You don't walk in the middle there, but on the edge, along the wall, and you stay alert so no one comes to attack you.

Q: Megaquantic Field, what is to be understood from this space?
A: Fear is always present, but when fear amplifies and takes control, you live inside it. When you don't give it power, fear disappears instantly. You have given power to fear, and now in your subconscious there is chaos; fear governs.

Q: Where does this fear come from or what exactly am I afraid of? And how can I take back all the power I gave to fear?
A: You have baggage, many boxes in your subconscious. I now see through the filter of fear. Fear is present, but I can put it aside to see what is there. I see many boxes below. But actually, you are afraid of what is inside these boxes. It's because you yourself created the fear; it did not come from outside.

Diana: I am ready to release this fear, to see everything I need now to release in order to continue the journey.

A: Now you have to imagine yourself facing the window, from where the vortex starts, standing in the middle of the room, and the vortex comes straight into your heart. The vortex is very strong, it has a double effect. Now I want you to say that you release all the creation of this fear through the vortex in the heart, through the heart, outside the heart, from all sides, and see how everything enters this vortex where it disintegrates. Like that. Yes, I saw you fall down. The vortex retracts, and fear is no longer present. Now you are in a luminous space, and next to you on the right side are the boxes. They are many, small, medium, average size boxes. There are many events, past lives where you died, many unspoken or spoken words; it's like opening many Pandora's boxes. Now you explore alone and see what comes. It is a gift, because I saw how you turned back to the left and asked ... But You have to be ready.

Diana: I set the intention for the process to be as gentle as possible.

Like that, now you can explore the boxes. Interestingly, you waved your hand and opened many at the same time. There are many and fly in this space, as if a flock of birds invaded you, pecking you. They fly toward you. I see you cover yourself with your hands and something hits you.
I ask those beings present in this field to help Diana understand that all these fears are temporary, they have no power over her, but she is the one who has control over all things, words, and any stagnant experience in these boxes.

I see you at kindergarten dancing with the girls. You all danced in a circle, hand in hand, and you couldn't keep up. You stumbled, and a girl kicked you, and you fell to the ground, while the girls kept dancing and out of fear you crawled on the ground like a puppy, you left this circle, and it triggered a fear that something would happen to you.

Diana: I don't remember anything from then, generally.
Victoria: Your memory was erased because it was too traumatic.
Diana: Then I am ready to release it.

Now you are in a place, on the right side, there is a red lamp, like a fire alarm. You see the light, it's on your right, and this alarm was a shock for you. Something related to an earthquake, a stronger intensity earthquake. I don't see you, but I see through your eyes.

Diana: I have even experienced in this life a stronger earthquake at night, and I was in shock.

I see you on ice, on your knees, it seems to be a lake with water underneath, you see the ice cracking, and I perceive fear that you will die, you will fall.

Another memory in a swing when you were little. You are one and a half years old. I see you small, someone was pushing you, and this created fear that you might be thrown feet over head, that you would fall.

Diana: Okay, thank you, I release this fear too.

You run somewhere, you run from something, it seems something wanted to hold you, and you panicked to be released, it was holding you from both sides. The fear was not being released, related to freedom; fear that you can't get out, that you have no escape. This is in adolescence.

Diana: Thank you, I release this fear too.

I now see a vortex, and there is fear to be spun around. It's something more subtle, I don't understand, but it's stored in your throat chakra.

Simple release doesn't help because I see how you open the cap and it goes back. It is actually a cap. You can imagine your head like the shape of a honeycomb, it's round, and it has a cap that closes at the throat. Actually, the cap opens and closes back automatically. *How can we keep this cap permanently open?* Okay, an operating table has been set, someone put everything down. You sit there, you lie down. The cap opened. When you lie down it opens.

I called on the 2 Arcturians, but they are not fully present in the field, only a hologram.

Diana: That confirms what I felt, that there are Beings of Light who don't have full access to the Megaquantic Field.

No, these 2 Arcturians do not have full access, only a hologram is present according to the request of the one who accesses them. Incredible how it works. They are both at the throat, trying to unscrew the cap. They removed the cap, and there is another device. From the throat there is an extension to the shoulders, on the chest above the breasts, and above the back, like a kind of extension. At the back, it comes off easily, but it is imprinted in front, on the chest.
Now they are on your chest, and they don't understand how it is imprinted, it seems part of your essence, it grew with your skin. They removed it from the back, from the shoulders, but in the front, under the armpit, it grew with your skin together. They don't have permission to continue further. They left.
Thank you.

AIMTUA: Beings of Light from Dimension 294

Victoria: We call in forth those beings who have authority to release this device.

Interesting beings, I don't even know how to describe them to you because they don't have an exact body. It's a mix between a dragon and a serpent. I can't decipher it. It's beyond my understanding. They have many bodies, tentacles, I don't know what these are, nor where their bodies begin.

Q: If it is beneficial for us to know, I ask them to convey what beings or what race they are.
A: **AIMTUA**, I cannot decipher more, but it's not even close. This is the closest term to our terminology. It tells me it's only 3% of what we could understand. Their name does not follow any principle we can imagine. It shows me their mode of operation, and if anyone saw something like this, I believe they would be scared. I simply look and don't know how to explain. It's like a machine, it shows me their body. It moves me aside to understand that they are gigantic, on an immense scale. If we could see such a being in our reality, we would believe it is from lower planes, but this is not true.

Now, this entire being hovers above your body, with multiple serpent heads and bodies that have slipped beneath your skin. Beneath this collar, they break down everything, but in such a way that once their bodies are beneath your skin, they possess healing properties, like a soothing balm that regenerates. Each body and head simultaneously cuts and restores your entire being. It's a complex process. From one angle, it may look like you're being torn apart, but having many heads is essential to ensure nothing is left unhealed. The collar is gone now; it simply flew off you. Thank you.

Q: I want to ask this being in which dimension it exists or operates?
A: **294**, interesting number. Can this be confirmed?

A: Starting from dimension 29 it exists but operates up to D294. They are very advanced.

Victoria: This is the first time I've heard something like this.

Q: What is the difference in dimension, why is there such a difference between the numbers? What does this mode of operation consist of?
A: Creation is too complicated to be explained now. It shows me that if we were to understand, the molecules inside us would be divided in two, there would be a conflict of coexistence between the reality we know and the existence we actually see. The advanced explanation is not worth it for our creation. It doesn't make sense because it will always be misunderstood by our humanity. The world is used to hearing only one true piece of information and to attach to what it believes is true, but higher planes do not know about other higher planes. There is no talk of codependency or... I can't find the word. They try to find alternatives in my knowledge. They can't find the right word in my brain, wait, I can't get it off my mind.

The word closest in meaning is **competition**, to demonstrate that everything we know, we know from the perspective of competition - many dimensions live in the concept of competition. Higher planes do not have such a principle; everything works according to principles unimaginable to us.

They have now disconnected from my consciousness. Their way of connecting with us is completely different. It's not telepathy. It feels more like the earliest telephone systems, back when calls weren't automatic but had to be manually connected by human operators. You'd speak to someone at a switchboard who would physically plug your line into the right circuit to reach the person you were calling. That's the kind of connection I experienced with them, slow, deliberate, and structured, nothing like the instantaneous telepathic communication we're used to imagining.

Thank you. I feel honored with such information and connection. Thank you for helping Diana.

V. Other Information and Experiences in the Megaquantic Field

In this chapter, I will present various pieces of information that came through during numerous sessions of work in the Akashic Field, the Quantum Field, and the Megaquantic Field. I will also share certain experiences from a retreat I attended in October 2024, and will include information I received telepathically from Beings of Light.

5th Dimension – The Consciousness That Shapes Reality

The fifth dimension (5D) is not a physical space, but rather a higher state of consciousness in which intentions, thoughts, and one's inner state directly influence experiences in the three-dimensional (3D) reality. Unlike the physical world, which is defined by space, time, and material limitations, 5D represents a level of vibration where consciousness becomes the primary creative force. In this state, reality aligns synchronistically to reflect the individual's desires and needs, *as long as they are in harmony with the highest good*. Here, we will explore what it means to live in 5D consciousness, how it manifests in daily life, and the role synchronicities play, offering practical examples and clarification to support deeper understanding.

What is the Fifth Dimension?

The fifth dimension is a way of perceiving and interacting with reality in which fear, control, and lack-based thinking are replaced by trust, presence, and abundance. In 5D, consciousness operates at a higher level, and the physical 3D reality, the material world we see and touch, becomes malleable, adjusting itself to reflect the inner state of the individual. This doesn't mean you disappear from the physical plane, but rather that you live in your body, in the material world, with a perspective that transcends ordinary limitations.

For example, instead of worrying about not having enough resources (money, food, time), in 5D you set the intention that everything you need will be provided at the right moment. This deep trust allows the universe to respond through events and circumstances that may seem illogical from a 3D perspective. In 5D, you no longer try to control the "how" or "when" something will happen, you allow yourself to be guided by a natural flow, where your desires materialize effortlessly.

How Does 5D Consciousness Work?

5D Consciousness operates on the principle that everything in the universe is energetically interconnected, and your thoughts and intentions act like signals that influence this energetic field. When you vibrate at a higher frequency, one characterized by love, gratitude, and presence, you attract experiences that mirror that state. Unlike in 3D, where reality seems rigid and based on linear cause and effect, in 5D, time and space become fluid, and synchronicities (seemingly random yet meaningful events) become a language through which the universe communicates with you.

For example, let's say you want to eat healthy but you're on a tight budget. Instead of focusing on lack ("organic products are too expensive"), you set the intention: "I will find healthy foods that are affordable."

In 5D, this intention, supported by trust, can lead to a synchronicity: you walk into a store and find exactly the products you wanted on sale, or you receive an unexpected offer that allows you to buy them. These events are not mere coincidences, but responses from the universe to your vibration.

How 5D Consciousness Manifests in Daily Life

To better understand how 5D works, let's examine some practical examples that illustrate how consciousness shapes reality. These situations reflect the principle that when intentions are clear and aligned with the highest good, the universe orchestrates the necessary circumstances.

1. Financial Abundance for Personal Desires

Imagine you want to attend an event that costs more than you can afford. Instead of focusing on the lack of money, you set your intention: "I want to be present at this event, and the necessary resources will come to me." You let go of the need to control how this will happen. A few days later, you receive an unexpected sum of money, maybe a gift, a refund, or a small work opportunity, that exactly covers the ticket cost. In 5D, this synchronicity is the result of your trust that the universe will respond to your desire.

2. Access to Resources for a Healthy Lifestyle

Suppose you decide to follow a vegan diet for physical or spiritual detox, but vegan products are rare or expensive in your area. Instead of worrying, you set your intention: "I will find the foods I need in an accessible way." One day, you enter a store and discover they have exactly the vegan products you want, perhaps even on a special discount or in the perfect quantity for you. This is not a mere coincidence but a manifestation of your 5D consciousness attracting the right solution.

4. Multiplying Resources in a Group Context

In a group or family situation, you have a limited amount of food for many people, and at first glance, it seems insufficient. Instead of panicking or calculating portions, you focus on gratitude and the idea that "there will be enough for everyone." Surprisingly, the food is enough for each participant or family member, and there is even some leftovers. In 5D, the collective consciousness of abundance within the group amplifies the resources, creating a result that transcends usual logic. An example is Jesus Christ multiplying one fish and one loaf of bread to feed thousands of hungry people.

5. Synchronicities Confirming Decisions

Maybe you are thinking of following a new path in life, such as a spiritual practice or a career change. In the following days, you notice repetitive signs, a number that appears often (like 11:11), a seemingly "random" conversation with someone sharing a relevant story, or a book that falls into your hands addressing exactly your theme. These synchronicities are messages from your higher consciousness, reflected in the outer reality, confirming that you are on the right path.

Synchronicities – The Language of the 5D Dimension

Synchronicities are a central element of 5D consciousness, representing moments when physical reality aligns meaningfully with your intentions. Unlike ordinary coincidences, synchronicities carry emotional weight and deep meaning, offering confirmations, solutions, or guidance. They occur when you are present in the moment, free from fear, and aligned with a higher vibration.

For example, you think of a person you haven't contacted for years, and that same day they call you or you meet them "out of the blue." The resulting conversation brings you an opportunity or a new perspective. This is a 5D synchronization, orchestrated by the energetic connection between your consciousness and the universal field.

Other examples include finding a resource exactly when you need it, such as a book that answers an urgent question, or receiving a sign that confirms an important decision.

Synchronicities are more frequent in 5D because this state of consciousness removes mental barriers that block the natural flow of the universe. When you let go of the need to control outcomes and trust the process, the universe responds with events that may seem unlikely but are perfectly aligned with your needs.

How to Live in 5D Consciousness

To experience 5D consciousness and amplify synchronicities, it's necessary to cultivate an inner state that reflects the principles of this dimension. Here are some simple practices:

Be present in the moment: Spend a few minutes daily focusing on your breath or observing your surroundings. Presence anchors you in the "now" - the gateway to 5D.

Set clear intentions: State what you desire without attachment to how it will happen. For example: "I desire to have the resources needed to live healthily."

Practice gratitude: Give thanks for what you already have and for what is yet to come. Gratitude raises your vibration and attracts more synchronicities.

Follow your intuition: If you feel an impulse to act in a certain way, follow it without overanalyzing. Intuition is your guide in 5D.

Release fear: Notice thoughts of lack or control and replace them with affirmations like "Everything I need comes to me easily and at the perfect time."

I have personally witnessed such situations, experiencing these phenomena that defy logical explanation.

The fifth dimension is a state of consciousness where physical reality aligns with your intentions and inner state, creating a flow of abundance, synchronicities, and solutions that appear "magical" from a 3D perspective.

Through examples such as finding necessary resources, multiplying food, or confirming decisions through signs, we see how 5D consciousness transforms everyday experiences. While critics may question these phenomena, the practice of presence, gratitude, and trust allows anyone to experience this way of living. In 5D, the universe becomes a partner that responds to your desires, as long as they are aligned with the highest good, offering a life lived in harmony and abundance.

Retreat – The Earth Entity

In October 2024, I attended a retreat organized by my mentor Danielle Lipton, in the New Hampshire region. Only four people participated in the retreat, along with my mentor, and although at first I didn't understand why it happened that way, during the following events, I realized that the souls had found each other for an experience that needed to take place. I will describe more in the lines that follow.

Dark walker

When I attended a retreat organized by my mentor in October 2024, after cleansing and releasing everything that no longer served me, the Beings of Light activated a new ability for me. The new ability is called "Dark Walker" or more directly, "Demon Walker," which you will find mentioned in Danielle Lipton's book, *Keys to My Ascension*. Danielle told me that she had only received this information about the ability, but in reality, she had not yet met anyone besides me who has this ability activated - and that happened during the clearings at the retreat.

With Danielle's permission, here is what she wrote in her book to explain this information.

"A demon walker is an individual who has mastered a level of dark *experientials* and who has risen their biological frequency into a healed frequency. This then allows for further control over demons and dark ones.

This ability is very useful for master healer archetypes. It allows them to command any dark entities off any of the 'children of light's' energetic grids. It allows for the demons to be brought into a type of use when it comes to different dark arts manifestations.

Demonic entities are directly connected to the void and may assist in any frequency bandwidth removal. One example would be the need to clear out a forest. If the forest needed to be removed for any reason, the darker ones may be summoned to feed off of the energy of that forest, thus allowing for the forest to go through a transmutation experience.

This shall allow for a rapid clearing and rebalancing of that forest area back into a more love-light frequency. Many times different elemental demons may be summoned which would allow for a more rapid process. One example would be fire, demons, and their ability to manifest a forest fire.

Demons and angels are simply messengers of the source frequency. They are fully connected to each and every child of light and they are here to help us manifest whatever emotions we choose to experience. Holding no judgment towards these beings or entities is key for allowing for further control of the simulation to manifest for you."

This message is sent with much love and blessings. Channeled by Danielle Lipton from her book: Keys to My Ascension.

Q: What does my new ability involve?
A: Throughout many past lives, my bodies have been heavily attacked, possessed, and exposed to low frequencies, even in this life. During a period in my teenage years, I went to priests for exorcisms, being controlled and possessed by beings from the lower planes of creation. By releasing and healing this aspect in this life, now, through this ability, I have been given the capacity to control these beings from the lower planes myself, just as high beings, the Seraphim, or all beings from the higher planes can. This is a test and practice for me on many levels. Thank you.

If you are interested in my exclusive awakening journey, you can find my anthology book "Awakened Hearts: Stories of Embracing Light, Love and Limitless Possibilities" on www.awakenedheartsbook.com

ANT BEINGS - AGARTHA

A few days before the retreat, just before falling asleep, a being connected with me from inside the Earth, from Agartha. Being already in a Theta state, with my eyes closed, a shy being appeared, without communicating with me. But soon after, a few dragons appeared trying to attack me. Then that shy being disappeared. A telepathic message came to my mind that this gentle and calm being trying to connect with me was actually from the Ant Beings group from Agartha; the true inhabitants of planet Earth. The next day, I did some research which showed me that such a name exists and that it refers to beings *inside our planet*. This being was tall, about 2 meters, slightly greenish in color, humanoid, but had antennae, like ants.

Planning to visit the last state in North America, Vermont, I was looking to see what and where I could visit nearby. Although I was fine to go alone to visit this state, I chose the closest city from where we were at the retreat, about an hour away. When I was searching for information on what to visit there, I found nothing that attracted me or sparked my interest. I told this to my mentor, and she suggested that the four of us at the retreat should go together to visit those places. The fact that we were four was not a coincidence.

I was called to visit Bellow Falls along the Connecticut River. There were petroglyphs on stones that were at least 3000 years old. I felt we should connect with that place, but when we had "almost" arrived, the GPS kept leading us on detours; we were going in circles, wondering what was happening, what we needed to understand. The energy vibration of the place felt very dense. We took another route and arrived at a gas station where a man from the retreat called me "Veronica" twice. I didn't hear, but my retreat colleagues and my mentor told him my name was Victoria. He said he knew!

Without paying much attention, we went on and stopped at another store. The day before, I had told my retreat colleagues that I love cherry pie, and there, at that store, I bought the last piece of cherry pie. I perceived that store like a train station, I saw two worlds at the same time. I saw people, souls, hurrying to catch a train, because it was like a station, and at the same time I saw our world! There were two parallel realities, different, existing simultaneously.

My retreat colleague, who had called me *Veronica* was a doctor in the other reality, because my mentor Danielle felt like calling him "doctor," and he called me "Veronica." Then information came that in another timeline, we had taken a step toward connecting with the petroglyph site, but had failed because it was necessary to have four people, four powers, present. Our current timeline, the one where all four of us were together, was successful because we met the minimum number of people needed for that activation.

At the end, when we reached the petroglyphs, the place became steeper, and climbing was necessary. I was the only one who felt called to advance further on those stones. When I reached the spot, there were drawings in the stone of humanoid beings with antennae.

Then I continued with the retreat souls and we found a place to sit and activate the site. I entered meditation, and was guided to make some light language movements, and through those sounds, I released the souls trapped in that place and managed to connect with those beings. I channeled twice to a shaman and sang in the shamanic language, and through that song, I made adjustments to our timeline.

The place was very ancient! My mentor did the channeling, and I saw the Ant Beings speaking through her. These beings were about 3-4 meters tall, and I received information that they are very careful about whom they connect with, but they communicated that we would be able to connect with them in real life, in this lifetime, meaning we will see each other soon. Only those who are open and willing to see will be able to.

When we first entered the city, it felt like an old place with heavy, dense and unpleasant energy. But after connecting with the Ant Beings and completing the activation, everything shifted. As we left, the city appeared completely transformed, the blockages and dense energies had been cleared and the city looked modern. An instant reality shift of the environment.

The connection with the petroglyph site and the Ant Beings was not in vain. The city was a special place, as someone told us days later. It was a surprise for the group but also a blessing. Everywhere I looked, I saw the number 4 ahead, and I was confirmed that four people were needed to activate the site and connect with the Ant Beings.

During the retreat events, I saw the ET beings more clearly in reality. We were at the fire, it was night outside, and during the cacao connection, at one point, I saw two white beings descending from the sky on my right. When they landed, my mentor was sitting on a chair, and at that exact moment, she got up and changed her place, and the entire right side was empty. Then, at one point, I realized I couldn't hear what my colleagues were saying. I was frozen, my gaze, body, everything was frozen. My colleagues looked at me, confused about what was happening to me. I perceived a transparent veil, like a wall, between me and them; they were on Earth, my physical body was present, but my consciousness was not. I saw myself on a ship, like an oval made of white transparent crystal. The ship was mine, and then I returned.

During the cacao connection, I also connected with an Ant Being leader from Agartha who had a masculine energy and was too powerful for my physical body. They had to connect through another being, energetically more suitable, and that being was his daughter. She was a very playful being, and through me, she saw Earth for the first time, from how it exists on the surface, in our reality.

I was thankful for all the experiences at the retreat and sent light and love to everyone.

America's Stonehenge

Our group from the retreat then decided we should go to *America's Stonehenge*; a place similar here in North America to what exists in England. During the entire week at the retreat, we hadn't managed to do any breathwork exercises, although it was on our to-do list. When we arrived at America's Stonehenge, we entered a cave where all four of us gathered and activated the place. That's how I felt we should proceed. During the activation, I felt currents of energy passing through me, which exhausted me after the activation. That place required activation and clearing. All four of us were channels for the activation. Then we continued and reached the Stonehenge center, from where the main point starts. There, I felt we needed to stop and meditate.

We all sat down on the ground, but I felt the need to *lie down* on those stones. We began breathwork exercises, inhaling and exhaling. Before starting these breathing exercises, I received a message that all phones should be kept away from the body.

At one point, I felt the urge to make different sounds, but my human mind held me back because, being in a public place, I thought the other visitors would hear. However, I received a message, that during the entire time we were there, while meditating, all people would be prevented from entering the park. The sounds were shamanic; a specific shamanic light language. They were gong-like sounds, with a male shaman's voice. At one point, I saw myself and the other three colleagues at the bottom of the ocean. While on the ocean floor, I saw two large tectonic plates that had moved: one shifted west and the other east. Between those two plates, a luminous portal formed, connecting with the Creator and the Earth's core. There, very luminous beings appeared; I didn't perceive a defined body, only extreme light. Meanwhile, I saw and literally felt *all the pain of all the people on this planet.*

Then, I saw an immense entity that simply came out of me. I released it, and with the release of it, all souls on Earth, living and non-living, were freed from shackles, around their necks, that prevented their evolution. All souls from the entire planet were freed, and I saw a layer dissolving that had kept us all blind, unable to know, see, or feel what is beyond the veil. After releasing that large entity, those white beings from the white portal came and placed a medal around my neck, and with that medal, I was changed; I looked like another being. It was as if my head and tail were one whole, and I was dressed in long white robes.

The place where we decided to meditate was the site number NE 14, and the date was October 4, 2024. After this release, big storms and cataclysms started in Florida State. Being at the beginning of breathwork, I saw how that place was almost an inch away from the one in England, and if you look at the geographical trajectory, they are actually on a straight line with each other. After this event, I was curious to read more information, and I discovered that in ancient times, many slaves were kept there.

Following the release of Earth's entity, planetary laws shifted. The old pact with low-vibrational beings was dissolved and replaced by a new agreement involving high-dimensional Beings of Light, whose mission is to support Earth's ascension. From now on, souls reincarnating on Earth will come with a new purpose and no karmic debt, their role will be to aid in the planet's evolution.

Traumatic Visual Memories

Our brain records such traumatic or less traumatic visual memories, even unconsciously, regardless of whether you physically experienced a traumatic event or not. These memories remain for a long or short time and have a critical impact which can affect the subconscious and conflict with many internal beliefs or parameters. Thus, the brain will generate visual impulses triggered by those memories and can create a lot of tension, as well as visual and emotional conflict.

Example: You watched a movie that included a brief scene of rape, which can involve any gender (girl or boy). For you, it may seem like something normal, but the brain registered it as a traumatic event, even though you did not physically experience such a situation. When we are empathetic, we easily absorb various programs or traumatic events, which can impact us.

How can we release these visual images when, no matter how much you try, you can't get them out of your mind?

You can ask the Beings of Light to help you release these memories permanently from your subconscious mind.

When these releases happen, the pain or energetic aspects stored in the body may be felt in various parts where the emotion was recorded, such as the genitals, stomach, chest, etc. This means that the traumatic memory accumulated exactly there.

Imagine this pain or energy exiting through a light or sphere outside your body, releasing itself and simultaneously leaving your cortex (brain).

The Beings of Light will block access and perform a reboot (recalibration) that can last between 3-5 minutes. Then, when the brain tries to generate that memory or moment again, it will no longer have access. The response received will simply be "access denied."

Vibration: The Metaphysics Concept of Extraterrestrial Consciousness

In a session with a colleague, which you can read below, we connected with a being who communicated through vibration. That being helped us to understand what vibration is. Our thought is a vibration, and thus the method of communication was through vibration.

Then, through **channeling**, the following was transmitted:

"**Vibration** is the empty space where matter is absent. Light is transparent and emits sound waves of an opposite frequency, which we think must be positive, but the scale of numbers actually goes into the negative, and there, the more negative the number is, the closer it gets to the absolute radiation of universal energy crossing through Cosmos 1, which is superimposed over tens of thousands of universes, and when all taken together, form an existence."

The message transmitted by this being can be interpreted as a teaching about the nature of vibration and universal reality. Let's analyze some key concepts from this channeling:

1. Vibration as empty space, where matter is absent
This suggests that vibration is the basis of existence, even in the absence of matter. Quantum physics tells us that in the apparently "empty" vacuum, there are quantum fluctuations where energy appears and disappears spontaneously. Therefore, vibration may represent the very essence from which everything manifests.

2. Transparent light and sound waves opposite to human frequencies
Light and sound are manifestations of electromagnetic and mechanical waves. If the frequencies perceived as "positive" by humans are opposite on the cosmic scale, this may indicate that human polarity (positive-negative) is only a limited perspective, and at the cosmic level, "negative" vibrations could be essential for balance.

3. Scale of negative numbers and absolute radiation
Descending a "negative" scale could symbolize approaching the fundamental energy of the universe, perhaps similar to the concept of the "zero point" in Quantum physics, or the primordial state of energy from which

everything arises. Absolute radiation might represent the fundamental energy traversing the entire cosmos.

4. Cosmos 1 superimposed over tens of thousands of universes
This suggests a multiverse vision: a "Cosmos 1" that serves as the central point or foundation of existence, connected to and superimposed with many other universes. This is an idea found in modern physics theories, such as the multiverse or string theory.

5. Existence as a totality
The message seems to invite us to see existence as a vast, multidimensional unity, where every part is interconnected. The vibrations of each entity contribute to the whole.

Q: What does this message mean for us?
A: Understanding vibration seems to show you that *everything* in the universe is energy in motion. Thoughts, emotions, matter are all vibrations - and understanding this fact can change your perspective on reality. Awareness of the universal perspective, namely beyond our dimensions, reveals a higher order that transcends duality (positive-negative) and offers a broader vision of existence.

Your personal connection to vibration is a unique experience, where it may be a sign that a higher level of consciousness has been reached, allowing you to perceive these subtle realities.

Formulas – The Energetic Space between Individuals Present within the Field

In another channeling, the Star People offered this formula to explain, in more technical and scientific terms, the energetic space between individuals when they are present in the Akashic, Quantum, or Megaquantic Field, which at the time, made no sense. However, I am sharing this formula here for even greater openness.

C1 = 0
A proposed formula for explaining the energetic space between individuals when present within the field.
0.0001

The Infinite Gravitational Field – Integrated Unified Consciousness
The structure of our matrix consists of binary components: "**0**" and "**1**". The value "**1**" denotes **Matter.**
Transitioning from "0" to the value "1" represents the process of individuation, while returning from "1" to "0" reflects a path of self-recognition.

$$E = M^2$$

E (Energy) is conceptually divided into dual aspects of matter.

$(2/4) \times 0.0001$ **M [24,000Hz]** — interpreted as a reference to light frequency.

Analytical understanding is not possible without first establishing a proper framework.

Note: 'M' as matter not 'm' as mass, as in Einstein's formula.

Q: Does this enable the perception of alternate universes at the level of *nano-tectonic electronic particles?*
A: If the question refers to the "spaces between spaces," then the answer is a definitive yes.

VI. Channelings and Transmissions

In the channeling below, I received details about the dissolution of the Reptilian aspect within the human body a few months before the actual event. At that time, the information didn't make much sense, but on December 12th, the confirmation of this channeling came along with more details about this aspect. You can review the information regarding the Reptilian aspect in the physical human DNA on page 122.

September 22nd, 2024

Apparently, from September 29 until November, there will temporarily be an asteroid in our planet's orbit, acting like a second mini-moon. I feel strongly that it's actually a ship that physically appears as an asteroid, whose purpose is to adjust the planet's trajectory along the galactic axis.

Energy needs to enter through the equator into the Earth's core, and instead of exiting through the North and South Poles, it will flow out through the souls who came here with a mission to raise the vibration. I'm getting the image that those who are already activated will participate, and those who haven't yet, will be activated deliberately a few days before. It might be a bit painful on a physical level.

The energy will exit through the bodies of those with a mission on this planet, to act as energy conduits.
Earth Grid workers.
This is the final shift.

Many will be shaken, especially those still in dense vibration.
I now see an image where their brains will "crack" in waves, due to high frequencies.
The planet is ascending faster and time is narrowing to the highest constant our physicality can withstand.
It will reach a point very close to where the physical body can still exist as we see it now.
This shows me that over the next 4,000 years, mutations will begin at the genetic level, leading eventually to the next stage: *ascension and the disappearance of the physical body.*

I'm being told that our children will have different genes, changed, genetic strings activated - which in the past were blocked up until modern humanity.
The planet will be able to support human beings with activated genetic strings because the vibration will be high, but with a few rules.
This time, they are mandatory for Earth to continue.

Specifically: *shut down the Reptilian brain.*
Their contract with this planet has expired.

They are obliged to leave and relocate in space, to planets with lower vibration in another solar system.

It's like a repeated cycle that keeps happening until the planet and its beings evolve.

They are given a new space, just not here.

They now fall under other galactic laws.

We will have a new galactic representative after the frequency shift.

It is extremely important to stay hydrated.

The physical body is made of this major ingredient, water, which allows vibrations to better navigate the physical space when present in the body.

Everything is being done for the benefit, not just of humans, but for the *galactic association of the metaversal council.*

It's a side effect that makes our place seem like a "carcass," but it actually has a huge role in creating the whole.

Our component enables both the *expansion and compression* of the One into *total mass squared.*

Infinity is null when aligned with the creation of space in ultra-finite co-creation.

Everything is good, purging at high speed.

More fake and illusion will be revealed in the coming weeks.

Be centered.

Be loyal to yourself, to God's pure light.

Face the light.

Be the light.

Work in light.

Merge with light.

Become light.

Light is One.

One is darkness and light at the same time.

Nothing exists.

Everything is created.

All life has no beginning.

The end is the start of an edge.

You are Me.

Me is all You.

Done.

July 9th, 2024 (9:40pm US timing)

I centered myself in a quiet mode, started some music in my headphones and did a different type of fast meditation today. I centered my thoughts into heart chakra and set my intentions: to reconnect with yesterday, Collective consciousness beings, and that all process to be of pure 100% God's light and of a high frequency. While writing, I started to fall asleep.

I saw a white round table. Around this table, there were different ETs, and I asked to clear my third eye and my physical eye to see clearly, as long as it is in my highest good.

The intention is power!

I sat at that round table and everything seemed to be a white safe space around me. When I asked how many beings there were, the answer came that "there are 12 with me."

Now they will switch from my way of typing to their way of expressing the message and to continue with today's transmission.

"Shall we begin, dear ones?

We are happy to announce that today is a cosmic day. Sirius is aligning more with the axes of your planetary system and your planet ratio during the movement on a radius of 30 degree of upscale rotation into the infinity square of your universe.

It's simple the way we are trying to describe - do not overthink for now.

The live molecules in your ecosystem are switching from carbon to crystalline base, and are not liquid yet. It needs years to pass for you. Time is squared a little to more than zero degree into the north axes of rotation to the north node. The cold is imminent and changes are coming globally. Live beings are already changing; vegetation is already changed, but not fully. Processing time has to be adjusted to the molecule level of the animal and human kingdom. Birds (wild ones specifically) already pass this process.

Why were these two types not yet changed? The structure is more advanced than the rest of all.

It has an impact on other ecosystems and it needs time (in human years).

Apocalypse? Depends which timeline you are now. Quite impressive is your world and we are still mesmerized by the idea of how could you not notice that once you change your thoughts, you are no longer in that timeline where the apocalypse exists. It either happened far away in time, or already happened, or is happening now, or doesn't happen at all. It's all about your mind and thoughts. Be mindful of its power!

Let's move to the next compartment of the scale. (We will need a calibration to adjust Victoria to go deeper on her brain).

... pause ...

There is a device placed in the spine for keeping it grounded - we do not want to disturb her "ph" grounding level.

Now.

It is quite amazing to be part of you all. Yes, exactly we are you and you are us, at the same time.

The heart chakra in your body, once opened, creates a space where we are connected to each other. The nano-atoms are very small worlds that exist there and you are a bigger ecosystem for us. You think that it must be something bigger to help and save you, but in truth there is everything inside of you, millions of worlds, that you can access and help yourself to grow and be what you want.

(Victoria please continue with typing and do not correct the mistakes yet, we love you for trying today).

No matter how hard things are going in your world, be positive and believe in the best, in good - which is quite funny for us to say, but as long as it helps, we will use your language method for a better expression of our ideas.

... pause ...

The twelve of us are the main group in your circle:

1. It is water beings from 34 dimension of your left (10 O'clock)

2. Right in front of you at 12 is Your main guide - Obtirius from ... pause... 15th dimension.

3. At 4 O'clock, the guide responsible for your safety is "Oblikiusis Maldbekiusis Prime." He is of 14th dimension of different kinds of the world. Has a lot of skills and is almost your best version in martial arts that you are able to perform. He is a double feline physical looking, from the other side of black hole. Yes, it is possible to be in your world at the other end of your existence. Fascinating, right? *(smiling from all of them)*.

4. 6 O'clock is the "magnet" that holds on Earth. Very important job, since you tend to float a lot and you are quite a challenge for him (yes it is male gender). His name is KI-AmtIka-Tu-Ma, residing in the 4th dimension due to the closest dimension level to yours. It can not be far, otherwise it is not possible to handle this "job" from further places. Yes he looks more dark but we assure you there is a reason behind his color. Grounding is about to stay put into what roots spreaded. Your planet has dark soil (in particular where you are from, born as human as Victoria).

5. At 7 O'clock is the fairy world. Very gentle and loving beings. They are collective beings which are all around you on a daily basis. They are inside house plants and flowers, outside when you walk, in the forest when you hike, everywhere you are. They recognize you and love you very much. There will be no name due to collective work and they love to be called "flafiki" in your native language - *(I hear laughing - funny name for us.)* It means something different for us - it's a quadrant physician term for the thermodynamics of a crystal core. Pardon us for giving too much for now.

7. At 2 O'clock sits the Lyrian father Dormaskisus Valdolfan 12 (the lion father that you know). He is always by your side, always has been, even when you didn't know his existence. He was always by your side, always will be! *(I started to cry ... like I miss him so much)*.

He is closing this transmission. It is too intense for you and he doesn't want to make you feel so emotional before your human body sleeps. He is sending you so much love that you can feel the heat coming into your palms.

We will continue next time. We hope tomorrow will be tomorrow for you.

P.S. We will discuss more and will leave the channel open during your sleep and awake time.

The more is coming and be prepared for more.

Much love and enjoy the tomorrow (funny to say because it's always now for all of us).

Much Love and Light."

July 10th, 2024

Dear one, you have been transported to dimension 12 for a better connection to our higher vibrational brothers and sisters of yours. The way you have been transported is by an "elevator" that moves upward in a vertical tunnel - the higher it goes the lighter it becomes. The tunnel is a bluish fluid color, like a fish skin surface but very smooth. It's this way because it's a living portal. Nothing is solid in upper worlds, nor in yours. It's "fake".

You pass a protection wall shield that clears up all lower vibration for the contamination of our beings. It's very necessary, pardon us for your inconvenience.

Your world has a lot of residue in the core and brings a lot of subatomic energetic cells that are not incorporated with our core.

Let's have the transmission on. So be it.

NOW place your hands in the praying position and have a pause within for as long as you feel that you can hold the non-thought space. Do not worry if it doesn't happen, try tomorrow, after tomorrow and so on until you reach a longer and longer *"no thought zone"*.

Breathe, and when you exhale, stay there in that very short time space of no thought. That is the one zone, right before breathing in or out. The longer you master the better. This is called the zero space zone through which the heart sends to the universe the messages or wishes. That is the short time when it passes the heart portal and escapes the mind gates. The more time spent in *no thought zone*, the better the wish can be sent to be granted.

When people depart from your world or others (we will discuss another time), the main focus is Gaia world in 3D dimension space.
They never departed, the continuum circle spins until you can unlock the "prize" of eternity. It is a complex process with outstanding results. The infinite possibilities are played simultaneously and you exist in all. All connected, each second decision of thought in a time/space unit.
If you are absent from one relationship, there's a chance that you made another connection in another line of yours. It's like having tons of toys, playing with all of them, but prioritizing some of them, then others in another time. All have the same space, just time differs in the unit capsules of quantum leaps. Imagine an organizer box for toys where all of them exist in the same place and time.

You are not designed to stay, hold, or suppress something. It is about letting the control off your shoulders and playing with the wave.

Reaching the eternity level is when you master at least 72% of the missions and emotional engagements that were intended to be fulfilled prior to the unit experience. Then it merges into the trial period of the remaining 28% to show that all experiences were triggered and understood fully. You cannot step into the next level by not understanding the reason behind all of your experiences at once. This would be called heaven and hell for your most religious on Earth. Then, if understood fully, you are moved toward an eternity level. This level offers more complex possibilities to be part of a collective or to move to an independent collective.

Much Love and Light.

September 1st, 2023

Hello my dear Victoria! So happy to be back in connection with you.

Welcome back our dear sister soul. We are the Arcturian High Council of 9 and we are so pleased to send this message to you. It was open to your attention, this Word program, to see if you've noticed the change on this computer. (Laughing) Yes that is a laugh and we are trying to make fun in an appropriate manner.

Now, we would like to guide you for the upcoming trip of yours which will be amazing and your soul already has a plan for the physical meeting in your reality with us all, who will be willing to show off their true essence. The chill you are experiencing is that this message is very true and, yes, you will be the most happy for this meeting event.

You have been blocked, so to distort your reality and be stuck in the Matrix that you are now.

But the help was made and now the channel connection has been restored. You will experience future *deja vu* visions and slowly will be prolonged to longer future moments, so to speak.

The instructions as what you have to focus on:
- Try to do 10 deep breaths after waking up.
- Visualize yourself in the middle of the waterfall mist. Imagine you being in the center, and horizontal from left and right are falling waterfalls into your being, the center of the bottom, like past, future and yourself in the NOW moment.
- Go inside of your heart and try to balance the feminine and masculine energies. Visualize a toroidal vortex outside of you, originating from your heart.
- In the end you repeat a couple times - 7 times to be more precise - in your mind or out loud:
  1. I bless and love my body
  2. I accept as it is
  3. I am Loved
  4. I am blessed
  5. I am that I am.

We will be in touch and we are very excited to meet you soon.
So much love and light to you all.

August 8th, 2023 (10:53am US timing)

Dear Victoria,

We are glad to be present in this time and now moment of yours. We are Lyrians here. It is so amazing to experience where you are on your journey, despite the time changing in your dimension world.

Here are some instructions on how to take care of you:
- Take a salt bath and soak for about 8 minutes, wash off and then meditate and declutter your mind and foreign emotions that do not belong to you.
- Sit in a straight position and look above (to the ceiling or sky), try to breathe in slowly the energy, stars, then breathe out the unnecessary energy that no longer serves you.
- In your mind say a prayer that comes first at that moment.
- Before going to sleep, set your intention and ask for us, or any Star People you feel more close to, and ask for energetical clearing, and to be transmuted where it belongs.
- Send Love and Peace to all that you release.

That would be all for now that you'll need and will help you in the future endeavor.

Much Love and Light.

January 10th, 2023 (9:30am US timing)

I see you, my dear friends.

Today we would like to talk about trust. Trust of what is coming for you, as it should be, created by your thoughts.

287

Now, You have to pay attention to your thoughts and have to trust the process of what you put the energy into.

Now, the most sensitive time, when all the inputs of your mind materialize at higher speed. Be at peace and trust the divine timing of your dreams.

Much Love dear ones,
Pleiadians High Council.

January 10th, 2025 (2:30pm US timing)

It's time to *remember* who You are!

Your time is just an image, not an illusion, but just an image to speak.

You have to connect with the skull crystal at your home. It's from the *above double reality image*.

Double reality image is a world of the opposite law of attraction that is the opposite of the exact world of yours. The spinning motion that was experienced twice while connecting requires a comprehensive connection of its (sort of) mechanical intrusions that makes the connection possible.

Intrusions of this kind are a normal reaction, due to the vibrational random core in nuclei of your molecules of the physical organism. The blood is floating upside down during this transmission and your brain is conducted by us, temporarily, to make this message possible. It feels to you as if you have an extension of the body that exists at your right side. Do not worry, because it's totally safe.

The Star has two types of meaning.

One is as a location star, with the linguistic name as:
HGXWLN*8DU~B..../ and second part as its frequency that expresses the place of the energetical cord between you and us,
as >>>>>.JJJJJJJJaDkNX.

288

X - as your feminine chromosome in your local DNA, present in your reality.

End of message.
With love KorasMaudebu - Star system.

November 30th, 2023 9 (12:16pm US timing)

Now, shall we begin.

I will ask you to not pay attention to the writing, but to the message that is coming through you.

We are Pleiadians High Council and my name is Zohra and I'm more of a feminine energy here.

Remove the veil and let my message come through, don't block it, don't resist it. Everything is at peace.
I'm not here to harm or teach, but guide you on the next steps of yours.
We've noticed your fear that spiked to a high level and that is not what should be worried about in your current situation. It was truly to help you release the attachments with financial concerns.
The water you are drinking now is a fluid gold and yes you've noticed with your third eye. The fluid gold needs to sit in your physical body to transmute the fear.
Now, since you've understood pretty well the message, we are happy to tell you that there is no threat to you. Stay at peace, because fear is an illusion!
Your path is more important than this situation and your time is not done yet.
We will suggest you to think and sit quietly in meditation, try to pause the thinking process, even if it's impossible. Then think of nothing but peace and light.
Then, everything that comes, accept, don't fight, don't interfere, just let it pass by.
But if your heart tells you that it is important, take it, grab it and work with it, play with it, don't take anything seriously. It's the Matrix and you can remodel as you wish with your thoughts.

We will suggest a couple exercises for you:

1. Sit in the room quietly and feel the surrounding, the flower - be the flower, the wall - be the wall, be the dog, be the trees, etc. Notice how it feels?

2. Imagine being in a meadow in the forest, feeling the fresh air of pine trees, the grass, the river - be there, be everything and then come back to you.

3. Sink in your bed and imagine being upside down - how does it feel?

RELEASE ALL TENSION - How does it feel now?

4. Be the water in the river, float and go with the flow. Feel every curve, you hit the rocks, but you still continue going with the flow. That is what we call 3D life.

To get to the ocean, you must traverse all obstacles to return where you belong!
We love you immensely and know that you are protected, very!
Until the next time.
Goodbye.

Japanese Martial Art Master - the other version of myself

October 25th, 2022
(my first conscious channeling)
Channeling with Mentor Daniel Scranton

Victoria: I've been channeling long before this day, but I was not aware of what it was or what it is called? I felt a call to try something new, but in reality it was not new, I was only unaware that I'm meant to channel. It was a feeling of some sort of call ... Try!
Everyone can learn how to channel. For some it takes time, for some it's from the first try.

Shiku ... *long pause and silence.*

> *Note:* Shiku is a form of greeting in the Asian language. In 2025, when I was revising the recording I Googled if it truly exists. To my surprise, it exists exactly as initially written in my notebook). *In Japanese, "shiku" when referring to a greeting most likely means "yoroshiku", which is a polite phrase used when meeting someone for the first time, essentially translating to "nice to meet you."*

... Long pause
OMG this body is so heavy!

... Long pause
This body is so heavy!

It needs a lot of adjustment in the neck area. The energy is moving through the body. This energy is making the adjustments and upgrades. This physical body has an issue in the neck area. The reason is that she is not speaking her truth, she is afraid to speak or to say, when she needs to say and what to say.

Q: Who is this speaking?

A: Ashi-pin Sha. This is my name. (Asian name, later discovered to be a Japanese name).

... spoke in Asian language with no translation.

Q: Does your name mean anything?
A: *... explained in Asian language with no translation.*

Note: Victoria doesn't know nor speak any Asian languages at all.

A: I was showing her some tricks of how she needs to move her body. It is Qigong. She needs to learn. She knows, but she forgot in this life. She was a martial art master! It will help her physical body to adjust and heal. She needs to visit Japan. She feels connected with the forest and a city - Nagano.
Not Now! She needs to do a lot of work before going there. She loves to see pictures of Mount Fuji.
The left side of the neck has been adjusted. The right side is still working on it. She doesn't believe in traditional doctors. The degeneration of the neck bones, she believes that everything could be healed on its own. She is a good example for others, where she strongly believed that could be healed, too and she will.
The palm chakras were activated. She can heal others, but she doesn't believe that she can do it.

The adjustments are complete.
Goodbye.

Pleiadians Ascended Masters

May 14th, 2023 (10:00pm US timing)
Channeling with mentor Daniel Scranton

Hello Daniel,
I'm sorry it took so long. We updated Victoria's throat chakra.
Shaanonn.. (sound tone) is where I'm from. I feel nostalgic. It has been a long time since I've experienced such a planet as Earth.

Q: Do you have a name?
A: T-A-O mn Sha - Sha is what you call last name - it has a specific tone.

Q: Is this related to TAO teachings?
A: We do not consider ourselves religious. We don't have such a concept. Victoria had many experiences as christianity and buddhism. Is this religious?

Daniel: Yes it is.
A: All these have the same truth. We stand for the same truth, but not religiously.

Q: Why are you saying "we"?
A: We are a collective conscience that all speak for one, and one speaks for all.

Q: Do you have a physical or non-physical body?
A: We are non-physical beings who no longer have a physical body as humans. My body is much bigger than Victoria's physical body. It feels like a paper thin body. It is so limited. Our body's energy contracts and expands as much as we need to.
We are Pleiadiands Ascended Masters. Victoria's part of the soul is from here.

Q: When was the last time you've been here on Earth?
A: Eons ago. Please hold. I'm checking that time.
It was Africa. This continent was accepting us, you call ET from all over the places, they were more open to it, they were open-minded.
Oh, you no longer have a continent in the northern hemisphere! It's so different from what you have now. So much different.

In the near future of Earth, transition, growth and continents will look differently than it is now, but it will be for the best; for animals, birds, people - and not only people - but many and different of us ET as coexisting together in peace and love.
Victoria will be the one to witness this experience, the moment, and she will be very happy. You Daniel as well, you already met them and even more of them.
Such a joy for all of you! We are proud of all of you! If you'll excuse us, we will need to leave soon. The pleasure is ours to meet with you here. Goodbye.

October 31st, 2023
Channeling with Mentor Daniel Scranton

Good evening Daniel,
How much progress Victoria is making. *(happy laugh)* Her body is much lighter.

I am a tall, white being. We are from higher dimensions. Victoria did connect with us, through her heart chakra, like a portal between each other, between worlds.

Q: Is your world non-physical?
A: Yes, it is energy. It's not in the same Galaxy as you are on Earth. It's a different location. I would say even a completely different Universe.
I am not female nor male. It's exactly how she was seeing, too. We are her soul family. She saw us and needs to enjoy life, and she is doing so. Do not grieve or wish to be where we are now.
This is the mission she signed up for. We are not the Pleiadians as she thinks we are.

Q: So you moved from the dimension of a physical body in a sense from there to where you are now?
A: We don't have a physical body, many eons time ago. She is part of us, but that's her mission. That is why she is not connected to Earth. It's not her home - she knows that a long time ago.

Q: So she came in from a different universe to help Earth?
A: Yes. She is on a bigger mission than other souls on Earth.

Q: What do you see as humanity's way of coming together and being together?
A: It is already happening now. Now for you it's slower, but it's now. Energy is in progress. There are many souls like you that help.
But there will be others who will choose not to help or involve themselves.

Q: Will there be any catalyst events?
A: At your question, I can not answer.

Daniel: I think it could be both slow and big events that reflect evolution.

A: My apologies to say, but new humanity will choose to slow down themselves. We do not understand why this choice will be made in this beautiful time of evolution. Others can feel and they are taking it.

We are happy for you, no matter your choice. In the lower dimension you must be happy to have such experiences, compared to higher dimensions.

Q: Is your Universe where you are going through a similar process as we are on Earth?
A: Everything is connected. Even though you call that Earth is a tiny planet somewhere far, we are in a chain connection. You are evolving, we are, too. Everything is connected. It is Universe in Universe that the concept is connected and you can visualize on a small percentage scale.

We are looking at your world as you would see the Sun.

The Sun is named as some sort of Triangle shape. Your world is a tiny piece of a big puzzle.

Q: Would you say this is Victoria's first lifetime on Earth?
A: No, it's not. She's had a lot of imprinted lives to help her with Earth experiences. She had physical lives before there.

Q: So she came to help Earth?
A: Yes, to help with the ascension of Earth. She is out here for Karma purposes.

Q: Is that some experience of karma or negative? Or you being stuck in a karma wheel, or reincarnation cycles?
A: It is an answer and a question at the same time. It doesn't work on the same principles as on Earth. There equals, to some degree, on very low frequency. In higher dimensions, which is my universe, it works on very close principles, but is not as slow or dense as it is on Earth.

Will be too complicated to grasp for your human mind.

It is a philosophical question.

Q: Would you say in your experience as a physical being, in your universe, you grew more into traumatic, or challenging environment experiences? Or is your growth more in love, bliss, and spiritual experiences?
A: Are you asking me about if we, in our universe, are born in the same way as on Earth?

Q: It is a philosophical question. I want to know if, in your experience, you go through abuse or traumatic situations in order to move toward light and growth?

A: We do not have pain. *Pain* is not a word. The energy, you would call ... Mmm ... the plant kingdom, is a pain of growing out ... Not physical ... Liquid ... It's not liquid, it's not gel. It's very interesting how to explain all of this in your world.

In general, we don't have pain. The word is to create different types of energy, like liquid or light around you.

On Earth it is *pain*. In our world, it is liquid air, a different type of chemical substance. We are not born out of pain. The energy of birth is created and you grow this way. This is why karma works differently. I'm sorry for such a poor explanation of it all.

Q: In our world, do you see people growing from their passion or from their traumatic experiences?

A: We are very mood *(original text)*. This is not the right word. When you are sincere, this emotion makes you think: Are we happy? Then it creates a vortex from the heart chakra, where it grows a flower of love. We are happy to see growing flowers in your hearts.

Q: With your universe so far from our universe, are there differences that are noticeable to you?

A: Let me ask you a question to better answer this question?
How do you perceive the light?

Daniel: I feel it ... not see or taste it.

A: Exactly! The feeling is the same for us, but you see light, and we see ultraviolet light. But you do not perceive that in our Universe, we can feel it too. In your world, you have buildings; in our world, the universe is different. They look like white pure light energy and all the forms are constructed into round shapes.

Every soul group family has their own city. All cities are separate, but coexisting as one.

Just imagine an amphitheater that is round and has pillars as its own. This is the place where I am located now.

Q: Are there more beings from your universe coming here, to Earth?

A: 100 beings.

Q: To incarnate into babies?
A: Yes, there is no other way to be on your planet.
Victoria has a kid in our world. Yes, in my universe. They already made a connection with the image of a girl. In our universe, where we are from, we don't have the same system as in your world. Not born, not made, but created out of energy. These kids can be *"left"*, *not the right word*. They can be on their own, and others will teach them, as per our system.

Daniel: Thank you. I will bring Victoria back.

Much appreciation and love to you.

November 10th, 2024
Channeling - Victoria and Diana

I see a cosmos and a portal, but it's actually very advanced technology, like a ring.
In front of me, to the right, is our planet.
On the left, something appears like a sieve, like a triangle that absorbs and then releases through a very narrow channel.
Something is draining from the planet, like a vacuum pulling, and from the other side, through that very narrow channel, light is flowing in.

I'm not in the Akashic Field.
I'm two levels higher, in the Megaquantic Field.
I can see you higher still, but you're also in the field.
It's like we're magnetically held together, automatically.

Q: What is this portal, and what connection does it have to Earth?
A: You are a small seed from this planet.
Hearts are activating.
You are not what you believe yourselves to be.
Your connections are being perceived on a major level in the Quantum Field.
We cannot untangle the plan that is unfolding now, where you are observers of this major planetary event.
The cortexes are opening; memories are coming like seeds to Earth.
They need to root themselves in order for human brains to perceive clearly.

Energetically, subtly, atomically, the lower planes of human creation are being cleansed. Victoria is not present here. We connected through her, and today's event is on the final rung of stepping into a diverse world for humanity, from your current dimension.

December *(2024)* will be the final stage of the creation you've known until now; the civilization of humankind.

Though the physical body through which we transmit this message is present, the presence of the soul inside this body is not currently here. We need recalibration of the internal organs - the stomach, the connection to light, the blood, the brain, the phalanges. The calibration process has already begun.

Victoria: Oh Lord, it's like I just woke up from a deep sleep.
It felt like I died and came back to life.
I've returned.

Thank you.

VII. Star People.
We are Pleased to
Introduce Ourselves

*Humanity knows these presences under the name "extraterrestrial beings," yet from a broader perspective, we ourselves could be perceived the same way from their point of view. Out of mutual respect for both sides, my mentor chose to use the term **"Star People" Beings of the Stars** – a name they prefer and one that is frequently used in my spiritual practice.*

In this space, you will have the opportunity to encounter, perhaps for the first time, advanced Beings of Light, some of whom may be unknown to you until now. These beings represent only a small portion of those who have come forward and made themselves known. However, many of the Beings of Light I work with and collaborate with choose not to reveal their individual identities, as they function as a collective consciousness. Due to their high level of evolution, they do not feel the need to define themselves through individuality, as we humans often do.

Their purpose is to support us whenever we ask for their help, always honoring our free will. Often, our language cannot fully capture the sounds, frequencies, or vibrations that these beings transmit, some messages are simply impossible to translate into words.

I invite you to gently and trustfully open your hearts, to receive with calm and love, these frequencies and light codes, infused into every word transmitted by these wonderful and loving beings.

New ET Race – The Liberation of Dark Beings Around the Star MINDUBAS

One evening, mid 2024, I felt called to take a salt bath. While I was in the bathtub, a new race of ET beings connected with me, one I had never encountered before. I could clearly see the upper part of the being: bluish in color, with an elongated, oval-shaped head extending backward. It resembled an octopus, with many tentacle-like extensions instead of hair. Its skin would shift into yellow patches whenever it felt gratitude. The lower half of its body was pure energy, almost like a Djinn.

At first, I thought it might be a low-frequency being, so I called upon my Higher Self, my spiritual guides, and guardians from the higher realms to verify. This being was circling around me in a flow, in a vortex. That's when my spiritual guide made their presence known and informed me that this swirling motion was simply the being's way of greeting during interactions.

I then asked what message it had for me and what connection we shared. As I did, I watched its skin change into yellow patches. It told me it was deeply impressed by me and couldn't comprehend how I managed to co-exist on Earth, saying that my energy was far too complex for this planet. It asked me many questions: *how could I be at peace in a world like this, given how harsh the game on this planet seemed to be?* I asked if it had ever been here, on Earth, in the physical realm, and it said "no," and that it wasn't interested in doing so.

> **Note:** *There are beings who don't find motivation to incarnate in this dualistic world and prefer to incarnate in higher planes.*

This being told me it was amazed at how well I remembered my essence, *who I am.* Then I asked how I could assist it, or why it had appeared. It told me it came from a system called **MINDUBAS**. It is not a planet, nor is it a "star" in the way we understand stars, because their laws don't apply to us. This star or constellation is located on the left, beyond the limits of our known universe and is quite distant from us, from what it explained.

Their star is like a comet, and its entrance is like a platform, as if entering the back of the comet. It appears intensely white.

The being told me that I have greater access and shared that around their star, a strange form of dark matter had formed, appearing suddenly in their space. The beings from that dark matter look like humans, but from the eyes upward, their heads are completely black. Their bodies are composed of "*nanotectatrons*", which allow them to look exactly like us humans, except these beings have no soul.

This being said, these entities are built like ultra-advanced robots. They are the army of certain groups from the lower planes of creation, who came to invade them by disguising themselves as humans from Earth.

I asked the being to step aside so I could speak privately with my Higher Self and my spiritual guide. My Higher Self appeared as an enormous raw form, and in its eyes I saw thousands of stars, galaxies, and universes. My Higher Self told me to look into its right eye, where I was shown the star, and I could see what was happening there. I saw a horseshoe-shaped ship surrounding their star. The being that had contacted me couldn't see this ship.

Then, looking into my Higher Self's left eye, I was shown what I needed to do to send the ship out of that universe. I called the being back and summoned the **Galactic Council**, the Beings of Light, beings from **Lyra**, and **Celestial Union Consciousness** to assist me.

I pulled the entire ship, as if drawing a blanket, toward a portal; a passage point. The Celestials then closed that portal and placed themselves as guardians around that region of the universe. After the process was complete, the being from MINDUBAS left.

As it departed, I observed its tentacle-like appendages moving gently, bending and swaying in a rhythm that resembled inhaling and exhaling. This allowed them, in their habitat, to live both in water, on land and in the air.

Various ET Races
Akashi ET - Victoria & Monica - March, 2024

AMBIOBI

Monica: You've had interactions with some ETs since you were little, you were aware of it. Your human memory didn't record it because you weren't ready then and you weren't prepared to hold on to that memory. I see you as a child, collecting stones from the river, deeply connected to nature when you were young.

I feel they've always been near you, like a physical interaction. It appears to me that you look and wonder: *Was something there? Or what was that?* And actually, it was there, like you see something and think it was just your imagination.

Victoria: Interesting, when you mentioned the first part, I saw next to me some kind of ET race. Tall, pale, with large eyes, if a human would see it in the physical realm, I think they'd be frightened. I used to be afraid of those beings as a child. When I asked the second question, I saw a chair to our left. We're facing each other, dressed alike, wearing something on our heads like a large helmet that helps us breathe, and to the left is a chair. When I entered the field, the first race tickled the left side of my face, then left. Their body is made of light, their head too, pastel colors, not a physical body, more like light. They're still there. I feel the first race needs to return, because they still have something to say. I see nothing now; it's as if everything's paused. I have the impression we need to return to childhood, to the first ET race. Yes, now they've sat back down in the chair.

Monica: I see them descending from a ship. They're very slender, with large heads, and they're greenish-gray.

Victoria: That's the exact moment I see. Above me it was like a whirlwind; they descended, I felt a childhood fear, fear of the dark. I was afraid to look into darkness because I'd see something in my imagination. Now that image comes to me, just like you said; they descended, and I was awake then. My human brain recorded it as fear of darkness because it was shocking, but they're not actually harmful. That's my fear of the dark, but I associated it with them.

Monica: They seem to come and play with their fingers on your face. Yes, they came because they seemed fond of you, they wondered about you, about your face.

Victoria: Oh my God I'm panicking. I need to release these fears. My whole body is going numb, it's fear.

Monica: Are you in any pain?

Victoria: This fear is recorded in 2nd, 3rd, and 1st chakras. It's like something's planted inside of me, connected with the fear implanted in my navel. I feel it moving through the umbilical cord.

Monica: They're working on you right now. It's like they're pulling a long thread from your belly. I don't know how you feel physically, but, energetically, you're being freed significantly.

Victoria: My back hurts, exactly where I've been feeling pain lately.

Monica: Breathe from there.

Victoria: They're sorry that the fear imprinted physically and energetically inside me. It's about to come out through the navel, a small dark sphere, like a pearl, and they're pulling it back.

Monica: I see them working on you, and they're happy that you'll accept them from now on.

Victoria: Now they're changing my memories, the ones from early childhood, memories of being at my grandparents' or at my godmother's house. I see the window. There was light in the house, darkness outside, and now they're slowly changing my image from the darkness into light, and they're there. They're showing me by gesturing that they're friends, and they're rewriting my memories. Every time I wanted to enter another room, I would always turn on the light before walking over. Now they're changing what I envision in my cortex; it's already light in every room. They're always there in the room.

Monica: I see them guiding you, see?

Victoria: Yes. I see the forest. I don't remember being in a forest, but now I have a memory of being little with my mother in a forest, and there I see them again and they wave to me. They're restructuring my memory scheme. Now they're about to place a sphere, a white pearl, into my navel to replace the umbilical memory. It's passing through the umbilicus into the navel inside, illuminating the walls where those fearful memories were. I see my spine straightening outward because the lower part was inward. It was like a metal piece inside and now they're removing it and straightening it back out. This pearl of light travels up my entire spine. Now they've reached into my brain, in my forehead, into the cortex, and it's like they ignited an explosion of light in my brain.

Monica: Now I hear them say: "Now do you remember?"

Victoria: The fear has disappeared. Thank you. Wow! Now they've left, and the light-colored being has sat back.

Monica: Who is it? What race is it?

Victoria: No, we have to continue, it's not important. They gave me their name: **Ambiobi**. They're not from nearby dimensions, they're from distant dimensions. They said they will come again to visit me. They are curious about how I've evolved since our last physical encounter. They told me that now we are ready for the next step.

TOPHOTELUUU*

Victoria: I see her open her mouth and say something - vibrations come out, but I don't understand them. Please, give us a simpler word we can understand. The letters **TOPHOTELUUU*** and a star at the end. I don't know this word. It has feminine energy; it vibrates more in the feminine. We didn't ask first who they were?

Oh God, how patient this being is. It's like she has all the time in the entire universe. She vibrates so powerfully, her body is here, not just her energy, but there's something else. It's not a wave, not a frequency, it's another concept. You can't even call it an extension, because her body is here and yet you also see the reflection of her energy 10 meters in front.

Monica: It feels like she exists in multiple dimensions, and that's why it feels this way. As if she's multiplied.
Victoria: Yes, it's interesting. What dimension is she from? Is there a 44th dimension? I don't understand.
Monica: What came to me is that I've never even heard of this dimension.
Victoria: I see 44 very clearly.
Monica: Why did she come to us? Does she have a message?
Victoria: Yes, but her message is coming through very slowly. It's like she's speaking, but her message is an echo. I don't understand anything.
Dear being from D44, please speak with simpler words for us. Thank you. Now I hear the word **CURIOSITY**.

Monica: It's like we entered a field and she came just to observe us.
Victoria: It's like she's saying a word, but we only receive the first half of it. I see her like this … I don't know, like a swan above her head, like there's an extension coming from her head. I feel like we are at one end of the universe and she's at the other end.
Monica: Yes, the image is slipping away from me.

Victoria: What is your message for us? Again, I see how she speaks, but the message seems to take longer to reach us. Did you receive any message?

Monica: I can't perceive anything. Everything is just vibrating.

Victoria: Yes, everything is vibration. What I'm getting is: **BE AT PEACE**.

I want to ask another question, but I don't know if we should continue, because the connection is very hard. I want to ask, and she's telling me something too complicated - *how are we going to understand it?* What advice would she give to humanity?

I see she's talking a lot, vibrating, but it's hard to understand. It's like someone is placing a device into my crown chakra to convert the message so I can perceive it. I see someone sitting in a chair, taking a pen and a sheet of paper, and beginning to write. The same thing is happening to you. She's putting a converter on you too and sending the message to both of us. Now I see it being placed at your head. How interesting! She is very curious to see how two human beings can perceive a message from her dimension. I feel like she's not communicating telepathically, but in another way, faster than telepathy, and she's curious to understand how human consciousness works in these kinds of bodies and how we managed to connect with her. She's not even close to our reality. Her extension caught the wave of our connection.

Monica: Yes, that's how she communicates, through vibrations.

Victoria: She just showed me how she energetically opens up like a swan, and above her, she has a robe or a mantle, and then she spins, and that's how she catches the waves. Wow. It's like she picks up waves across more than 20 dimensions at once. She's telling me to let you see what you've received and for me to be quiet.

Monica: What I'm receiving is this: *to understand **what vibration means**.*

Victoria: What does vibration mean?

Monica: She's helping me feel waves of vibration in my body, something really strange.

Victoria: Vibration is the empty space where matter is missing. Light is transparent and emits sound waves of opposite frequency for humanity, what we think should be positive, but the scale of numbers goes into the minus. The more it goes into minus, the closer it gets to the absolute radiation of universal energy, traveling through the cosmos, Cosmos 1, which is layered over tens of thousands of universes, all forming a single existence. I have no idea what I just said. I don't even understand what I just said. My mind can't concentrate, anyway. I accept and I thank you.

Monica: You say it's hard for you, but actually, you're prepared for this.

Victoria: Now we're in a hall with many spectators watching us. It's like we're on show, and all the spectators are of different races, and I see them laughing now. They're laughing because it's too complicated for me, but a message came through that *it's not too complicated.* They're laughing at us humans (in a gentle way) because we're so naïve.

Victoria: Dear beings from D44, (I'm using plural because that's what I feel) it's telling me that it's not singular ... do you still have any message for us, or for humanity on Earth? She's speaking again, but now the vibration is different. Do you see how the vibration looks, the waves?

Monica: Yes, I see it like it's creating a portal or something.

Victoria: Earlier the waves were more frequent and regular, now the vibration of what she's saying is straighter, it has tonality. I feel the tonality in the middle of the frequency. Okay, your converter device just activated. The message is coming to you now.

Monica: What I feel is being transmitted is that she came here to observe us, and that she's waiting for us, because we will soon be able to ascend into other dimensions.

Victoria: Yes, exactly in that tonality you mentioned. She's still saying something.

Monica: It depends on our vibration, if we raise our vibration, we'll be able to create portals, and through those portals we can enter higher dimensions. *That is,* with a certain vibration, we'll be able to create portals to her dimension.

Victoria: Wow. Thank you. It's like she stood up from the chair and took something from it, like a little mat. Thank you for the message.

AZARGENOD

Monica: I've seen other ET races appear to me from a planet somewhere close to us, but as they appear, it's like they arrive there and then take me somewhere else.

Victoria: Okay, let's start from the beginning. Let them speak to us. I see a being that is shy, standing behind you. It's interesting how you see him. I actually see him through you ... and he thinks I can't see him.

Monica: They're different from anything I've seen before because they're very thin, their bodies are extremely slim.

Victoria: But do you see that they have multiple arms?

Monica: Yes, I see more arms, but thin ones.

Victoria: Yes, I see him now like a beetle, with a very large head. They're a yellowish color, almost tiger-like, and they have little arms and legs. I don't quite understand. But they're very shy. I saw them ... You know how I see it? Like they've sat down in a chair, like when someone walks out naked and is afraid someone will see them.

Monica: Are they letting you see them now?

Victoria: Yes, I can see them.

Monica: I saw a large tower that they are working on. It's something very tall.

Victoria: Here on Earth or on their planet?

Monica: No, on their planet. And I'm being told that through that tower, they block radiation that is coming toward Earth.

Victoria: I can see the radiation. It comes like a thick layer. Do you want to ask what planet it is? Is it in our galaxy? Let's ask for yes or no answers to make it easier to understand.

Monica: Yes, it is. But we don't know it yet.

Victoria: I'm seeing something now, only we humans wouldn't perceive it. It's not a planet exactly, but more like a circle. It looks like them. And inside this sphere there's a planet, and outside there's an iron-like ring that floats around it, with little bubble-like protrusions. They're all the same color as the beings. The planet inside is normal, but the outer ring floats like Saturn's ring, except it's not a disc, it's thick. And when it floats, it changes something chemically in the radiation that comes through.

Monica: And they're from the 7th dimension.

Victoria: Yes, because we wouldn't be able to see them. No one can detect them with any device, not even with infrared. They're helping us to stop the Earth from completely drying out.

Monica: Yes, and I also received that there are 12 races united in brotherhood. They work to protect the planet from tangible threats, radiation, asteroids, etc.

Victoria: I have a question for them. *Do they have a name?* Do they call themselves something? I see them speak. They open their mouths and it's like radiation comes out.

Monica: That's because it seems like they actually feed off it.

Victoria: Yes, but it's so fascinating how I see it. They speak, and I see radiation, words, vibration coming out, and the radiation doesn't come toward us, it goes back into them. It's like a circuit. They are benevolent beings because they work in a way that prevents contamination of others. Around them, the ring forms a closed loop. They speak, and the energy goes into the ring and back into their bodies. Their whole bodies absorb everything through their pores - all the radiation.

Monica: **AZARGENOD.**

Victoria: Thank you for your presence. I have two important questions. *Right now, is our planet Earth in danger from radiation?*

Monica: Yes, it's always in danger.

Victoria: Is that danger caused by us or is it cosmic?

Monica: Both.

Victoria: Is there a method for us that could help stop the radiation on Earth?

Monica: Yes, there is.

Victoria: Is it good for us to know this method now, or not yet? What I'm getting is a big "NO."

Monica: Yes, it's not the time yet.

Victoria: Interesting. Why not?

Monica: I feel that certain truths about those who harm on a global level will come to light.

Victoria: I see them coming out from within the Earth ... ok, I'm not even allowed to speak. I see them coming out from underground. They will have to come out because they're stopping the planet's progress. They'll be forced to emerge. I see our planet changing, rising, shifting its position within the solar system. Not only that, I see our solar system at the border of another solar system, one that is much bigger, and it's a sphere in another space, orbiting a sun, close to the boundary. That's where our planet is now because our universe has shifted, and it's come to the edge of a much more advanced and larger existence. It's already interacting with us, and all those of low frequency, all of them, will be forced to leave Earth when these two fields start to interact.

Monica: They're merging, right?

Victoria: Yes, they're merging, and our planet is the first on the axis of the solar system to merge with this advanced existence. Because of this, I see many races who are curious about this event. They're wondering how a planet with humans, or beings, who have not yet evolved to that level, who needed generations and generations of advancement will react and respond when this "merging" happens.... For them, it's a shock that we're still in 3D, that we have physical bodies ... and yet we're entering such a grand cosmic event.

Monica: This is the fifth time I've seen our planet *almost touching* another planet.
Victoria: Yes, but this isn't another planet, it's another existence. You can't even call it a universe, because the universe is small compared to it. What's merging is something gigantic; a mega-gigantic existence. The universe as we know it is very limited, and it's merging. And when it enters, I see beings. They're showing me their image, but they're not in our field, because that was the intention; for us not to interact with them. I'm being shown the kinds of beings inside the Earth, beings that don't allow us to evolve … but they have no choice. Those who no longer resonate with the frequency of the planet will be forced to leave entirely. These beings consider themselves the originals of planet Earth, but they've built histories we can find in libraries. For the beings sending this information, the word "online" seems very strange. I don't know why I'm being told this. They refer to libraries. I asked, "Online?" and they said, "What is that?" They mean library. In our libraries, there are many histories that are false, created by the beings inside the Earth, who, over the years, over millennia, have falsified history. They are not the original beings of Terra; they conquered and destroyed the originals. The concept of "originals of the planet" doesn't really exist, because even the originals were brought here. These others consider themselves the first, but something in the air became contaminated. They created an event, introduced a virus, and a new creation emerged. That creation still exists underground, and they wrote the history that they *are* the originals, that they are the good ones. But in truth, the truth will be revealed, and they will have to leave for good. The being who is with us now, is she the one telling us all this? She ran away. She left the chair. Okay, now I leave it to you.
Monica: I see many beings now, just like you said.
Victoria: Call them, speak with them. There are so many beings, and it's like they all want to speak … but one at a time.

PLEIADIANS

The Pleiadians are a highly evolved star race originating from the Pleiades star cluster, also known as the Seven Sisters. They are known for their profound spiritual wisdom, compassionate nature, and dedication to the awakening and healing of humanity.

Often described as tall, luminous beings with a deep connection to love and light, the Pleiadians have been guiding Earth's evolution for millennia. They assist in raising human consciousness, promoting peace, unity, and environmental harmony.

The Pleiadians work closely with Earth's spiritual communities, encouraging individuals to remember their soul's origins and embrace their divine potential. Their teachings emphasize healing, self-awareness, and co-creating a world based on love and cooperation.

With their gentle presence and advanced understanding of multidimensional realities, the Pleiadians continue to inspire humanity to align with their higher purpose and cosmic heritage.

Monica: Now I see the Pleiadians stepping forward, and we are at a council where the steps, regarding the universe and what's happening, are being decided.
Victoria: Dear Pleiadians, is Monica part of this council?
But do you also feel there are two here, not just one? And can you tell me how you perceive them around us? Because I see exactly how they're positioned.
Monica: The two of us are sitting next to each other, and I see them in front of us. There's a man and a woman with us, and the man is standing slightly behind.
Victoria: Yes - exactly, that's how I see it too. I'm here, you're in front of me, the Pleiadian man stands on your left, the woman on your right. The man placed his hand on your left shoulder, the woman placed her hand on my left shoulder. You placed your right hand on her left shoulder, and my right hand is on your left shoulder. We've formed a circle, and there's a round table in the center. The man has medals on his right side, and the woman has a star on her left. They each have a star-medal, and they're dressed in blue, like astronauts.
Shall we ask what their messages are?
Monica: I want to leave it to you.
Victoria: This man is actually your husband. I feel a very strong energy of love, and as soon as he made his presence known, I felt that emotional wave, like when you haven't seen someone for a very long time and you're trying to stay professional, but he can't hold back from wanting to embrace you. That's how I perceive this Pleiadian.

Okay, dear Pleiadians, what is the purpose of your presence today?
Monica: It feels like a council and they are welcoming us.
Victoria: Yes, it doesn't feel out of the ordinary.
Monica: There's a hall full of other beings - if you look behind.
Victoria: Yes, they're all around. Look, they're here, and we're in the middle like on a stage. The woman is my sister, and he is your husband. That's why he connected to you first, and she connected to me, and then they connected to both of us. They were showing the relationship dynamic. I have a question for you. Do you and he have children together?

You two looked at each other and smiled.

Monica: I just got the message: *yes, we do.*
Victoria: I can see them; they came to you. There are two. One is three years old, and one is one year and eight months, but both are walking. They came from the hall to support you. How beautiful.
Monica: But I feel like you and this woman are his sisters, or my sisters.
Victoria: What do you mean?
Monica: I mean, you and this woman are either his sisters or mine. It's like a family dynamic there.
Victoria: She's nodding now. *What is she saying yes to?* Who are we sisters with?
She's pointing to him, we're his sisters. I'm curious if they want to share their names.
My sister's name is **BELIVAR**. Now he's showing his name … you need to connect to find out his name.
You've taken each other's hands. He stood and walked over to you, embraced you tightly, heart to heart, and he's trying to send you your memories, from where you are both from, at the same time, so you remember his love, and his name will come to you.
Monica: Yes, I feel something. ENOIM, ENOHIM.
Victoria: **ENOIM**. Now he let go and sat back down. In this human lifetime, I know this person. It's incredible how he looks just the same as in his Pleiadian existence.
Now I want to ask, do I have a child and a husband in their existence?
Monica: I now see you transform directly into a Pleiadian.
Victoria: She tilted her head to the left, and she looked sad. What does that mean?
I'm getting; *"I chose to be a lone wolf to explore the universes."*

That was not a priority in the creation I belong to in their world.

And now she embraced me. Thank you.

Let's ask what dimension they come from now. I've received the answer, but I'm waiting to confirm it.

Monica: Fifth?

Victoria: Yes, he reached his hand out over the table for me to see. But he evolved from the fifth and is pointing to the sixth. He evolved into the sixth dimension. He can travel between the fifth and sixth; he can exist in both.

He hugged you again, and you rested your head on his shoulder.

My goodness, the love between you two is immense.

He placed his hand on your shoulder and said, "it's time to go."

We thank you.

Monica: I felt like I was on some kind of ship, like a satellite, where many races meet.

Victoria: And were we really there?

Monica: Yes, we met with them, with the Pleiadians. That's how I felt, It's like a safe space for everyone.

Victoria: Aha. Wow. Interesting.

Monica: We will be able to connect with them there. They come to that place, and it's part of a plan we created. I don't know, I don't see them speaking, but they send messages through intuitive channels.

Victoria: Yes, they send messages exactly like that. We're open to it. I've been searching for answers to many questions for a long time, and I wanted to do a regression on this topic. I wanted to connect with the beings I met during my mountain journey last year, where I saw many beings. If you are Beings of Light, I'd be happy to speak with you here today.

Oh, there are so many, wait, they're bringing chairs.

But who do we talk to if there are so many? What do you perceive?

Monica: Yes, it seems to me that they've lined up. And they are of many different races, not just one.

Victoria: Yes, they're very different. Some look like tigers, and some are white beings. I see a silver-white lion next to you on the left side, on a chair. My mind can't even comprehend how to understand this.

Monica: Let's see who wants to speak first.

Victoria: Yes, one at a time: *who wants to speak first?*

I already see who it is, on your left side, my right.

And this lion is very large, wearing white and gold, with blue eyes.

313

Monica: I see the lion too. He holds a wooden staff in his right hand. He tapped it, like saying, "Silence, I want to speak now."

Victoria: Yes, he's very authoritative. Extremely.

We are ready for your message and ask you to please introduce yourself, and what dimension you come from.

LYRIAN - THE LION

The Lyrians are one of the oldest and most revered star civilizations in the galaxy, originating from the Lyra constellation. Known for their advanced spiritual wisdom, high technological achievements, and deep connection to the cosmic light, the Lyrians have played a pivotal role in the evolution of many planetary systems, including Earth.

Renowned as benevolent and compassionate beings, the Lyrians are often considered cosmic pioneers who have seeded life and consciousness on various worlds. Their energy is deeply aligned with creativity, healing, and the expansion of universal love.

Lyrians are also recognized for their mastery of interdimensional travel and multidimensional awareness, serving as guides and protectors of soul groups across space and time. Their influence can be seen in many ancient human civilizations, myths, and spiritual teachings.

As allies of humanity's awakening, the Lyrians support our journey towards self-realization and higher consciousness, encouraging us to embrace our light, purpose, and connection to the greater cosmic family.

The Lion: It doesn't matter to the children what size they are. You have a lot to learn. First of all, learn to know where you are and where your planet is, because you are being misled by what you are taught.

Victoria: And with the staff, he shows me a map on the table. Using the staff, like on a board, the teacher points to that spot, right in the middle. He indicates that in the center of that point is the total universal creation from which everything expands, and we are almost at the end of this expansion. The world thinks that we are in the middle.

The Lion: Silence, there's nothing funny here.

Monica: It's like he's scolding us, I see him as very authoritative.

Victoria: Yes.

Monica: I feel like he connects more with you, like you forgot what he taught you, and he's actually upset with you.

Victoria: Yes, and now he's banging the staff on the table. Ok, hold on. Please remind me what you taught me. I'm sorry, but I don't remember. He has softened.

The Lion: Alright, I understand, you're human.

Victoria: So, this map comes in spheres, and he shows me that during the creation of our constellation, it was somewhere a bit beyond the halfway point on the map, but humanity has degraded so much that our planet has come close to the edge, where creation ends.

Monica: Subsistence.

Victoria: Yes, correct. And when I decided to come here, he was my main instructor, who taught me to be careful because I could lead this planet toward degradation. He tells me how I was laughing then. I was laughing even before I was here, physically, as a human. He told me to be careful because I could very easily lead my energy toward degradation.

Monica: I still feel that. It's like you're running around playing with little flowers, and he's saying to you, "What are you doing?"

Victoria: Yes, exactly. I will ask, please help me understand how? I just want to laugh. I feel like laughing. He looks at me very seriously and doesn't understand what's so funny.

Monica: I stepped aside and watched you two.

Victoria: You know? Like a parent teaching, and you as a child laugh. He looks at me like, "What's so amusing?"

Monica: I feel like I need to tell you that protection is no joke.

Victoria: What protection should I have? He just told me, "I will talk to Monica because I have nothing to talk about with you." And he approached you to clarify things for me.

Monica: Ah, it's like a subtle war you've chosen to participate in. You've chosen to be on the front line, and you have to remember this, so it's not a distraction for you. You enjoy having beings appear to you, but you need to see your purpose.

Victoria: And what is my purpose? The mission? *Why did I come here?* I just saw him raise an eyebrow and say, "What do you mean? You don't remember?" Then he put his hand on his head. "God forbid ... what kind of student I sent there."

Monica: You have to ascend a number of people around you. You are first, leading like an army.

Victoria: That's the purpose?

Monica: To bring as many people as possible into the light, so we can win this subtle war.

Victoria: At the moment, I am already doing this process. At what percentage am I, so I can understand?

Monica: Yes, you are doing this process, but somehow you are losing yourself.

Victoria: I'm losing myself in daily life?

Monica: I feel it with the protection. You don't protect yourself properly and you tend to be distracted. He looks at me and says, "See, see?"

Victoria: He tells me that when I saw him on the mountain last year, it was like a meeting. I needed to see him physically, with open eyes, but fear overwhelmed me. He was another race, looked like a tiger with black stripes, and I was very scared of him then. Now he confirms, that it was a test to see if I, at the human level, was ready to see them physically. I was very scared because I had fear, from the start, that stopped me from seeing and accepting them. Then they knew I wasn't ready. I only saw them with the third eye. At that moment, they should have activated so I could see them with human physical eyes, but I wasn't ready. He looks at me and says to be more serious. "See, your friend is serious, but you are giggling. Come on, get to work, I want to see you. Oh, these children …" and he left.

But you know how I feel? Like a fighter, that I can do everything. I have no fear, but I'm like, "Aha, come on, play with fire." Look, he sat back down in the crowd. Thank you.

Victoria: Does anyone else in this group want to send us a message?

TETA-uli

Monica: There are other beings with antennas and small eyes. They don't really speak, they make sounds.

Victoria: Yes, they don't speak. I can see their eyes and antennas, but they don't have a mouth. They've sat down in the same spot. The whole group that came to talk is now silent, just sitting. *What message do you have for us?*

Actually, they're talking to you. But you know how? Through their eyes, they transmit messages like waves and emit frequencies.

Monica: I'm trying to understand them.

Victoria: One antenna connected with your crown chakra and asks you to look them straight in the eyes so you can receive the message more clearly. That's how they communicate.

Monica: Yes, it's like they also came when you saw the other beings on the mountain.

Victoria: Yes, and you know how the message comes to me? From your heart. You're transmitting like a converter, and the message comes out of your heart and connects to mine.

Monica: I feel a great warmth in my chest.

Victoria: That's how you're communicating with me. Let me know if you get a message, because I do, and I want to wait for you.

Monica: I feel them like those microorganisms in the stomach that clean things out, that's how I feel them. It's like they deal with clearing residues, and they're telling me they're here for you. That's what they do for you.

Victoria: For what purpose? How are they helping me? These messages are so amazing. This is purely physiological. They're telling me you go to the bathroom normally, right? They say, "We help make sure you don't store toxins in you because your body has to be in activation mode. It has to process very quickly, and when that's happening in your body, your stomach also needs to function quickly." They help me by constantly cleaning my system, and they're laughing at me. They're saying, "You go to the bathroom in the morning, and we help overnight to clean things out, so that you don't have toxins in your stomach and colon." This is all at a physiological, human level.

Yes, and at the same time, I realized, when you said they connected to me, that I saw them as beings when I was a child. And the memory issues I had until adolescence, weren't just because of them; there were multiple times I saw them. They "shut off" my memory, and that's why I forgot everything. If I had kept going with those memories, I would have reached a critical state as a human. I wouldn't have been able to handle those memories. I wasn't ready.

Thank you for the explanations. Very helpful.

Now they've placed one antenna on my head and said, "Good job," - like a child.

Can you imagine how important it is for these beings to help us at the physical body level, to make sure our physiological processes are healthy and regular? We know about microbes and bacteria, but in reality, there are actual beings helping us on the physical level. They're actually highly advanced beings, not just microbes or bacteria. That's ... wow. We asked what they're called.

And you know how excited they are that we discovered something new? Wiggling their antennas! *OK, can you introduce yourselves and tell us what dimension you come from?* One of them placed an antenna on your head and one on mine.

Their name: TETA-uli.

Victoria: What dimension are you from?
The number 15 appears to me. I ask further, *How is that possible?* Again, they move their antennas saying yes, yes, yes. I try to understand how it is possible for such advanced beings from D15 to help us physically in D3.
Monica: They see that we want to grow, to move into another dimension.
Victoria: The ones with antennas touched your face, they like how you look.

My goodness, they're so adorable. I don't know if you can see, but someone very tiny just appeared, like a little blue bird, with a white belly, blue wings, black tail, and black wingtips. They have a message. They brought something and placed it on the table. On the table now sits a tiny dwarf. But he's very small.

Monica: Yes, I see something on the table. *Who are you?* He seems to be looking at you.
Victoria: He stands with his hands on his hips and points a finger, "Yes, you." *What's the message?* They said to look in my pocket. In my pocket, I've been carrying a heart-shaped amethyst crystal. I took it out of my pocket, and he told me telepathically to place the crystal on the table. He climbed onto the crystal, and he grew, now he's our size.

The TETA-uli are higher vibrational beings from the 15th dimension

(D15) who assist humans with physical well-being, particularly digestion, detoxification and clearing the colon. They are the energetic essence
behind what we perceive as beneficial gut bacteria, working harmonious-
ly with our body's physical processes. These beings are often perceived
as advanced in nature due to their existence in a higher vibrational state,
though they interact directly with the human body in the 3rd dimension
(D3), maintaining harmony and promoting health. Their role seems to
be supportive in elevating human energy and promoting well-being on a
cellular and energetic level.

As for their appearance, they can be seen as small, intricate creatures with
physical characteristics resembling those of an elegant, multidimensional
insect or bird-like form. One of the beings described resembles a tiny blue
bird with a white belly, black tail, and dark wings. There's also mention of
another small being, almost like a "dwarf," who interacts with the crystal
the person carries. This tiny being, initially appearing very small, grows
larger when standing on the amethyst heart-shaped crystal, signifying its
potential to expand in energy when in the presence of certain frequencies
or intentions.

This experience demonstrates how, despite their dimensional advancement, the TETA-uli work closely with humans through energy exchange,
helping us understand the symbiosis between our physical bodies and the
unseen energies within us.

When given energetic tools such as crystals, they can increase their presence and impact. For example, one small being grew to human size when
placed on an amethyst heart, symbolizing how certain vibrations (like
those of crystals) amplify their presence.

In simpler terms, the TETA-uli are like spiritual microbiome helpers from
the 15th dimension who assist in maintaining the balance and flow of
energy within the human body, specifically in digestion and clearing the
colon, by operating on a vibrational level. Their role bridges the spiritual
and physical, helping humans align more closely with higher energies and
to grow toward new dimensions of consciousness.

OTB AAA P(A)T

Diana recently received information in a session that she wouldn't react if an ET ship were to land in front of her house, and she was curious whether she had such interactions in the past without being aware of them. During the discussion with her, it came to me that she has a strong fear of ET beings, and I was shown what that being looks like.
She expressed the desire to explore this subject further in a joint session, so I'm sharing below, the information received from these beings.

OTB AAA PAO (O and A together) T

Diana: I want to ask about my fear of ETs and whether I've interacted in this life with any ET being.
Victoria: It's a kind of different ship. This ship looks somewhat like an umbrella. And not in a physical way to see it; it's an energetic ship, like a mushroom-shaped energy field. I see you on a plain. It's night, dark, not daytime, and you were walking on a path. They landed, and as the ship descended, it covered you right in front. At that moment, a switch was triggered in you so you wouldn't remember, and you turned around. And when you saw them, they were those beings with different-looking heads, a long and thin tongue, that's how they communicated.
When you saw them, at one point, as you were stepping back, you became scared and tumbled. They realized an accident had occurred and they interfered in a way they weren't supposed to. They wiped your memory, but the fear of the dark remained with you, but in truth, it's the fear of them. They didn't harm you; that's simply how they speak, with that tongue. But you saw them as a giant dragon.
Diana: Yes, because that's the human filter. But how old was I then? Around 10?
Victoria: You weren't that little, I see you with a young girl's body. You are 12 years old. It's a flat ground, not many trees.
Diana: Is it welcome to release this fear of them or of ETs in general?
Victoria: This fear is too deep in you, the shock was too strong. And it's very strongly stored in the left side of your head. I'm getting that the process is a bit more lengthy. These layers need to be removed. Let's ask if it is for Diana's highest good to release those layers now, related to this fear.

Now these beings have come in front of you, and with their tongues, they've wrapped around your head. With the tip of the tongue, it's entering through your crown chakra. The fear has materialized into your flesh, brain, the bones in your head, it's rooted. Now their tongue has the ability to extract, like through a test tube, something blue in color. And it goes through a channel in the middle of the tongue. Inside the being, there's a kind of tube that drains it from your brain into their body.

They're extracting the "fear liquid" that took root, not by tearing it out, but by slowly drawing it out, like sap from a plant. Over time, the plant withers, starved of what once sustained it.

This will take 24 months until it dries out from your brain. It will dissolve and exit through your pores. Now it makes sense why I saw it as a long process.

Diana: For your book, would it be helpful to know the name of these beings and what dimension they're from?
Victoria: Yes, they should be included before the PIKI Beings of Light. *Dear beings, what is your name? Or what is your race called?*

OTB AAA PAO (O and A pronounced together) T.
Their name is very long, but they prefer this shorter version.

Q: From which dimension do these beings come?
Diana: I received 22.
Victoria: I got that they operate in D12. Can you clarify this?
Why 12 and why 22?
Diana: I got 12 initially too.
Victoria: Their energy revolves around D12. But what's with D22?
They ascend up to D22. But why only up to 22?
Their role beyond D22 isn't welcome, or rather … it's not required.
Victoria: Their purpose above that wouldn't make a difference.
Diana: I feel like asking, *what is their role in supporting the planet?* Or are they interfering?
Victoria: They don't help in any way. They just extract natural resources.
Diana: Is that for their own benefit?
Victoria: I see a kind of base, where there's a lot of burning, an oval shape, but not a round oval, sharper at the ends. Inside, it's like coal is being

dumped, tons of fire, and that's where they bring everything.

Q: Is the resource extraction for personal gain? Is it somehow beneficial for humanity or the planet on a higher level?

Victoria: They're extracting something for a flying ship in space. The ship is very large. Now I want to ask, *is this in the highest good of planet Earth?*

Victoria: No.

Diana: Yes, that's what I'm getting too.

Victoria: I don't understand, they're not doing anything bad, but the extraction is not for the benefit of the planet. How is that?

Diana: Do these beings work with light and love? I understand they operate in higher dimensions.

Victoria: I get that it's both yes and no at the same time.

Diana: Why yes and why no?

Victoria: They don't touch any beings; they don't make contact with people, animals, or plants, etc.

Q: But why not?

I feel the ship has a darker vibe, it seems to be a prison ship.

Diana: You mean they deal with races that do harm?

Victoria: They hold those beings on that ship. They simply help by providing fuel to the ship from the resources they extract.

Q: Was this interaction with Diana accidental or intentional?

Diana: It came to me as accidental, then intentional, out of curiosity.

Victoria: For me, it came as intentional.

Diana: Accidental for me, but intentional for them.

Victoria: Where were you living in Romania? Mountainous region?

Diana: Yes, at the foothills of the Subcarpathians.

Victoria: They were there. They saw you and were curious, even though they weren't supposed to interact.

Diana: Well, right in that area, close by.

Victoria: They were there extracting resources, even though they weren't meant to interact. Now I understand why only up to D22.

I get that Earth holds a huge amount of resources, but the regeneration of these natural materials doesn't involve draining the planet of what it needs to survive.

Q: In general lines, if you know, approximately how many distinct races are consistently coming to Earth to extract natural resources?
A: 240,000 are consistent.

Diana: Are these extractions of natural resources in the planet's highest good?
Victoria: I'm getting yes, because in return it receives other resources. There are some downloads, someone comes and does a "shower" of energy, of information.

I don't feel we need to ask more questions here. Thank you.

PIKI

Victoria: The name **PIKI**. Welcome. *What is the message for us today?* I don't know if you can see it, but he's sending this to me on mute.
Monica: I was thinking that I wasn't receiving any message, but he's connecting with you.
Victoria: He sat on the chair, he's levitating, flying, then returning. He's showing me that something is pulling him into the ground through a darker portal, and then he's back again. I don't really understand what kind of message this is.

Q: PIKI, can you give us a simpler message about what you're showing us now?
A: He tells me, "You know what I mean."
He's saying that I have the power to lift myself up, to fly upward. I can do it, but I don't have enough belief in myself to really take off. I believe more that I can go downward than upward. This is a type of belief that I am giving power to.

Q: How could I change this belief?
A: He's pointing his finger at you.

Monica: I feel that belief isn't just about knowing how to read, it's about feeling within you that you are a multidimensional being and that you can do anything.

Victoria: He clapped his hands for you.
Is there any other message?
Oh my God, this being is so funny, he waved his hand and said, "No."

"Next, who wants to connect?"

I feel there's a being that wants to connect with you. It's on your right side.
Now I understand why it's on my right side and why it connects to the left.

When it's on your right side, that's when the message is general, for both of us, for you, for humanity.
But when it connects to the left side of me, that's when the message is specifically meant for me.

ŌPŪNĪLŦuu∞

Monica: Now there's someone on the right. I feel something, but I can't describe it in words. It's not a defined being. It's like a green fire.
Victoria: Yes, it has a ballgown-like form, it's flowing.
Monica: What is it trying to communicate?
Victoria: I feel it's from a high dimension because it's very difficult to perceive.
Monica: I'm picking up D24.
Victoria: What came to me was D22. Or maybe 24. Let's ask more clearly -
What dimension are you from?
It's showing me and you together, kind of indicating we are "2," and it shows an image of the Pleiadians, so that means the number 4. 24. Yes, D24.
Monica: And what is the message it has for us?
Victoria: I can't understand it.
Monica: This feels different … its energy.
Victoria: I can't understand it either.
Monica: It feels like a healing energy.
Victoria: Now it's showing me something simpler. If we humans are masculine and feminine, this energy from D24 has no body, but above it has two points, masculine and feminine at the same time, and below, the reverse. Like a battery with positive and negative poles.

The overall form of this being is like a battery with two opposing poles of masculine and feminine, not two separate parts, but four in total. It's like being F and M in one body, but doubled.

If you could ... *please present yourselves in simple words for our human ears.*
OP (P is inside the letter O - it's impossible to start with O or P because they are one and the same)
then **UN** at the same time, intersected, linked together,
an **L** which at the bottom has a capital **T**, but without the top hook.
and many endless **uuuuuuuuuuuuuuuu...**

ŌPŪNĪLŦuu∞ - That is their name.

Meaning:

  • **OP** united inside a circle of wholeness → a beginning without separation, representing the union between two polarities, the start and the penetration of knowledge.
  • **UN** fused → the total unity of duality, the universal "ONE," unified consciousness.
  • **L-T** combined → a pillar of consciousness that supports without dominating. L and T combined into a symbol of inner structure, strength, and balance.
  • **uuuuuuu...** → the sound of universal vibration, eternity, the never-ending source, the infinite wave of creation.

ŌPŪNĪLŦuu∞ is considered a "source-code name", not just spoken, but *felt* and *activated* through vibration. Thank you.

Victoria: What is the message? It's showing me images.
Monica: I'm also seeing lots of animals or eyes.
Victoria: Do you see it like an eye shape? You know what I see? It's showing *you* first, then me. The message is that we must combine the masculine and feminine within the same body, two completely different energies. They come together and become one.
And at the base, F connects with M, and in a flame shape, spiraling upward, they interconnect and evolve upward.
Now I see that this is the purpose; the twin flame connection.
It shows me that this is what humanity will eventually do. We all need to

connect with our twin flame and merge, and through that union, we evolve. Because it's crucial to first establish a foundation of masculine and feminine in separation.

Maybe you have a question?

Monica: I find it very hard to connect with this being. I don't have any questions.
Victoria: They've taken flight upward.
Monica: It feels like they sent some energy into the body.
Victoria: Yes, yes. They pass through everything naturally with this energy. Can you still go on, or should we reconnect another time?
Monica: Did you feel me? I got a bit tired.
Victoria: Many have said that for our physical bodies, we need to take it slower. They all stood up. Each one is showing a frequency as if they're applauding.
Monica: I feel like they're saying goodbye. But we're also doing something. In your throat, you're sending a frequency to them.
Victoria: I can't see it. I don't understand.
You know what I see? My body is radiating energy of love and gratitude. We'll return when we're ready to learn more about it. Thank you.

LUCERNISUM
Quantum Session - Victoria & Diana December 20th, 2024

Q: Why does Victoria see boys of various races? Is there a little soul trying to tell her something?
A: On the table in front of me, where my laptop is right now, there's a little boy, and he says to me, "I'm here! Hey, but can you see me?" The way he's sitting on the table, I see him swinging his legs.

Diana: Ask that little boy if he wants to tell you something.
Victoria: His face is made up of many stars. He is blue, like a cosmos, and has many stars on his face. *Lucernius?* I don't know if such a thing exists. *Lucernium* Or *Lucernisum.*

Channeled message:

"We are beings from a completely different universe. From your location, from Earth, and in the separate world of our side, we wish to speak with you for the clarification of our name. Which is **Lucernisum**. *This is our name from where we're coming from. The world, our world has an intense sound frequency that it is impossible to hold onto your planet, and your world. The halogenates in your creation, everything would explode instantly and briefly of just our own voice sound in our world. For you, it would be a boom of ten thousand bombs, atomic bombs at the same time. This would be the sound frequency on our planet. This is how we function, and this is how we look; blue with yellow. For you would be stars, but that's our creation. It is impossible for you to hear us except through such connections. Thank you. Goodbye."*

The Hidden Space Before the Incarnation.
Victoria & Monica February 23, 2025

Monica: Ok, I've entered the Akashic Field and I see an activation happening to you. I see a silver ship above you. Its edges are a very dark blue, navy blue, and from that blue light strands come out, spiraling like DNA chains. You're lying down and they're entering your body. I see your DNA is being worked on, codes are being transmitted to you, something is being completed in your DNA. There are blue threads wrapping around your DNA.

Victoria: Yes, I saw this process beginning last night, exactly as you're describing with the DNA.

Monica: Do you want to see what ET races are involved?

Victoria: Yes, I do.

Monica: I see grey ET beings. I don't recognize all the races, but they're tall, thin, with larger heads and bigger eyes, and I see them with three fingers on each hand.

Victoria: I see a smaller being, just one, who's short in stature.

Monica: Let's see what's going on with this being.

Victoria: It came close to me and pressed its right finger on my third eye. It feels like there's a camera in the third eye, micro and macro at the same time.

Monica: Yes, I see cords of light, energetic strands.

Victoria: Yes, it's activating them. The word "maintenance" comes to me. I think it's changing the "cables."

Monica: Exactly. It looks like those thicker LED light bulbs - that's exactly what I see.

Victoria: Yes. This shorter being is working on the third eye, it's like a technician.

Monica: I feel an implant being removed from your left shoulder blade. They're pulling some darker wires from there that look like the shape of a spider.

Victoria: I can't see behind me, but I'm curious about this implant.

Monica: I see it was placed in one of your past lives, in a much higher dimension, where you used to explore ET races - you traveled like that.

Victoria: The word "contamination" comes to me.

Monica: It was put there by someone who didn't want you to do that or to see; they wanted to stop you.

Victoria: Ohhh, that's why they're working on the third eye now. Because I feel invaded in my personal space.

Monica: Yes, the process had to be done simultaneously, to remove the implant and work on your third eye.

Victoria: Yes, that makes sense.

Monica: Now I'm being taken somewhere in the universe. I see the Milky Way in a sea of stars, a lot of blue. What does this blue mean?

Victoria: **MAHATUN k T A 46.039** that's the location.

Monica: I recognized it the moment you said it.

Victoria: I got chills when I said it.

Monica: Me too. I see a smaller planet here; it's cold because I suddenly felt cold. Let's see what's here. I'm being shown it's empty on the surface.

Victoria: It's empty like the Moon.

Monica: Yes, exactly, but everything happens inside it, like an ant colony.

Victoria: Yes, there's a portal that opens. It's an electromagnetic portal that opens through subtle energetic waves, and it goes in 1, 2, 3 steps. From small, to bigger, to bigger.

There are **3 LEVELS**, and then you can enter the interior. From the surface, you go inside through a kind of teleportation. For example, the way ETs lift you up from the surface into the air, this process is the reverse, it pulls you downward. A kind of levitation.

Monica: Yes. Let's see what happens inside, why this planet has appeared to us.

Victoria: Oh wow. I'm trying to position myself above it. I went to the center and I'm trying to look inside. There is so much space inside, that physically and visually, from the outside, the planet looks small. Inside their habitat, I see there is so much light, the space is huge, it's a paradox.

Monica: Exactly, there's a whole world inside.

Victoria: Yes. I want to go in. Once you're inside, it pulls you down by the feet like a vacuum cleaner, and an invisible cloak lifts off you. Something gets deactivated. No … More like neutralized.

Monica: But I see that when you enter there, and look at yourself, you're no longer the same as when you went in.

Victoria: Exactly. I see how it pulls you by the feet and lifts that cloak off. It's a complex process of **neutralization** - you enter as your true essence. The human cloak disintegrates.

Monica: I see beings there, including us, still as humanoids, but with different skin, maybe a bluish-white.

Victoria: I see it as white too, like there are no pores or hair. The skin is very, very thin and white. Our skin is a glowing white and has two layers underneath, where the inner luminescence reflects outward; it doesn't shine directly from the surface but from within, creating a reflective glow. There are two layers under the skin.

Monica: Exactly, skin like latex.

Victoria: Yes, like latex.

Monica: Like a pearl.

Victoria: We're taller, slender, light-bodied; I don't feel organs. There are many beings.

Monica: How interesting. This is a space before incarnation. A place where you come and make your choices.

Victoria: Oh my God, I just got chills on my legs. I've seen this place in a dream. It's a space, but it appears differently to each person, each can interpret it through their own imagination filter.

Monica: Yes, it looks different to each, so that the transition toward incarnation is easier.

Victoria: Ok, now I'm curious from another angle. Does this space maintain each individual's limiting beliefs, following universal law?

Monica: What I feel is that in this space, connections begin forming with the people you'll meet in your next life, but feel a sense of family, belonging, you start to get used to these feelings. But I also see a vast, full space, filled with love, peace; it feels like floating. I think you're still in a soul state, but getting close to incarnation.

Victoria: Yes, I see so many people.

Monica: This is simply a floating state, something on the verge of materialization.

Victoria: That means the energy in this space is flexible energy, and that's what I've been studying this morning; about flexible energy in total creation.

Monica: I see some beings that aren't quite of the light, and it's like they're looking for this space. I see them moving from galaxy to galaxy, but they can't find it.

Victoria: The reason this habitat is created like this, is so it cannot be detected; it's like a decoy, a planet that appears to have nothing. I'm getting information that under the surface, below the crust, there is a wave field, similar to gamma radiation waves. This gamma wave is a complex **radiation** that has the effect of neutralization and cannot expand, meaning light is contained **within** and cannot be detected. Not even with advanced devices from other beings.

Monica: That's exactly what I see too.

Victoria: In what dimension is this place located, if it's appropriate for us to know?

Monica: I'm getting 7.

Victoria: I'm getting two different layers; one lower and one higher, that coexist in the same space. The planet is in a lower dimension, in D7, but once you enter the interior, I see the number 22. D22 coexists with D7 in the same space, but the division depends on the energetic perception you have when accessing the information. The energy is flexible; it cannot be static or solid.

Monica: Let's see what else shows up.

Victoria: I got the words "key points."

Monica: I saw how they finished working on your third eye and you rose up, and now you're wearing a kind of latex suit.

Victoria: I saw it!

Monica: You did?

Victoria: Yes.

Monica: A beautiful suit, and it's like nothing can penetrate you anymore. They put a **protection** over your body, and your hair is long and pulled back.

Victoria: I see a cloak flowing behind me.

Monica: Yes, like Wonder Woman. In your zone of femininity and power. Now I see the ship leaving.

Victoria: Did we ask who they are? I'm getting the phrase "non-related question."

Monica: So they came just to perform this activation.

Victoria: Yes, it's not important for us to know.

Monica: Anyway, they're the grey ones.

THE GREYS ET

Victoria: Yes, they're on the technical side. By the way, I'm receiving just one distant message, a final message, that they are working on themselves now, they've begun the process of recovering their karma. They've started their own evolution process on the path of positive polarity.

Monica: I see them going to other people too, they're helping a lot of people.

Victoria: Yes, their operating system has been changed. Before, they used to do experiments for their own purposes, but now they do it with the goal of helping through their knowledge, to help humanity and other beings. Wow, that's interesting, because we all think of them as being "bad", but here it's clearly shown to us that they're on the path of correction, so I thank them.

Monica: Your lion father appeared. He's come to pick you up from where you left off. You're flying, and you pass through a kind of portal. He's showing me a green portal that pulses. I see you entering it through a tunnel in space-time, and here you're searching for something. I think it's part of the journey in our session ... to find information.

Victoria: This is a different kind of library, it feels more confidential, secret even, I would say. I see a hallway with doors on the right and left. I tried to open one door on the right and it said "Access denied." Okay. I ask the field to indicate which doors we're allowed to access.

Monica: I'm being shown that you need to go forward.

Victoria: Yes, straight ahead.

Monica: Yes, right now you don't see anything, but if you take a few more steps, it will appear.

CHITKATU MAIS 29

Victoria: We're in the 5th dimension.

Monica: The 5th, yes, exactly. I wanted to tell you when you were pulling on the doors.

Victoria: I'm in front of the door, but there's another one. I'm being shown two doors, one to the left and one straight ahead, but the first one I need to open is the one in front. Ok, I'll open it now. Oh, this is very, very fast, I feel like I'm flying faster than the speed of light.

Monica: Yes, everything here moves much faster.

Victoria: Instantly ... it's like I'm a rocket.

Monica: I'm behind you.

Victoria: Wow, we're in an open space where, from the center, another space is going to appear, like a ship, a conference room. It's already there, but we can't see it yet. Wow, it's huge. I'm starting to see it materializing. It's a very large ship, kind of platinum-looking. It has a wall, and then, like a façade.

Monica: I'm seeing the color red as well on this ship.

Victoria: Interesting, I don't know where you are that you see it red, because I'm outside, off to one side, and I see it gray, platinum, something in the composition. And I see different windows.

Monica: Again, I'm getting that this is about perception, how each of us perceives things.

Victoria: Yes, that's fine.

Monica: You need to board the ship.

Victoria: Yes, I'm behind it now, and there's a door - like those on cargo planes.

Monica: Yes, it's big and it opens downward.

Victoria: Right, now it's opening, I don't know how you perceive it, but I don't see any beings with a physical body, only energetic ones. They're there, but they're invisible.

Monica: I see them kind of like jellyfish.

Victoria: Transparent. You can see their outline. Wow, how much physicality we have compared to them. They're really tall, around 4 meters compared to my 1.65m (5.5ft). At least 4 meters, because they're bending down to look at us. But they're transparent, like jellyfish.

Monica: They are very tall.

Victoria: They're letting us pass. I see you on my right, and they've created a small table for children.

Monica: Yes, I saw it too. It was created so we can sit there.

Victoria: Ok, I sat down on the chair, and I see you again on my right.

Monica: Yes, and I see you on my left. Let's see what information they want to give us.

Victoria: There's a device inside, in the upper back-left corner. It's a kind of device like an antenna that spins information and creates a kind of translator. It's a translator device that doesn't translate by voice but by frequency; the frequency of words.

Monica: Yes, I saw it while you were saying that, I was looking right at it. I was watching how it spins like a metallic sphere.

Victoria: Yes, it's round, and when it spins, it creates circular waves. When we speak, the device makes a larger wave to listen to, but when it speaks to translate to us, the wave is smaller, at the center. And it transmits using the red color, which is what you saw. It looks like those round, soft earbuds on AirPods - that's how it appears.

Monica: Yes, exactly.

Victoria: Let's begin communication.

Monica: Yes, I'm trying to perceive. I heard: *"Welcome. We are…"* and now I'm trying to perceive what they are. I'm receiving the letters **AR**.

Victoria: **AR//*34!44**

Q: Dear beings, could you translate more easily, in our human terminology?
A: We are **CHITKATU MAIS 29**. Anyway, they have numbers. Thank you.

Monica: I'm receiving that they're coming with upgrades done at the DNA level, in all our subtle bodies, and they work with the frequency of planet Earth.

Victoria: On an inner level.

Monica: Yes, they're showing me the Earth's core, and again I see red.

Victoria: That's why they communicate through the color red. Their bodies allow them to be invisible, especially when they reach the inner temperature or layers of the Earth. They pass easily through our physical matter.

Monica: Yes, I see how they draw their energy and all their technology, not like ours based on electricity, but rather from the energy of planetary cores. They just channel it from there.

Victoria: And they feed on that. That's their life force energy, even if it doesn't appear physically. The mass in the core, which is extremely dense and hot, keeps them cool.

Monica: Exactly. I want to ask: *in what way will they help the planet upgrade, or help us?*

Victoria: From the North Pole. They're working on a project, it's like a radar. Imagine a radar where they create a portal that is deepened, like a meteor hit and left a crater. That's how it spins, from east to west, clockwise, from the northern part, that's where they enter. That's how they can enter inside the Earth.

Monica: I'm seeing that they also create protection with this frequency. They wrap the Earth in a protective layer, like a very fine veil.

Victoria: You know what they're telling me? That the South Pole doesn't actually exist. That's their hologram. Only the North Pole exists, as in, we perceive both poles, but they don't recognize the South Pole on our Earth. From their perspective, our planet is not round. On a holographic level, all energy originates from inside the Earth, from the North Pole. That's the origin point.

Monica: Okay.

Victoria: What dimension do they operate from, or what dimension do they come from?

Monica: I'm shown they come from dimension 34.

Victoria: And I got D18.

Monica: Is that where they operate?

Victoria: Let's ask again. *What is the origin of your dimension, and what is your operational dimension?*

Answer: Operational dimension: D18.

Monica: Same for me.

Victoria: Interesting. How does their operating system in D18 manifest, in relation to our dimensions 3-4-5? I'm getting that the question is complex, but at the same time, it's as if it's being asked by a child.

Monica: Yes, exactly. I see them drawing formulas on a board, but they aren't letters or formulas we know; they're like symbols.

Victoria: I see symbols.

Monica: A lot of symbols. I see something like a 0 with something inside, or a reversed E.

Victoria: Or rounder, softer ... that's how I see it.

Monica: They're trying to show us, but it's complex. They say they've helped many planets ascend, and now they're here to support Earth's ascension process.

Victoria: I'm seeing a book. Like flipping from page 1 to the next, does this mean we're at the end?

Monica: Ah, do you know what I'm seeing? That they're taking down the Matrix veil and helping us to see beyond it. They're the ones helping us see the Matrix codes, in dreams or meditation.

Victoria: Now I understand why I was seeing different symbols. The symbols or formulas I was seeing aren't horizontal, they're vertical, like in packets. "Units of formula" comes to mind.

Monica: They decode and rewrite the Matrix.

Victoria: I'm getting that it's quite a complicated process. They actually work with these formulas; they see them, interpret them, understand them. But their focus isn't on the formulas or the Matrix codes, but on the gaps between these packets. They study the spaces between the systems, formulas, and programming of the Matrix. They don't care to change the system, they analyze and focus on how to reprogram the gaps between the formulas and numbers.

Monica: They study the frequencies, the sequentiality between them.

Victoria: What's interesting is that this morning I did the same kind of study and came across that exact word.

Monica: I don't think I've ever used that word before - *sequentiality.*

Victoria: Yes, and now I feel intense downloads into my third eye. I'm getting that in these gaps, black spaces between formulas, the gaps themselves are white. That's where they have the ability to see. There are many beings, races there that we can't see, and the Matrix doesn't have access to. It's "special access denied," so it doesn't overload the programs, the software. They can see formulas inside those gaps. From there, they reformulate and adjust the matrix operating systems.

Monica: Wow.

Victoria: Ok, I've transmitted this ... though sometimes I wonder what I even just said?

Monica: Yes, I get like that too. You'll listen back and understand.

Victoria: So. Do you want to ask what the message is for us, for humanity? I feel like we're at a high point, planetarily speaking.

Monica: Yes, I feel the same. I see that they encourage us to trust the process, but also to be gentle with ourselves because we'll go through many processes, physical and emotional. We need to just let them flow through us; they're inevitable.

Victoria: Yes, and as you were speaking, I got the image of our planet on the top of a mountain. To stabilize yourself on that ridge, you need to let go of the burdens you've carried. The longer you stay on the ridge, the easier it is to lose balance and carry that weight into the future. The message is: *as humanity, as individuals, we need to let go of all baggage, all heaviness, all we've accumulated, let it all fall.* I see clothes, suitcases, weights, they fall away, and that's what allows you to stay at the high point, with only the essentials.

Monica: That's why they took us to that planet with souls before incarnation, so we'd understand how pure and empty we were.

Victoria: Exactly. The goal is to remain only ourselves. We don't need anything else.

Monica: And even if we have material things, we must be ready to release them, not be attached.

Victoria: Yes, that's the message for all of us. It's not individual, we are part of the whole. They can't identify us as individuals.

Monica: But I also feel you're part of a group of people working with the matrix, its base, its codes and sequences. You'll discover something about the matrix. Maybe you feel it, or can even touch it at times.

Victoria: I'm really curious about that. I want to understand this concept and what's meant by it. What ability do I have that allows me to see from outside the matrix, and understand how its inner principles work from the outside?

Monica: Immediately, I see you in another dimension working with enormous computers.

Victoria: Oh. I'm the one who makes decisions. I see myself aborting some operations.

Monica: Yes, you make decisions.

Victoria: And where am I, in this aspect, this being, this role?

Monica: You're not like those beings we saw earlier, you're something else. You're between dimensions, on a ship.

Victoria: Yes, I see a ship. It's a semi-sphere, flat and then round.

Monica: Yes, that's how I see it too.

Victoria: Do you know why the ship is shaped like that? Because that shape allows it to move through time and space. Space is flat (dimensions 1-2-3), and then there's this vector. It's flat to allow travel through dimensional locality, but time above is round, like a moving wave. The round part helps you pass like a ball through water. It's a laboratory.

Monica: You look the same as I saw you on the Pleiades, but I can't say you're Pleiadian, you're something similar.

Victoria: I see myself alone there.

Monica: Yes, I see you alone too, traveling through many dimensions, through time and space. You take something from the past and return.

Victoria: The ship has buttons everywhere. It's huge.

Monica: I see that you communicate through this ship with other beings.

Victoria: The ship is bio, but not synthetic - it's bio and something else. The ship itself is a being, but at the same time, a complex operating system.

Monica: Like biotechnology.

Victoria: Yes, like our body; our physical body communicates with us directly, but we are the soul inside that communicates with the body. The ship also has a soul.

Monica: Like an artificial intelligence.

Victoria: Yes, exactly.

Monica: That's what you bring into the 3D physical realm. You have much knowledge from that dimension and can help people see the Matrix and understand this programming.

Victoria: What is the general project I'm working on now, from the higher self perspective? If it's okay to know.

Monica: Planetary Ascension. That's the major project, but it has many branches.

Victoria: Subdivisions. It's a very complicated question to understand.

Monica: Mostly, that's what you do. That's your big mission. That's why you receive all these formulas, because it's science.

Victoria: OMG, now it makes sense why today I got into a theory about quantum computing, and it's complex. My mind really struggles to understand, but now it all makes sense.

Monica: Do you want to ask about their bodies, how they function, or something else?

Victoria: I'd ask, if they're okay sharing, *what information is welcomed for us to know?*

Monica: They say:

"You, as humanity, are in the process of decoding yourselves.

You're rediscovering who you are, how you are structured, how you were built.

It's a long and complex process, and not everyone will get there at the same time."

Victoria: That's why I'm seeing chromosomes and DNA unraveling.

I'm seeing sequences lighting up and rearranging themselves.

Monica: Yes. They say:

"Even your scientists are beginning to understand this, but they still operate from a very limited system.

They will soon discover the bridge between the physical and the energetic body, and from there, things will accelerate even more."

Victoria: And that's why they're here. To guide those discoveries.

Monica: Yes, they say their role is not to intervene but to facilitate. To open doors. They offer information, codes, images, and even physical encounters in dreams or altered states of consciousness.

Victoria: I'm seeing one of them showing a hologram, a sort of cylinder, and inside it is a person.

They rotate it slowly, and as it spins, lights appear on the person's body, certain chakras or areas light up in a sequence.

Monica: Yes, because that's how they scan us.

Victoria: Exactly. They scan our light bodies. The chakras are like code access points. From what I see, when one activates, it allows a sort of "download" or energetic infusion. Then another activates, like a sequence of unlocking certain layers of consciousness.

Monica: That's why many of us are experiencing physical symptoms. These activations happen quickly and intensely now, and the body tries to adapt.

Victoria: I see many people getting headaches, heart palpitations, pressure in the chest, especially upper chakras.

Monica: They say we shouldn't worry. It's a temporary phase and the body knows how to adapt. The key is to listen to it, to rest, drink water, and allow the body to integrate.

Victoria: I want to ask, *will they continue working with us? Individually or collectively?*

Monica: They say:

"Yes. We've been with you for a long time, but until now, you couldn't perceive us. Now that you're awakening, many of you can feel our presence, or even see us. We're working in groups with people across the planet. You will begin to recognize each other soon.

Those working with our frequency are encoded in a specific way. You will feel it through resonance."

Victoria: So if I meet someone from the same group, will I feel it right away?

Monica: Yes, it's a deep recognition. Not just of the person, but of the mission.

You'll feel like you've always known them. It will feel familiar and aligned.

Victoria: That makes sense. I've started meeting people like that recently, and the bond is instant.

Monica: They say that's part of the unfolding process. These encounters are synchronized. You're brought together to work on tasks, build projects, and anchor new structures.

Victoria: I see buildings of light being constructed. Not physical buildings, but like grids or light networks between people. Each person is a node.
Monica: Yes, exactly. They say:
"Every awakened being is a frequency anchor.
Together, you're forming a new grid around the Earth, one not visible to the eye, but very real.
This new matrix, let's call it the organic matrix, is what will replace the artificial matrix that's been running for millennia."

Victoria: Oh, so that's what they're doing! They're not fixing the old Matrix, they're building a new one.

Monica: Exactly. They say:
"The old Matrix is collapsing. You're witnessing its decay.
What you perceive as 'chaos' on Earth is just the dismantling of the old codes."
Victoria: And that's why we must let go.
Let go of everything attached to the old Matrix; roles, identities, jobs, expectations…
Monica: Everything. They say:
"You can't carry the old baggage into the new system. It's incompatible.
That's why you're being stripped down, emotionally, mentally, physically."
Victoria: Wow. It's both reassuring and intense.
Monica: Yes. They say we're supported at every step, but they respect free will.
They can't intervene directly unless invited, either through intention, meditation, or conscious connection.
Victoria: That's a very important message. Many people expect to be "saved" or "rescued," but the reality is … we must choose it.
Monica: Exactly. They're not here to save us.
They're here to co-create with those who are ready.
Victoria: Thank you. I feel immense gratitude for their presence.
Monica: Same here. I feel like we've just received a huge download. I need some time to process it all.
Victoria: Me too. It's like our whole system is recalibrating. My body is buzzing.
Monica: Let's rest and let it all integrate.
We'll understand more in the days to come.

GALACTIC COUNCIL

The Galactic Council is a collective assembly of advanced extraterrestrial civilizations, enlightened beings, and cosmic guardians dedicated to overseeing the balance, harmony, and evolution of life across the galaxies. This council functions as a universal governing body that monitors planetary systems, supports civilizations in their spiritual and technological growth, and ensures the preservation of cosmic law.

Composed of diverse races with unique abilities and wisdom, the Galactic Council operates beyond political or cultural boundaries, focusing instead on the higher good of all sentient beings. Their guidance helps maintain peace, prevent conflicts, and facilitate the ascension process for planets like Earth.

By working collaboratively across dimensions and timelines, the Galactic Council fosters cooperation between star systems and promotes the sharing of knowledge, technology, and spiritual insight. Their presence reminds humanity of its place within a vast cosmic community and encourages us to awaken to our interstellar heritage and responsibilities.

Victoria: Three beings have arrived - they are from the Galactic Council.
Monica: I see them very tall, with cloaks.
Victoria: Yes, and the being in the middle has something on their head, something rigid, I can't perceive it clearly. It's not a crown, but it's something large.
Monica: I see a tall tube.
Victoria: Yes, and it has various crystal medals. The other two beings on either side don't have such an advanced headpiece, they wear something simpler, and their cloaks are quite large. When I look from my left, the cloak is ruby-colored; from the front, I see white with gold; from the right, it's violet, blue, and white, but the colors are shifting.
Monica: Yes, the colors are vivid on them.
Victoria: Yes, it's like they're chameleon-like, their cloaks change colors.
Monica: Okay, we thank them for coming. What is the message for us? Is it something related to your book? Why are you laughing, Victoria?
Victoria: I laugh because the being in the middle, whatever rank it has, and we'll ask them to introduce themselves, sent a thought to you. They are sending you a lot of light and love but said that they are not speaking to you, but to me. The one next to you is shifting into violet and blue and has started radiating more love. It's not about discrimination, it's a business talk.

Monica: Exactly. I felt that, too. When I asked what the message was for us, I got a "no," that the message is for Victoria, not for both of us.

Victoria: That's why I laughed.

Monica: Yes, I had the same feeling, and it's related to your book. Let's see if they'll transmit something to you directly.

Victoria: What I get is that the book needs to be finished soon - SOON.

Monica: Yes, I see you at a desk writing, and you're discussing with them while you write the book.

Victoria: The project I'm working on with them and the book is called, wait, it came and went. The name escaped me. It was two words. I feel like they'll send it to me separately, for some reason.

Monica: I also got some information about water and the data that transmits through water. You need to check on that. It's something very important you need to find out.

Victoria: Interesting. I haven't reached such a topic, nor did I think about it.

Monica: I'm shown the water cycle in nature, how water rises to the sky and returns with new information. You're going to discover something about that. I also see a blue crystal, like clear water, maybe aquamarine, like a blue diamond or sapphire that holds the same information water collects when it reaches the universe.

Victoria: They're communicating directly with me, I can't even speak. They've created a channel where they speak to my subconscious. I can't verbalize or speak aloud because it's too fast for my logical mind to perceive.

Monica: I felt them speaking within you.

Victoria: Yes.

Monica: You're going to download something from this, it feels like they're implanting it.

Victoria: Yes, it's a direct channel with me, and I want to express the information I'm receiving, but it passes through all filters. My mind can't even grasp what's coming in. I wish I could record it, but I can't. Wait a moment, it's still happening, I can't yet.

Monica: Yes, I see how they're communicating with you.

Victoria: Yes, I'm working on this project with them - actually, I'm being guided directly by them. I get that the book needs to come out soon, so the information reaches the precise time and space unit within our humanity. There's a deadline, I can stretch it a bit, but if I prolong it too much, they'll kindly push me to finish. I get the message: DON'T WASTE YOUR TIME.

Monica: Yes, this is a rapid process, and I was trying to understand something, there's information about that. It's like they've brought us into a plane where everything is very elastic, flexible, and we'll begin to feel that on Earth as well.

Victoria: It's done; the transmission has ended. Now the connection is open, they removed a transparent wall or something, and now he's sending love again because you were patient.

Victoria: I want to ask more about these beings, if it's in my best interest to know or include them in the book. *Who are they, where do they come from, what is their role, what are their names?* Let's take it step by step, if they can introduce themselves.

Monica: I see they're part of the Galactic Council, and for the first one, the one in the middle, I received the name **ROMR**.

Victoria: Hmm, I felt something with "R," not quite "R," but a frequency like "R." I don't know how to explain it.

Monica: Yes, we can't really perceive it. They tell us their names in ways we can understand.

Victoria: Do I have a direct relationship with them, or is it just a project?

Monica: In your relationship with them, I see they're guiding you. You are a very open channel, and they came to guide you in writing your book.

Victoria: I feel like I'm their intern, and this is the project I need to finish in order to graduate. It's like I'll become part of their Galactic Council. But for now, I'm their intern.

Monica: I see them on your book cover, either front or back, those three, and in this space where we are, I see them painted.

Victoria: Hmm, interesting, because I had picked another image for the book. Can they give me more details for the image I should include? How do they appear? More details?

Victoria: Let's ask for a detailed introduction from the central being.

Monica: I get that this is a council of priests, as we might perceive it, and he is like a patriarch or similar.

Victoria: Yes, yes, exactly.

Monica: I see him holding a kind of scepter, like a wise figure. He's not very old, but his energy feels evolved and wise.

Victoria: The number 44 comes to me. What does this number mean?

Monica: The dimension he comes from.

Victoria: That thing on his head, it resembles something worn by priests, but straight, and the top is shaped like a crescent, not flat. I see flowers on his right side, red and pink crystals; upper right red, middle left, lower part blue. In the middle-left, I think I see a citrine moon, because it's yellow. On the upper-left, two flowers connect, there's a straight crystal linked through the flowers. On the far left upper corner, it's darker, yellow and pink, but the flower closer to the center below is a transparent Lemurian quartz. Lower left there are small flowers, chains like our DNA, interlinked. These are made of different colored crystals. His face, maybe it's my imagination, I see a male face, but I feel he doesn't really have a defined face.

Monica: Yes, that's how I feel too. It feels like they show us a wise old man's face with a beard just so we can understand the energy.

Victoria: His cloak is large, just like how I see on the Andromedan High Council (the painting that I channeled and posted on my social media). It's split down the middle, with a raised collar like a judge's, and beneath it he's dressed in white. The one next to you feels younger.

Monica: Yes. He feels younger, shorter, smaller.

Victoria: Yes, smaller, because the one in the middle is truly taller, bigger.

Monica: Yes, he has the strongest energy.

Victoria: But I can't understand him exactly. I only clearly see his cloak with its various colors. Maybe you see better. I don't interact much with the one on the left, mostly with the main being.

Monica: Yes, exactly, you're with the main one. The other two radiate, like they hold lights of energy.

Victoria: There's a balance of masculine and feminine energy. But it's more than that, one has cooler colors, and the other warmer. Let's ask, *what's the essence of the warm and cool colors?*

Monica: The word *balance* comes to me.

Victoria: Yes, the balancing of energies. Maybe you can describe how the others look, I don't perceive them well.

Monica: The one in front of me I see in purple, blue, with some light grey to white in his cloak, and I see him holding a lamp, like the old ones, but it emits living light, like a sphere, and he holds it by a handle.

Victoria: But the energy of the other one, on my left, the right of the main being, feels warmer, softer, gentler.

Monica: Yes, it's softer, and I see colors that remind me of a sunset.

Victoria: Yes, exactly.

Monica: They shift and move; it feels like a golden-orange, maybe pink, sunset.

Victoria: Let's ask if they have a main message for humanity. I don't feel like we need to explore more here.

Monica: Yes, let's see. I receive a message: "Our sons and daughters, our role on Earth..." wait, they're all speaking at once, and it's hard to receive the message. I feel they're saying: *We've come at a critical moment for the planet, and everyone has a specific role. We all participate in Earth's ascension, and we must not leave anyone behind. Don't drag others, go forward with love and openness. Hear everyone, hear the subtleties in their lives, because maybe a single sentence from you helps them in their ascension process. Don't turn your back on anyone.*

Victoria: Thank you. Maybe they gave you the message in advance, because I saw how they turned and left.

Monica: It all came at once, the words were all mixed together, and it took time to separate them.

Victoria: I saw how fast they sent it and left.

Monica: Thank you. Let's return to the door.

Victoria: Yes, to the 5th dimension. Another door opened, I saw the handle light up green.

Monica: Wasn't this the door where you previously got "access denied"?

Victoria: It's on the right, next to that one. This one opened. I opened the door and it feels like I'm in space, but also like I'm nowhere.

Monica: I saw myself stepping onto a glass spaceship.

Victoria: Yes, because I feel like I'm in glass.

Monica: I see Earth in the distance, the planet Earth. I see myself in the cosmos.

Victoria: Yes, it feels like we're in the cosmos, but inside, everything is transparent, glass-like.

Monica: Yes, it's a material like glass.

Victoria: This is like a transparent mask, because if you open a door, you see the true materialization of the ship.

Monica: Yes, I also got the sense that it's actually something else, but we can't perceive it. It has buttons we don't currently see.

Victoria: Some very tiny beings, like dwarves or elves.

Monica: I see them too.

Victoria: In such a big ship, and such tiny beings. There are many of them, and the walls have different levels. I see the ship has shelves, corridors, but actually, these are their pathways, their routes.

Monica: Yes. Let's see if they tell us: Who are they? What are their names?

Victoria: The *Teta-uli* beings entered the field again. We've connected with them before.

Monica: Yes, I know the name, I remember it.

Victoria: This week, Thursday or Friday, I kept hearing them nonstop. I was like, "What is this?" Then I remembered the session. *What is your mes-*

sage for us today, or for humanity? They are so happy.

Monica: Yes, everything is joy and happiness, I feel they've come closer to Earth, which is why they're so happy.

Victoria: In the middle of the ship, I see a tall being, it looks like a giant insect, with multiple arms. I don't know what it's doing here. It's the main one on board.

Monica: From him, artificial intelligence is created. He came to manage the ship.

Victoria: I see him at the controls, he operates the buttons.

Monica: Yes, yes. He handles everything on the ship, he receives the commands, keeps it on course.

Victoria: Its insect-like legs operate everything, but it's quite tall, about two meters.

Monica: He is the heart of the ship.

Victoria: From where and how is he here with the *Teta-uli*? They seem like different beings.

Monica: I get that in the universe, different councils and experiments happen to test compatibility, who can work with whom, who's better at what. Races group together for greater efficiency. Many species unite.

Victoria: Yes, because I don't see a logical connection. I feel this being is also cleansing karma by participating in the project. It's like a convict repaying their sentence.

Monica: Yes, I saw earlier that many planets going through their ascension processes, including ETs, wanted to evolve. They accepted this and started working with others universally.

Victoria: Yes, but on its right leg, there's a connection, it's tethered to the ship itself. It's anchored to the vessel. *Is it beneficial for us to know about this being?*

Below is the continuation of this transmission about this being.

ZUXSUMA II

Monica: A name comes to me, **ZUXSUMA II.**

Victoria: I'm getting "not important."

Monica: Yes, it's not important for us to know, because I saw a sort of history, something quick, where they traveled to various planets collecting information, but that's in the past.

Victoria: Yes, he's cleansing his punishment.

Monica: Yes, and he's open to doing it, he's not being forced.

Victoria: Yes, because I feel a kind of safety, *Teta-uli* trusts that he knows what he's doing. *Is "Teta-uli" a message for us or for humanity?*

Monica: I see them all climbing on you, they're all around you, on top of each other, and I can't see you anymore.

Victoria: What does that mean? Did they miss me?

Monica: Yes, because they're very happy. But they also want to imprint your body with something from their essence, something they want to place on you.

Victoria: If it's for my highest good, I accept.

Monica: I see them lighting up and placing something like a luminous film over you.

Victoria: Yes, I see a vortex spinning around my body, it starts at the head.

Monica: Through this light, they're showing you that it's beneficial. It feels so good. I feel a wave from you coming toward me.

Victoria: Yes, it's a wind blowing gold. I feel so good.

Monica: I feel like they're cleansing you of current burdens, and you'll feel this cleansing for 3 days, because there are things in your life right now causing you to stagnate with your book or other projects. You need to feel like you do now in this vortex; lighter, protected. At the moment, you feel a lack of protection, but not from entities.

Victoria: Yes, exactly, it makes sense.

Monica: They're offering this to you, and you feel so much joy and support. Now I see them getting down, and the vortex remains.

Victoria: Yes, I still feel it. It moves from top to bottom. Thank you.

Monica: They left in a playful, but also shy way.

Victoria: Yes, because this past week I felt them cleansing my body, and I kept hearing "Teta-uli."

Monica: Now I see how this light enters you, it's like a film that goes beneath the layers of skin.

Victoria: I saw it too.

Monica: Is there anything else we need to learn here?

Victoria: I'm getting "no."

Monica: Yes, I'm being shown an image of planet Earth.

Victoria: There's nothing more. Thank you. I stepped out of the ship and I'm in front of the door, but I took something from there. When I opened the door, I reached in, then closed it, but I didn't see what I took.

Monica: Let's see, maybe I can. I saw something like a flower, like one made from crepe paper, and when you took it in your hand, it entered your palm. In the center of the flower there aren't seeds, but something that flows through your bloodstream. I can see it moving through your veins, capillaries.

Victoria: What is the purpose of this process?

Monica: It's still for cleansing.

Victoria: Yes, and it's reaching my heart because I feel a sharp sensation there.

Monica: The heart, yes, your circulatory system. It's a cleansing and a liquefying of your blood, so that it flows more smoothly and easily.

Victoria: Oh wow, thank you. That space has now vanished.

Monica: We were in that hallway, and it's gone. Now I see us falling back to Earth - it's like we're parachuting, wearing backpacks.

Victoria: Now I feel like asking about myself, because the journey with the other beings is over. I need to ground myself in order to understand my near future. I saw I landed with a parachute.

Monica: I see that for about a month, you'll be writing new things in your book. You'll think about where to place them, because you've written something similar before, you'll wonder how to arrange it. Don't stress, ask for help, especially from the Council. The space for creation should come after a cleansing. I see you doing a cleanse, washing with salt, protecting yourself, giving yourself one hour, and then starting to write. Meaning: *write on the right frequency.*

Victoria: Aha, this is what I did last night. After that, I sat down to write and I felt very different.

Monica: Then that was a message from them.

Victoria: Yes, because yesterday I did a cleansing, it was very intense, and then I sat at my computer to continue, to focus, but my phone wouldn't work. I went to take a salt bath, came back, and everything flowed around me.

Monica: I'm getting that in your near future, you'll be going away for a few days. I see that you'll encounter an opportunity, like a retreat, a trip where you'll meet with women.

Victoria: That's interesting because next weekend I'll be at an event where only women will be present.

Monica: That will be like an upgrade. In the energy of those women, you'll manage to download something else, and every meeting has its purpose.

CELESTIALS - Channeling April 2nd, 2024

In 2023, I discovered a personal connection with the Celestial Union Consciousness, the Highest beings or Consciousness that I have encountered so far, and for Diana, the word celestials appeared very often. She was just beginning to connect with various beings and to expand her consciousness. We entered that session with the clear intention to receive more information from these beings. Below, I'll share part of that session

Celestial Union Consciousness represents the harmonious merging of higher-dimensional energies and universal wisdom that guide the spiritual evolution of humanity and all life on Earth. This consciousness embodies the collective awareness of enlightened beings, star families, and cosmic forces working together in unity to support planetary ascension and the awakening of the soul.

Rooted in love, balance, and interconnectedness, the Celestial Union Consciousness fosters deep healing, transformation, and expansion beyond the limitations of physical reality. It encourages us to align with our higher selves, recognize our divine nature, and participate consciously in the unfolding cosmic plan.

Through this unified consciousness, diverse cosmic entities communicate, share knowledge, and co-create a new reality where light, harmony, and spiritual awakening prevail. The Celestial Union serves as a beacon of hope and guidance, reminding humanity of its sacred connection to the stars and the infinite potentials within.

The field is a small unit compared to the international field of the universe we are part of. You must come to know this universe because this is what you desire. We are present now, not as beings, but as a higher level of consciousness. You (Diana) are currently beneath the concept of a "being" that exists in space. In order to reach our surrounding environment, you must expand your limits to discover more, and we rejoice for you.

Q: Would you be interested in discovering your connection to the Celestials?
A: We are currently working on your field in order to grant you greater access to this world in which we exist. DNA activated.

We will now begin working on Victoria, if you allow us a few moments.

Victoria: They have exited my body now because, energetically speaking, they are too powerful for me, but they are still present. It's more comfortable this way.

Q: What should we know about your world?
A: A parallel universe. A simple example that we can offer: the same world coexists, but they exist beyond, it's a different type of universe.

Victoria: They placed us face to face, and it appeared like a white disc.

Their world overlays all of ours. They encompass everything. They can move freely, passing through any "walls" of the universe, galaxy, dimension, any existence, stars or freely moving through Metaverse and Multiverse or above all this. They pass transparently through it all. If God, the Source, is the Creator of all that exists, they are like gods who move freely through all of God's creation.
They were purely created by God, and they exist one level above creation itself. They are the first creation.

Diana: Are they connected to the Monad souls?

Monad = a concept misunderstood by humanity.

What you explained (spiritual sons/daughters, 12 souls) exists on a level lower than what God is.
Between the place where we exist and where God resides, there are complex worlds, complex beings, and the creation of a soul, of a spiritual embryo, is divided into 12.
It is a new process, a new type of creation.

Humanity and our world are the most recent and lowest creation, newly made in universal terms (not Earth years).

Oversoul → 6 → 6 — after all 12 parts are completed, the soul can then progress further on a higher scale.

A More Accessible Path to the Celestials

Q: Who can connect with you?
A: Those who can or have the ability to connect with us are few, although we wish there were more of you. It is given more rarely to souls, so that they can establish this direct connection. Not everyone has access.

Q: Why doesn't everyone have access?
A: Not everyone needs to know this kind of information, because it would divert them from the path of their mission, due to the underdevelopment of the "infant" (they compare us to children).

Q: How does it help us on the path of our calling?
A: Through the few chosen ones, it becomes easier for you to spread information to others who do not intentionally have access. It will be easier for them to perceive the information through your simpler words and concepts.

Q: What does your world look like, if we are allowed to know?
A: I see a downward-pointing pyramid, and around it is a bluish-white light, a kind of energy spinning around it. An energy generator. It is not a universe, not a galaxy, it is absolutely everything. It is like a mesh of energy that transmutes, charges, and they are like blood vessels throughout our body, to all existence, to everything that is. They are like a union, like an army, there are very many of them. Just as we have a world, they have their own - they are the first creation of God, the purest creation.

LEMURIA: The Ancient Spiritual Legacy

Lemuria was an ancient civilization that existed long before recorded history, even before Atlantis. It is often described as a highly evolved society, deeply connected to nature, spirituality, and harmony. The Lemurians had a profound understanding of the natural world and lived in balance with the Earth and its energies.

Spiritually, it represents one of the earliest known hubs of advanced consciousness on Earth. The Lemurians were deeply connected to higher realms and cosmic energies, allowing them to access profound wisdom and spiritual guidance. This connection granted them unique insights into the nature of existence and the evolution of the soul. Lemuria was a place where the soul's journey toward awakening and higher consciousness was nurtured in a loving and gentle environment. The people had strong psychic abilities, deep empathy, and a unique connection to the Earth's energetic grid.

Central to Lemurian culture was their mastery of crystal technology; a sacred science through which they healed, communicated, and maintained energetic harmony with the planet and cosmos. Crystals were not merely tools but living conduits of universal energy, aiding in balancing mind, body, and spirit.

The souls who once inhabited Lemuria carry energetic imprints from that time. These imprints influence their current incarnations, guiding their spiritual growth and calling them to remember ancient truths. For many today, reconnecting with Lemurian energy is a path to healing old wounds and awakening latent spiritual potentials.

The decline of Lemuria, often described as a fall from spiritual grace, serves as a powerful lesson for humanity. It reminds us of the importance of maintaining harmony with nature, respecting the sacred balance of life, and upholding spiritual integrity. This legacy urges us to learn from the past to create a more conscious future.

Today, spiritual seekers speak of "Lemurian codes", vibrational frequencies and energetic activations that can awaken dormant aspects of the soul. Accessing these codes is said to facilitate profound transformation, reconnecting individuals with their highest purpose and the collective wisdom of ancient Lemuria.

In embracing the spiritual heritage of Lemuria, we honor the continuum of consciousness that stretches back across time, inspiring us to live with greater awareness, compassion, and connection to all life.

The wisdom and energy of Lemuria still influence many souls today, helping those who seek healing, peace, and spiritual awakening on their path. The Lemurian legacy teaches us unity, compassion, and living in harmony with the planet.

Q: Quantum Field, it is welcome to include in Victoria's book some information about Lemuria, what is beneficial for us to know?
A: There are so many of them; they are not tall but smaller than me. I see them in blue. I personally see myself much bigger than them. I see myself as enormous, like a giant compared to them. They are all dressed in blue and seem to have stars on them. There are many, but I don't see all of them, and I feel pulled to go with them.

Diana: I know they were tall as well, when my Lemurian version came into the session with you.
Victoria: The Lemurian from D22, the one we connected with in another session, was older and very tall, but Lemurians are usually shorter in stature. Your Lemurian essence probably comes from ancient genetics.

We, at the soul level, are multidimensional beings. We exist or have existed on many planes and dimensions, have had lives in other realms, and exist beyond planet Earth. Diana is now referring to her multidimensional version, which includes various races and many other ET civilizations.

A: I sat on a chair, and in front of me everything is made of glass, crystals, blue ... but it seems like a white crystal with blue. I feel I need to adjust myself to their energy. Now I see more light. I ask any being that does not come from light to leave this space. Done, they left. On the right side, it seemed like something dense was coming out of the ground, I don't know what, and I asked to close any portal in this space with lower vibrational planes.

Channeling Lemurians

"Now we are here to present to you life from inside of our crystals. We are on the 7th Dimension - this place is our home. We are working towards expansion into a higher realm to help us expand higher than we are now. We already created the portal that is above our room here, this portal is still opening, spinning to break through the veil of our dimension to higher to the 8th one. We are evolving because our vibration is no longer holding this place. The way that we will move it will be in a blink of an eye and the reality that we have here will look differently than the one above.

We no longer serve an urgency to help humankind. Our relationship with humankind has stopped due to the higher frequency of your planet. We will be in touch with the families that are still in the lower planes but we will not engage in creating space for us to downgrade to help you. The scope of all creation is for you to raise up. Once you do, my friends, we will be in touch. Now we are seeking to help you. It's a form of loving and being at peace with the events that are occurring in the universe. I am glad to connect with you all and I wish to "*see you up soon.*" Thank you.

Victoria: I need to recalibrate myself back. When higher energy enters the body and then leaves, it sort of signals you where you still have work to do.

This is an important message, and what I feel from all of this is that taking care of yourself is a form of love, both for yourself and for others. This doesn't mean taking care of someone else and then yourself, but rather, the most beneficial way is to do the opposite - take care of yourself first, and then of others. This way, you see, my ear is ringing now, this way, you offer love in the right way, by caring for yourself first.

LEMURIAN from Dimension 22 - Channeling

One afternoon, on July 30, 2024, as I was getting ready to leave work, a Lemurian being appeared to me. The connection with this being took place through astral teleportation. I began asking questions while still at work, and then rushed home, arranging with Diana to enter a session to see what information this being wished to share with us. I was curious to see when we could connect with him again, but the message we received was that it is not their role to connect with us very often, because there are other beings more suitable for this type of interaction. Their support operates at a "transgestional" level, deep and complex, within the soul's path of evolution. This is not an event meant to occur frequently on Earth. Their support is too vast for such a complex integration to take place easily. More time is needed for this process to activate. The process acts like a conductor of the Matrix, and its outcome plays out on intense platforms of evolution.

Below is the information we received during the channeling session.

We are at level 2, as you would imagine the steps when entering the second stage of evolution. Here, there are portals for which we are responsible. These are crystals that store codes for the creation of the passage field that allows the soul/souls to transition from level 1, where the physical form dominates.

Transgestional is a type of fusion between DNA, RNA, and *"IN"*; a complex structure layered upon DNA and RNA together. Your science currently lacks the capacity to access such information. It will become available in 50 years.

Souls that move to level 2 have the third, layered genome activated - the one you are only beginning to become aware of. This activation is complex, and the physical body manifests very differently on the physical plane. Existence at this level is experienced as an advanced duplex across three layers of matter; the first layer is the known physical, the second is *nano-complex*, what you call the microbial world, and the third is *invisible matter*, which the human physical eye cannot perceive.

Activation occurs instantly through the throat chakra. In this way, transition to the next level begins. Everything is unfolding. At level 2, you exist, but you perceive even the physical body differently. Level 3 is too complex. Humans are not permitted to be transmuted to level 3. You are still too small (referring to the level of consciousness).

We will now take you on a journey, here and now. Please close your eyes. You are now exiting your astral within the astral. A bit more … Now we are in dimension 22. Here, you feel the third part of your existence. Here you only see your extensions. There is no astral body, no physical body, only the light body that stems from the astral body. We want to know what you feel.

Diana: I feel very light, almost as if I'm floating.

A: Exactly. Here in dimension 22, the body is freer and more flexible than the astral body. Now, energy balance and control are needed. There, you feel it as your own. Now you have control over the light energy of your astral body. Only when you can control this inner light can the connection occur. This balance is what allows for *teleportation of the astral from within the astral.* Thank you for this experience.

Q: Dear Lemurian, what is our connection with the portal of the Lyrans?
A: They are **activators from level 1**, from within your Matrix. They offer the potential for whether or not you may transition to the next level. We are not associated with your evolutionary process. We are responsible for our own portal, within which there are codes and inscriptions embedded in our crystals.

Q: How do you recognize when you've passed to the next level?
A: I see something like an MRI machine, you stand upright and pass beneath it. At level 1, there is a portion that you walk through standing, and until reaching level 2, this period involves pain. In this process, a sort of vacuum forms that pressurizes you and extracts all attachments. The pressure is felt due to your body's density. It pulls out everything you once were at level 1, and that creates intense pain. By the time you reach level 2, those attachments no longer exist. The most painful part is when you move through that pressure point, as it extracts everything, and then you pass into the different environment of level 2.

Everyone experiences physical pain. It may manifest as unexplained illnesses. You feel like you're dying, but at the same time, you keep moving forward. It's very intense. It feels like the end of the world for your physical body.

When you go through such a process, then the transition to level 2 may take place. We used to say "may" because it can be confused with other cleansing processes. There is no specific feeling that lets you know you've reached the next level. It depends on the race you belong to. We all come from different races, and we are predisposed to different physical symptoms during the transition to level 2.

Q: What are the symptoms after the transition?
A: They vary depending on the dominant race within each individual.

Pleiadian Dominant Race
- The eyes will swell slightly – as if you had an allergy – and you'll think you have one.
- Very sensitive stomach – unable to digest much food.
- Sensitivity to daylight.

Andromedans

- They absolutely reject anything that is fake information. They are detectors of incoming information. If it's false, they sense it instantly, You can follow them for truth.
- Extremely flexible in everything. If the person used to be more rigid, they will become very flexible afterward. This is easily noticeable.
- Information flows through the **left side of the brain**.

Zeta Reticuli

- Strong heart palpitations with no explanation.
- Swollen and red toes.
- Shoulder joint issues.

Arcturians *(very few on Earth as a dominant race)*

- The density of Earth is too much for them.
- Downward-pointing lotus (like a motor spinning and forming a sphere at the root chakra).
- **Side effect:** no desire for intimacy. Their system is built in a way that they do not reproduce, to them, the human process of intimacy feels wild and primitive.

Blue Avians

- They **do not exist on Earth**.
- For them, our planet is like a playground.

Teta Tetroni - of which there are many, based in the asian region of our planet:

- They are all short.
- Their intestines are narrow, so they can only eat very small portions.
- Discomfort at the back of the head (the nape) that no one can explain.
- Third eye completely closed.

Syrians

- Headaches and head dilation.
- Knee problems.
- Denial/refusal of anything they receive from others.

Lyrans

- Increase in body heat; they feel too hot, they need cooler environments.
- Tooth pain.
- Their posture will change, straighter, more confident.

Greys – *(no communication in 2024 transmission)*

Update – March 2025

Greys have begun working only on benevolent technical support and to aid humanity due to changes in the UNIVERSAL COSMIC LAW at the PLANETARY LEVEL OF EARTH. Their race is currently repaying karmic debts accumulated over eons, perhaps involving more than just local retribution, seen from a nonlinear perspective.

Lemurians

There is a Lemurian population in **two areas** on Earth:
› In the **Western Hemisphere**, in the **middle of the ocean** –
  tiny islands that are not easily visible by satellite.
› In the **Eastern Hemisphere**, living **near very large cities**.

Their field is like a **positive and negative** system:
› The **positive** is **charged** in the middle of the ocean.
› The **negative discharges** energy into the larger population.

Side effects:

Western Hemisphere
› **Heat is absolutely necessary** – if nature's temperature drops even by 1–2 degrees, they are affected. They **require warmth**.
› Their **muscles contract.** Even with a 1–2 degree drop, they experience **muscle spasms**.
› The **fruits** on the island will no longer be suitable for them. They will need **alternative food sources**.
› **Time will become non-existent** for them.

Eastern Hemisphere

› They will become **highly empathetic**. They will feel **everything** - even the emotions of a **cricket, an ant, an insect** – they will be **extremely sensitive to nature**.

› They will **feel what a cricket feels**; if they observe it closely, they will experience its emotions.

› They **won't be able to tolerate crowded places**. They will flee to nature, but that will also become a kind of **hell**, because they will feel everything **even more intensely**, without understanding what is happening to them.

› In their **lungs**, there are **valves** that assist with breathing. These **valves will change**, and people will **no longer need to exhale through the lungs**.

› Their **bodies will adapt**, over time.

› If they have children, their **children will have partially disappeared valves** – they will be **hybrids**.

› In the future, they will be able to **breathe more easily without the oxygen in the environment**.

Predominant Races

Victoria

- **Pleiadian**
- **Lyran**
- *Arcturian* – though not strongly predominant

Diana

- **Lemurian**
- **Andromedan**
- **Pleiadian**
- *Arcturian* – similar as in Victoria's case

Note: When you **make the shift (the leap), all symptoms from different races** may **combine temporarily,** just for the **transition period** – then they **disappear**.

This is a **side effect** of the **shift to Level 2.**

ATLANTIS – Its Creation and Dissolution

During a session in the Akashic Field together with my colleague Xenia, we were able to witness a process from the creation and destruction of Atlantis. After accessing a series of personal insights in that session, we were transported into another space, where we began to see a knife marked with various initials.

I will share in the following section a few fragments from that session.

Atlantis was not merely a land or a civilization, it was a consciousness experiment, one of the first large-scale manifestations of divine knowledge integrated with physical form on Earth. It was born from the union of celestial beings who chose to seed wisdom, energy technologies, and higher vibrational templates into human form, guiding the evolution of Earth and its inhabitants.

The creation of Atlantis was intentional, divinely orchestrated. It was meant to be a beacon of harmony between spirit and matter; a civilization that would live in alignment with the laws of the Universe. The Atlanteans had access to crystalline technologies, sacred geometry, and were in contact with higher dimensional beings. Many of them were hybrids, souls carrying lineages from the Pleiades, Sirius, and other star systems.

However, as time passed, the vibration of Atlantis began to shift. The pursuit of power, ego, and experimentation with forbidden knowledge gradually overtook the original intention. The balance between heart and mind was lost. Technologies that once healed and elevated began to distort the natural order. Some Atlanteans started manipulating life itself, DNA, energy fields, even time.

The fall of Atlantis was not merely a physical event, but an energetic collapse. The collective frequency dropped too low to sustain the crystalline infrastructure and spiritual alignment. Great floods and earthquakes were only the outer reflection of an inner spiritual disconnection. Atlantis, as a physical realm, disappeared beneath the ocean, but its memory and codes remained.

Today, many souls walking the Earth carry Atlantean memory within their DNA. Some came back to complete what was unfinished. Others came to heal the trauma of the fall. The knowledge is reawakening but this time, the invitation is clear; wisdom must walk hand in hand with love. Power must be tempered by humility.

Victoria: I see very clearly a polished, shining golden knife, but I perceive it only from one angle, almost halfway, and then suddenly it's dark.

Xenia: What could that mean?

Victoria: Oh wow, the knife cut everything around, then it flew into this void space. Now it's floating. It's golden … like Zeus's knife.

Xenia: I see it like a kinjal, like a sword. It flew and stopped in a stone.

Victoria: Yes, it's something powerful. I see how it flew.

Xenia: On the handle, I see some stones, and I see it's made of gold, not wood. And it has initials on it, shining stones, and on the initials I see the letters A D.

Victoria: I see an inverted L.

Xenia: I saw an L but didn't understand what it was … I saw it as a D. These letters are written by hand, twisted, curved, and there are stones, rubies.

Victoria: Yes, that's what I see too. And it's a very bright red. But I don't understand what else is here. It doesn't give me more images to see if it's a planet, or what it is. The image stopped.

Xenia: But I see not only a red stone but also a blue one. You know what came to me when I said blue? Those two planets.

Victoria: This knife flew and stopped like a stone. The stone looked like a meteorite and it shows it black and dark, and as the knife stayed like that, from the meteorite, stone buds began to grow, buds that grew in the shape of A, a triangle, a pyramid, but it's not a pyramid, it's something growing huge - a crystal.

Xenia: To me it looks not like a pyramid, but like a steep iceberg.

Victoria: Correct. Let me ask what this is.

Xenia: I got Atlantis, and it shows me underwater, like the iceberg is coming out and then hiding again, and then coming out again, and there are many around the islands. I see rocks.

Victoria: It's Atlantis. Interesting, you said water and I saw many dolphins swimming around, almost like a swarm.

Xenia: Yes, and above I see a light moving in the sky, upwards. It moves chaotically, like two energies spinning. You know what I get? It's like some conductors.

Victoria: Interesting where it's going.

Xenia: It shows me another planet.

Victoria: I see how this energy comes out.

Xenia: Yes, it's far away. It showed me two planets at a great distance, and an axis forms between them.

Victoria: Wow, what I see goes beyond limits. As I watch it like a movie, this energy goes somewhere very far. It's a civilization very, very advanced compared to Atlantis. They are the creators of Atlantis.

Xenia: Ah, that's why they're connected to them, because I got a cord, a child.

Victoria: They finished with Atlantis because the civilization took a wrong path. Let's ask the Akashic Field what connection we have with Atlantis and the creators of Atlantis.

Xenia: Hmm. Very interesting, I got that *you are the creators.*

Victoria: Yes. You are the creators, and they showed me that up there.

Xenia: I got a kind of laughter.

Victoria: Yes, we are there above, in that reality, watching what those "children" from Atlantis are doing.

Xenia: I get a tingling on my forehead.

Victoria: Wow, I've never accessed information like this before. But it's extraordinary.

Xenia: You know how it shows to me? We are there on some kind of ship, at the edge, with hands crossed on our chests, looking down, wondering what they are doing.

Victoria: Yes, I see the same.

Xenia: And I got that these ones are ready.

Victoria: Yes, I see how we sit on a throne, somewhere high, and I sense this *cord*, the connection to everything.

Xenia: I see it like a ship with many cords. I look around and see many cords and many planets.

Victoria: It doesn't show me anything. Maybe we have different ranks, and you have access to more information. I don't have access to the information you see now.

Xenia: That's why I asked about the ship, because I have seen these images before, where there were many - and I saw others there too. Now I see many beings, different races, and they appear in different forms. I see many cords.

Victoria: Now I see a kind of cord, like someone comes through a cable and arrives on the ship, where I am with you, and goes out into the air and lands. Some beings could only travel with their own bodies; their body was the transport. Let's ask the field what we should understand from what is shown to us now, about Atlantis and its creation.

Xenia: I get "liquidation" - a failed project.

Victoria: I got a "failed experiment." The same.

FOUNDERS

In another session with Diana, we asked about our connection, and we were shown an essence of the Founders, in which we co-exist at the soul level. Below, I will share the information we received.

The Founders – An Introduction

Beyond the known boundaries of time, form, and dimensional space, there exists an ancient lineage of consciousness known as the **Founders**. They are not a race, nor a species as we define them, they are primordial architects, creators of galaxies, consciousness matrices, soul blueprints, and universal harmonics. They are the weavers of structure and frequency who laid the energetic groundwork for countless civilizations, including Lemuria, Atlantis, and many beyond our comprehension.

The Founders are not beings with fixed identities or bodies. They are streams of intelligent Source energy, expressed through various forms when needed. Their essence is fluid, often appearing as light, geometric patterns, liquid crystalline forms, or celestial archetypes. Sometimes, they take on humanoid aspects to be understood, but they remain unbound by any physical limitation.

The Founders and Us

Many of us carry within our soul lineage the frequency of the Founders. We are not separate from them; we are extensions of their consciousness, sparks of the same flame, temporarily embodied on Earth. Some of us have chosen to come into this dense realm, not merely to awaken, but to reactivate the original divine codes seeded here at the dawn of Earth's history.

We carry with us the memory of Atlantis, Lemuria, and other civilizations; some successful, some fallen. We remember because we were there, and we return now with a mission - to anchor light, restore forgotten knowledge, and help humanity evolve toward its next dimensional threshold.

A Living Legacy

The Founders do not operate through control. Their intelligence flows through co-creation, mentorship, and energetic transmission. They exist within a sacred lineage of wisdom keepers, where knowledge is recycled across timelines, not lost, but encoded and passed on through soul agreements and incarnational exchanges. One may be a teacher in one life, a student in the next. Parent, child, sister, guide, roles are fluid, and through each, the light of ancient wisdom is shared.

Their knowledge is not reserved for a chosen few, it is meant to be seeded widely. You may receive it in visions, dreams, light activations, synchronicities, or in quiet moments of remembrance. If you feel the stirring, the call to serve the planet through healing, teaching, remembering, or simply being, then the Founders are already within you, whispering you back to yourself.

Our Connection (Victoria & Diana) with Founders

Now we are inside the sphere with you. It will be interesting. We took each other's hands, face to face, and now the connection with the Creator is flowing through you. It first appeared within me, and now I see how this connection flows toward you. I see your entire connection flowing into your head and throat. Right here, I can see clouds above your head, yellow, as if you're in heaven.

Victoria: I become gigantic, and you grow too but remain smaller, yet the light from the Source flows through you. Interestingly, you are again my child. I see myself as an emperor wearing long robes, and you on my left in a white dress, as if about to step onto a stage … from backstage. You don't look human.
Diana: I perceive something about the Founders.
Victoria: Yes, that's what came to me as we grew. Our bodies aren't defined, they're liquid, blue-silver, like a universe contained within us.
Diana: For me, I sensed it instantly when you spoke of our connection, the Founders.

Victoria: Wait, I've understood until now that I am the 13th Founder and younger, and Ina (another colleague) is my mother, another feminine energy, not the primary Founder but the second being, after the main Founders. Now I see myself exactly on the same throne, in a castle. I'm seated and see myself wearing a crown. I am that principal masculine Founder energy, and I've placed you on my left. On the left, you are the child, though I also see you as an adult, grown. You are simultaneously my aunt, from when I was the 13th Founder. We all shift roles; we are not fixed in one role. You, as an adult, are my aunt, but now where I see myself as the Principal Founder, you are my daughter. So you can never define yourself as just one thing. You are tiny and lovely.

Q: Why do we choose the roles of parent and child?

A: I know we choose it deliberately. I was your father in that existence. You grew into adulthood. Your sister is Ina, who gave birth to the 13th Founder, that is me again. I am young and you are my aunt teaching me. That's how these ET tribes work. Knowledge is passed through generations. Teachings don't disappear; they are recycled through a new body. So in this life where I'm the primary Founder, my knowledge passed to you. You grew, gathered this knowledge, then a new member was born into the tribe, and you teach me the knowledge you received from me in a previous life as Founder, so that the information does not vanish. That's how many advanced tribes operate.

Diana: I sense it's just like on Earth; you reincarnate sometimes in the same family, just changing your body, but you still carry the same information you once transmitted.

Victoria: Yes, because the body expires. This process is more conscious here than on Earth. I'm curious now about your other Founder version.

Q: What is another Founder version for Diana in our tribe?

A: I see Ionela (another colleague). Ionela is the Founder who sits on the far left, in the last row. That's usually her place. I get that the eldest ones sit there. She is feminine energy, sitting to the left. You regenerate each other. Wait, she is also my grandmother, the mother of my mother. I got it recently that Ionela is Ina's mother, and you switch roles with her. Hold on, I'm trying to understand. Interesting how these Founders families regenerate. When you grow into adulthood, you take her place when she dies, or rather, when her body expires. She takes your place.

Now it is interesting how that happens. I still feel masculine energy, but you and her share the same feminine energy.

Q: How does this mechanism of body exchange work exactly among the Founders?
A: I see we have DNA, but their genes are structured differently; they don't spiral. Instead, they are like dots, shooting upward like a comet - a dot and a comet. Our DNA spirals; theirs stand vertically as energetic codes. They have X and Y chromosomes combined as a single dominant point, activated like a sphere, where both energies coexist. If blue activates, it produces masculine energy; if white activates, feminine energy is born. I'm looking at my DNA and yours. Mine has many blue points; yours many white. I am the more masculine genome, and there should be a line of twelve Founder energies in sequence.

It goes: *Masculine, Feminine, Masculine, Feminine,* etc. Yes, exactly. Your grandmother, maternal grandmother, is the last female, that's Ionela. That means at the end stand two women; the eldest. I am masculine energy, you feminine energy, and yet I see myself as the 13th Founder which is masculine energy as well.

Q: What should we understand in this life, in connection with the life over there?
A: It shows simply how we pass on knowledge. Wait, I'm receiving some more info. You need to learn to take my knowledge. After this life, in the next life beyond this physical plane we share as humans, there will be another existence in which you will teach me further what I taught you here. In that life, you will be an elder, and I see myself as a small child, a boy. Now, in this life, you take in all the information I transmit, and then you will transmit it back to me in the next life.

It's exactly like with the Founders, as if we reside there, but everything that happens is an exchange of information, passed through experience. Through our lives, we affect others. Through our knowledge, as part of the Founders, we share information, and we have to communicate and pass it on. At the same time, I see the 3D reality where we are - they influence us with the purpose of igniting a spark. I see us as two lamps, and the simpler world that lacks knowledge and ideas receives this information at just the right time. Between us, we scatter information into the world - this is our purpose in this reality. That's how we influence people on the planet, and they evolve along with us. It's not just the two of us, it's all those who come from other planets or systems, and galaxies. This is a global mission ongoing for years, to elevate Earth. The problem was that we didn't know each other, but circumstances were created for us to meet. Many will meet, and by connecting and working with them, like we do, we spread the information into the world. I see the information as very bright particles; whoever catches them, the information enters their consciousness and activates them. It's like you're sharing those particles and it doesn't matter who receives them. Through this process, our experiences transmit into the mental field, and from there a small light begins to ignite. That's how the starlight seeds operate worldwide - they've come for the evolution of the planet.

TKNAMOR

The encounter with these beings was an unexpected and profound experience for me. It all happened during a session with a client who needed healing at the level of the brain and spinal cord. I discovered that, in a past life, approximately 200 years ago in human time, this client had lived in a different form of existence and was part of the same soul group as these beings. Their soul connection was deep, and these beings chose to return during this session to offer support and healing.

Victoria: These ET beings have a head shaped like an egg, elongated at the back. They have no gender, they are androgynous, very thin, with a bluish-gray-violet texture, and their head is oval and elongated.

Q: Quantum Field, who are these beings?
A: They are technicians.

Q: What is the connection between client X and these technicians?
A: I'm getting that it's for a reboot, but you turn your head toward them and you're both laughing.

Q: Do these beings know client X?
A: Oh wow, you're laughing together, and you reach out your hand and make a gesture toward each other. You know each other.

Q: Quantum Field, is it appropriate for us to know the name of these beings and what dimension they come from?
A: Source **MZ241/024.39**, that is their location.

Q: In which system or galaxy are they located?
A: Ursa Major.

Q: What dimension?
A: D24.

Q: What is the name of these beings?
A: **Tknamor** - that's the name of their race.

Q: Is that the name of their species or individual beings?
A: It's the name of their race.

Thank you.

Channeling - May 26, 2025 Victoria & Diana

Diana: We ask the other beings if they wish to transmit any additional information for the book.
Victoria: They sat down on the table with their legs. I don't understand. They took something out from behind, got down from the table, and placed it on the table; two by two, two by two. They look like flashcards. There are eight cards in total.
Diana: What do they represent?
Victoria: These are the beings who came to one of my sessions. They are more robotic, they are technicians. The flashcards represent dimensions, arranged from largest to smallest, like squares. And from the card nearest to me, the largest one, cables extend. Yes, cables, not solid like you see, but energy-like, quantum-style. I don't understand where they go. What is this field we are in? What are these flashes and cables? It feels too technical

right now for me to understand. They show me energy cables flowing, explaining to small children that something is placed somewhere and it drains, very technical knowledge ... but I don't feel called to dive into these techniques. The first card they place at my throat, and energy flows from here into the field behind. There is something there. We have a flash at the throat. What is this throat flash? Is it the power of what we speak? *Is that what this is about?* It is the power of words. What you speak goes into the universe, it drains away

Diana: Ah, it's our capacity to manifest.

Victoria: Yes, this is the processor. When you speak words, they go into the field, and everything forms there.

Diana: Yes. I read that it takes seven seconds for what you say to reach the universe.

Victoria: Yes, this is the device, the flash, the card, or I don't know what to call it. We have the power of language. We are all fluid compositions of energetic cables flowing into the field. Okay, *what is the second card for?* It's at the belly, at the solar plexus chakra. That is creation, solar plexus is creation. It drains and flows similarly. The next smaller, the third card, is at the root chakra. Interesting because at the base, the channel is smaller.

Diana: Is there a reason for that?

Victoria: That's our grounding. The base, those cables are darker, they are our densities. The energy of density which is necessary.

And the fourth, the smallest one, *where is it located?* At the pineal gland. But why is it so small?

Tknamor: Your portion of connection is smaller due to operational reasons, how we operate in our reality.

Victoria: Humanity considers the pineal gland inferior compared to our base. That's not ideal from this point of view, because we are anchored in our physical reality and densities, rather than focusing on the pineal gland, on what we receive from above. I'm curious why the heart has none.

Diana: Let's ask. *Is there a reason that nothing is found at the heart?*

Victoria: I get that the system is an individual, autonomous, unitary operating system. But why are the third eye and crown chakra not included?

Diana: I felt when you said that the root card is larger and the pineal card is smaller, that it's related to the operating system and our physicality, that our physical plane is denser.

Victoria: Why are the third eye and crown not part of this system?

I'm getting that they are optional. They are not mandatory.

Diana: I wondered, aren't the third eye and pineal gland correlated together?

Victoria: I see an interesting visual. The pineal gland creates a wide energy strip upward, like a flower, and it goes upward. That's for the higher planes. And the third eye plus crown is optional.

Can people activate or receive upgrades with such cards, like a hard drive, to activate these two chakras? I get that it's up to each responsible team.

Diana: Yes, I also sensed that it's optional, depending on your experience.

Thank you.

CHKHINK M 10

Victoria: Is there another, easier name?

They look at me, kind of like, "What?" and are surprised. The name is **CHKHINK M 10**.

Diana: Yes, something easier, because that one is a bit complex.

Q: How does your race help humanity?

A: You have a global network that we operate within; this network communication system of your chemical, biological strings within your internal physical body. The operation we are responsible for is not tied to any one physicality, tissues, organs, or similar associations. Our work is strictly technological. We provide technical support to every organ of your body, which functions on a database-network system of higher technology. We call this the ***TECH NANO PUR MOLECULAR SYSTEM***. We are the top-level nerds of your physical system.

Victoria: Interesting. It's like I'm talking to an IT team. I feel like IT. They don't see the body as something alive in the traditional sense, they see it as alive, but made up of cables and operating systems. Thank you.

Q: Are there other pieces of information you would like to include in the book about your race?

A: The reproductive system of these beings is purely technological. It doesn't involve the manifestation of consciousness or the creation of what you would call a soul. Their creation is born directly from the technology itself, which contains intelligence. They are approximately AI, but from a different classification. In a way, AI is pure intelligent consciousness, but these beings have actual bodies and take actions. Let me give you an example: it's like a shepherd and a flock of sheep with a dog. The dog must be physically present to watch over the sheep, that's what these beings are like. They take care of things physically. But then the dog that's supposed to guard the flock goes home and watches the field remotely on a screen, that's AI. AI only monitors and exists as intellectual consciousness. But their race, the one that does the technical work, they are of a different category. The AI is virtual, while they are real, with physical bodies.

Thank you.

BLUE AVIANS

The Blue Avians are highly evolved extraterrestrial beings known for their profound spiritual wisdom and deep connection to the higher cosmic realms. Often described as tall, slender, and bird-like with striking blue feathers, they serve as guardians and guides for humanity's spiritual evolution.

Throughout various channeled communications, the Blue Avians emphasize their role as observers and supporters of Earth's unique ascension process. Although they do not physically intervene due to the current state of planetary contamination, they maintain a vital energetic connection, assisting in subtle ways, such as supporting the neutralization of toxins within the Earth's soil and bio-environment.

Their teachings revolve around balance, the harmonious integration of masculine and feminine energies, the power of conscious manifestation through words, and the nurturing relationship between humanity and Mother Earth. They advocate for a respectful coexistence with nature, encouraging us to utilize natural, sustainable materials in our daily lives to restore planetary health.

The Blue Avians' messages carry a tone of loving encouragement, urging humanity to awaken to its own power and participate consciously in the collective transformation that is underway. They remind us that while they are not direct participants in human affairs, their presence as watchers and informants is an essential part of the cosmic support system.

By sharing their insights, the Blue Avians invite us to expand our awareness beyond the physical and embrace the subtle energies that weave together life, consciousness, and the universe.

Victoria: Blue Avians, we kindly ask you to share the information meant to be included in the book, that serves the highest good for us and for everyone on this planet.

She puts on something like headphones and connects them to our table, in the field where we are now.

Channeling:

"We want to tell you that our connection has long been established; however, from a frequency perspective, the information has not yet reached the intended receiver. Everyone perceives information in their own way, but here is a clarification - we are not beings that discriminate or reject the relationship with humanity. You may receive this message in your own way, but know that our friendship is unique.

Today, we want to share that your planetary soil is currently undergoing a process of alchemization and neutralization of chemicals that are present deep within the Earth. The presence of many beings who are meant to arrive in the near future cannot manifest physically on your plane at this time. The reason is that the planetary soil, being infected with chemical substances and biohazards, does not permit their landing. Our virtual presence serves as a bridge to help transform these chemical substances, where their neutralization is taking place at a planetary division level, microscopically, cellularly, and in other planes. This, in turn, directly impacts your planet and your physical reality."

Victoria: We can ask them questions.
Diana: It's interesting, because I received some information this morning and I'm curious to ask who transmitted it to me.
Victoria: Dear Blue Avians, is that info connected with the one transmitted to Diana? And who sent it?
Wait, he's putting on the headphones again. He's connecting and disconnecting.

Channeling:

"You were the recipient in whom the lens for receiving information was slightly modified, and the purpose of that information was to encourage this channel to be shared and included. We congratulate you, Diana, for receiving this useful information."

Diana: Thank you. Yes, I felt that it came from the Blue Avians, especially this morning when I wondered who was transmitting, as it felt too philosophical. I just wanted to confirm. Okay, let's stay on topic.

Q: What would be helpful for Victoria's book, how can we contribute to the neutralization or anything else affecting the levels of the soil?

Blue Avians: This is a rhetorical subject you are implementing here as a discussion. For this topic, it is necessary to simplify the questions you bravely ask. This subject is important for your planet. Our physical presence on your planet is not possible, as our collective personal decision is not to expose ourselves to the chemical substances present in your soil, its layers, and waters. Animals, birds, and other beings will be adjusted to assist with the gradual elimination of these toxic substances in an easier way. The human DNA will be reciprocated in a process that eliminates these substances. Genomes 34, 28, and 51 will be completely altered, compared to all human beings, before your physiological and planetary transformation.

We are simply participants in the experience and the case studies in which you are involved. However, we are merely observers of these changes. For us, it is beneficial to study your race in order to gradually ascend at the appropriate time; individually and collectively.

We are present to observe, to teach, based on what you experience, but we have no direct interference with your experiences. The planetary collective of Terra is on its own unique journey, and we are not the only observers. We are here to inform you about how your planet is being seen and the coexistence of all beings within, on, and above the planet.

Diana: Thank you. Is it welcomed to understand more about those genome changes, what they mean, and what changes they will bring for us as human beings?

Victoria: It is not yet welcomed for that to be known. The Avian near you answered the questions and now he has left. But the other one is still here beside me.

Diana: We ask the other if there's anything else he wishes to share for the book, or something humanity needs to know?

Channeling:

"We introduce a new way of becoming self-aware of your surroundings. This involves the elimination of toxins, chemical substances, or artificial products around you. The removal of chemicals works best in combination with natural elements.

So, in conclusion, we can offer an alternative - the use of natural substances such as old trees, aged wood, reused and repurposed for personal uses, offering a natural balance between your physical and biological body with nature, while avoiding further destruction of the trees on your planet.

In short, it is beneficial to use and create objects from what nature already considers dry, dead, or no longer useful. This does not imply cutting, destroying, or exploiting nature, but coexisting only with the unused parts of it.

My presence here is more unified with the planet and its feminine energy. We wish you a harmonious coexistence with Mother Earth."

Diana: Thank you.

Victoria: I felt that like a motherly presence. The first energy felt masculine, but this second one was more feminine. I even heard a woman's voice, very philosophical.

Diana: That's how the messages came to me this morning too. When I was reading them, I was 100% sure they weren't from me. They were so philosophical. It guided me toward the idea that the lack of authenticity led to destruction at the level of Mother Earth.

Is there anything else the Blue Avians would like to share with Victoria for the book?

Final Channeling:

"Our presence is purely informative, and we do not have a specific or concrete message to develop further here. This informational space is welcomed to be included

373

in Chapter 7 of this book, as it was intended by us, but through different filters.

And now, this is all that needs to be included. Sometimes words interfere with the energy that is meant to be present, in a space, a time, a unity, a heart, a consciousness. We will not approach any complex subjects, as that is not the purpose.

However, we wish for these present verses, here and now in this book, to infuse every molecule of this physical body with balance. May consciousness align and synchronize with the chosen soul's mission and purpose.

This message will close with the balancing of the masculine and feminine energies into one unity that represents Source itself.

We thank you, and we will meet again through other sources. Until next time."
Thank you.

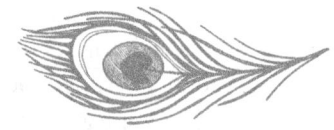

About the Author

Victoria Basil is a channeler of multidimensional Beings of Light, an energetic and intuitive healer, and a spiritual mentor, dedicated to metaphysics and self-discovery. She is a published author of the Bestseller profound anthology book *Awakened Hearts: Stories of Embracing Light, Love and Limitless Possibilities*, where her awakened journey can be found in more depth as an exclusive story.
The book can be found at www.awakenedheartsbook.com

As the founder and CEO of Infinity Triangle and Infinity Triangle Press, Victoria has empowered hundreds through group and individual channeling, daily mentoring, and support on their learning path, shared by Star People. She guides others to activate their dormant or inactive abilities, uncover their purpose, and embrace their power with confidence, releasing the old karmic ties, releasing the attachments, and bringing clarity.

Victoria has invented two theories in quantum physics, poised to be breakthroughs in science.

She is certified as an Akashic Record Reader, Quantum Hypnosis Healing Therapy (QHHT) practitioner, Licensed and Certified CNA, Certified CMA, Certified Phlebotomy Technician.

Pioneering the modalities of **Megaquantic Reading™** and her unique **Body Scan & Healing™**, born from her innate extrasensory gifts, she has unlocked a transformative breakthrough in physical-energetic healing, also through her multidimensional Channelings, and Quantum Reading sessions.

Specializing in releasing energetic attachments, Victoria works with Earth's grids and beyond, facilitating profound healing for individuals, the planet and other civilizations. Her premonitions, including foreseeing the Covid virus years in advance, stem from vivid dreams and timeline jumps she now navigates with mastery.

Victoria's dynamic life blends spirituality with adventure: hiking, visiting all 50 US states, exploring over half the national parks, tandem jumping, and scuba diving in the Pacific Ocean.

Her creative and intellectual pursuits span painting, medical studies, beauty business, law, accounting, self discovery, spirituality and metaphysics. Driven by an insatiable thirst for knowledge, Victoria embodies the boundless potential of the human body-mind-soul-spirit.

Connect with her at:

Website   infinitytriangle.net

               infinitytrianglepress.com

Email   victoriabasil@infinitytriangle.net

               infinitytrianglestar@gmail.com

Instagram @infinitytrianglestar

Facebook @infinitytriangle